The Shakespeare Handbook

Literature and Culture Handbooks

General Editors: Philip Tew and Steven Barfield

Literature and Culture Handbooks are an innovative series of guides to major periods, topics and authors in British and American literature and culture. Designed to provide a comprehensive, one-stop resource for literature students, each handbook provides the essential information and guidance needed from the beginning of a course through to developing more advanced knowledge and skills.

The Eighteenth-Century Literature Handbook
Edited by Gary Day and Bridget Keegan

The Medieval British Literature Handbook
Edited by Daniel T. Kline

The Modernism Handbook
Edited by Philip Tew and Alex Murray

The Post-war British Literature Handbook
Edited by Katherine Cockin and Jago Morrison

The Renaissance Literature Handbook
Edited by Susan Bruce and Rebecca Steinberger

The Seventeenth-Century Literature Handbook
Edited by Robert C. Evans and Eric J. Sterling

The Victorian Literature Handbook
Edited by Alexandra Warwick and Martin Willis

The Shakespeare Handbook

Edited by

Andrew Hiscock

and

Stephen Longstaffe

continuum

Continuum

The Tower Building   80 Maiden Lane, Suite 704

11 York Road   New York

London SE1 7NX   NY 10038

www.continuumbooks.com

© Andrew Hiscock, Stephen Longstaffe and contributors 2009

British Library Cataloguing-in-Publication Data
A catalogue record for this book is available from the British Library.

ISBN: 978-0-8264-9521-1 (hardback)
    978-0-8264-9578-5 (paperback)

Library of Congress Cataloging-in-Publication Data
A catalog record for this book is available from the Library of Congress.

Typeset by RefineCatch Limited, Bungay, Suffolk
Printed and bound in Great Britain by MPG Books Ltd, Bodmin, Cornwall

Contents

Contents

Detailed Table of Contents

Acknowledgements

It has been a pleasure to work with so many dedicated scholars in bringing this volume to fruition. We would like to thank all of the contributors for the commitment to and enthusiasm for Shakespeare studies which they brought to this project. The series editors Philip Tew and Steven Barfield have remained expert and patient guides throughout the preparation process for the *Shakespeare Handbook* as has the editorial team at Continuum, Anna Fleming and Colleen Coalter. Our sincere thanks to you all. This volume would not have been possible without the sustained and careful attention which Linda Jones at Bangor University devoted to the preparation of the manuscript. She performed an invaluable role in acting as adviser as well as correspondent for everyone working on the *Shakespeare Handbook* and it was and is much appreciated. Stephen Longstaffe would like to thank the University of Cumbria for granting him a term's sabbatical to work on this book, and for funding trips to research libraries. He would also like to thank colleagues, friends and family Penny Bradshaw, Brian and Norah Longstaffe, Amanda Flattery, Margaret Flattery and Robert Ward for their help and support. Andrew Hiscock would like to express his thanks once again to his colleagues at the School of English, Bangor University, but most of all his long-suffering family, Siân, Bronwen, Huw. This volume is dedicated to the Hiscock and Longstaffe family members.

Andrew Hiscock and Stephen Longstaffe
October 2008

General Editors' Introduction

The Continuum *Literature and Culture Handbooks* series aims to support both students new to an area of study and those at a more advanced stage, offering guidance with regard to the major periods, topics and authors relevant to the study of various aspects of British and American literature and culture. The series is designed with an international audience in mind, based on research into today's students in a global educational setting. Each volume is concerned with either a particular historical phase or an even more specific context, such as a major author study. All of the chosen areas represent established subject matter for literary study in schools, colleges and universities, all are both widely taught and the subject of ongoing research and scholarship. Each handbook provides a comprehensive, one-stop resource for literature students, offering essential information and guidance needed at the beginning of a course through to more advanced knowledge and skills for the student more familiar with the particular topic. These volumes reflect current academic research and scholarship, teaching methods and strategies, and also provide an outline of essential historical contexts. Written in clear language by leading internationally-acknowledged academics, each book provides the following:

- Introduction to authors, texts, historical and cultural contexts
- Guides to key critics, concepts and topics
- Introduction to critical approaches, changes in the canon and new conceptual and theoretical issues, such as gender and ethnicity
- Case studies in reading literary and theoretical and critical texts
- Annotated bibliography (including selected websites), timeline, and a glossary of useful critical terms.

This student-friendly series as a whole has drawn its inspiration and structure largely from the latest principles of text book design employed in other disciplines and subjects, creating an unusual and distinctive approach for the undergraduate arts and humanities field. This structure is designed to be user-friendly and it is intended that the layout can be easily navigated, with various points of cross-reference. Such clarity and straightforward approach should help students understand the material and in so doing guide them through the increasing academic difficulty of complex, critical and theoretical approaches to Literary Studies. These handbooks serve as gateways to the particular field that is explored.

All volumes make use of a 'progressive learning strategy', rather than the traditional chronological approach to the subject under discussion so that they might relate more closely to the learning process of the student. This means that the particular volume offers material that will aid the student to approach the period or topic confidently in the classroom for the very first time (for example, glossaries, historical context, key topics and critics), as well as material that helps the student develop more advanced skills (learning how to respond actively to selected primary texts and analyse and engage with modern critical arguments in relation to such texts). Each volume includes a specially commissioned new critical essay by a leading authority in the field discussing current debates and contexts. The progression in the contents mirrors the progress of the undergraduate student from beginner to a more advanced level. Each volume is aimed primarily at undergraduate students, intending to offer itself as both a guide and a reference text that will reflect the advances in academic studies in its subject matter, useful to both students and staff (the latter may find the appendix on pedagogy particularly helpful).

We realise that students in the twenty first-century are faced with numerous challenges and demands; it is our intention that the Handbook series should empower its readers to become effective and efficient in their studies.

Philip Tew and Steven Barfield

Foreword – *How to use this Book*

The *Continuum Shakespeare Handbook* has been designed to be read in a number of ways. The chapters can be read in sequence, from cover to cover, with each chapter adding to your knowledge of Shakespeare's times, his works, and contemporary understandings of both. However, each person studying Shakespeare has his or her own particular interests, and the early chapters have been designed so that you can 'dip in' to areas that may be of particular interest to you – and you can do this without reading all of the preceding material. You may wish to use this *Handbook* to research broader questions of religion, textual production, or urban culture in Shakespeare's England, or to find out more about particular critical approaches. There are regular 'cross-references' in brackets within the volume to help you follow your interests across, as well as within, chapters.

Shakespeare was a prolific writer and you will find references to and discussions of many, if not most, of his known works. However, the centre of gravity for this volume as a whole is the exploration of the following texts: *1 Henry IV, Twelfth Night, the Sonnets, Hamlet* and *The Tempest*. Shakespeare's works were variously published at the end of the sixteenth and the beginning of the seventeenth centuries in quarto and folio publications – for further information about these, consult the glossary towards the end of the volume which is arranged in alphabetical order. As the volume unfolds, you will notice, for example, that the first published quarto version of *Hamlet* is referred to as Q1 and the first published folio version of the play is referred to F1. When quotations from Shakespeare's works are being referenced in the critical discussions, they all refer to the following edition: Shakespeare, W. (1997), *The Norton Shakespeare*, ed. S. Greenblatt et al. New York and London: W. W. Norton (abbreviated as *Norton Shakespeare*). Thus, when you encounter a short reference such as *Pericles*, 1. 1. 82, p. 2720, this locates the quotation to Shakespeare's play *Pericles*, Act One, scene one, line 82. Where relevant, the *Handbook* will also draw your attention to a particular page in the *Norton Shakespeare*, in this case the reference draws your attention to p. 2720.

The *Handbook* opens with a historical discussion of the reception of Shakespeare's writings, beginning with his contemporaries and finishing with an account of the growth of 'professional' Shakespeare studies up until the 1980s. Succeeding chapters focus more squarely upon 'our' contemporary responses to plays and poems, amongst critics, the wider reading public, acting companies and theatre audiences.

Part I
Shakespeare's Time

1 Introduction: From Shakespeare to Shakespeare Studies

Andrew Hiscock and
Stephen Longstaffe

Shakespeare among his Contemporaries

In a prefatory text to his own drama *The White Devil* (1612), John Webster clearly indicated that Shakespeare was a force to be reckoned with by his fellow dramatists.

> [. . .] for mine own part I have ever truly cherished my good opinion of other men's worthy labours, especially of that full and heightened style of Master Chapman, the laboured and understanding works of Master Jonson: the no less worthy composures of the both worthily excellent Master Beaumont and Master Fletcher: and lastly (without wrong last to be named) the right happy and copious industry of Master Shakespeare, Master Dekker, and Master Heywood, wishing what I write may be read by their light [. . .] (Webster 2006: 6)

The cultural shaping of the ways in which we engage with Shakespeare's work thus began during his own lifetime but, as we see in Webster's survey, the 'copious industry of Master Shakespeare' was perceived as one of many strategic contributions made to the London drama scene in the early 1600s. In 'To the memory of my beloved, the author Mr. William Shakespeare' which appeared at the beginning of the *First Folio* (1623) of Shakespeare's works, Jonson celebrated the 'Soul of the Age', but Webster was much more representative of the seventeenth-century referencing of the dramatist in making him rub shoulders with his competitors like Ben Jonson, Francis Beaumont and John Fletcher. Indeed, it is worthwhile noting that in a satirical verse by one John Tatham which prefaced Richard Brome's play *A Joviall Crew or the Merry Beggars* (1652), '*Shakespeare* the *Plebean* Driller' is lumped together with 'elaborate' Jonson, and Beaumont and Fletcher who might passe 'in a dark night' (sig. A4ᵛ). Again and again it becomes apparent that for early audiences and readers, Shakespeare did not stand (as he would in later centuries) like his own Julius Caesar, 'bestrid[ing] the narrow world Like a Colossus' (1. 2. 136–37).

Interestingly, this state of affairs was often reproduced when 'Shakespeare the poet' was discussed by his contemporaries. A fellow poet, Richard Barnfield, places him in 'fames immortall Booke', alongside Spenser, Drayton and Daniel, in his lyric 'A Remembrance of some English poets' (1605: sig. G2ʳ). The so-called 'water-poet' John Taylor adopts a similar strategy in a subsection entitled 'Phylosophers, Hystorians, Chronographers, Poets ancient and moderne [. . .]' from a much longer poetic address where he celebrates Shakespeare in the company of poets such as Chaucer, Sidney and Spenser: '*Spencer*, and *Shakespeare* did in Art excell' (Taylor 1630: 322). (Taylor refrains from discussing him in his brief survey of contemporary dramatists in the same poem.) However, it seems that there were other ways in which to reflect upon Shakespeare's achievement, apart from simply celebrating his fame and genius as compared to his contemporaries. In the elegy 'The memory of my beloved [. . .]' noted above, Jonson compared the Stratford bard to the great dramatists of antiquity. The scholar Gabriel Harvey cherished the cerebral author of *Hamlet* and placed it alongside the narrative poem *The Rape of Lucrece*, finding that they both contained that which might 'please the wiser sort' (Chambers et al. 1932: 56); while in her collection *Sociable Letters* (1664), Margaret Cavendish, Duchess of Newcastle, turned particularly to questions of characterization and identification: 'Who would not think he had been such a man as his Sir *John Falstaff*? [. . .] one would think that he had been Metamorphosed from a Man to a Woman, for who could Describe *Cleopatra* Better than he hath done' (Cavendish 2004: 177).

The Seventeenth and Eighteenth Centuries

It was in the later decades of the seventeenth century that a more sustained examination of Shakespeare's achievement (and thus the birth of Shakespeare studies) may be said to have begun in earnest. Like his predecessors in the seventeenth century, when John Dryden turned his attentions in print to the achievement of Shakespeare, he could on occasions limit himself to a celebration of the dramatist's towering genius. Yet he did acknowledge that Shakespeare's plays might require 'refining' for his latter audiences, and set to work in 'adapting' *The Tempest* (with William Davenant) as *The tempest, or, The enchanted island a comedy* (1670), for example, and *Antony and Cleopatra* as *All for love, or, The world well lost, a tragedy [. . .] written in imitation of Shakespeare's stile* (1678). And in this he was not alone: Nahum Tate sought to 'rectifie' the failures of 'Regularity and Probability' with his own *History of King Lear* (1681); and Colley Cibber offered *The Tragical History of Richard III* (1700) with Shakespeare's lines italicized – so that there should be no confusion. There was certainly no confusion for the writer Fanny Burney when she perused Cibber's offering in 1773: '[Shakespeare], with all his imperfections, is too superiour to any other Dramatic Writer, for them to bear so near a comparison: &, to my Ears, every Line of Cibber's is feeble & paltry' (Burney 1988: 242).

In terms of notable critical scholarship of the age, in his *Essay of Dramatic Poesie* (1668) and his 'Essay of the Dramatic Poetry of the Last Age' (1672), Dryden shows himself much more concerned with the unwieldy creative energies of Shakespeare and his contemporaries, which, he affirms, might have realized their full potential, if they had been held in check with an attention to theatrical decorum. Elsewhere, in his preface to yet another Shakespearean adaptation, *Troilus and Cressida, or, Truth found too late, a tragedy* (1679), Dryden pursues a careful analysis of the ways in which the dramatic techniques of Shakespeare and John Fletcher might be compared and contrasted. However, he acknowledged more generally that

> The Poet *Aeschylus* was held in the same veneration by the *Athenians* of after Ages as *Shakespear* is by us [. . .] our reverence for *Shakespear* [is] much more just, then that of the *Grecians* for *Aeschylus* [. . .] [yet] it must be allow'd to the present Age, that the tongue in general is so much refin'd since *Shakespear*'s time, that many of his words, and more of his Phrases, are scarce intelligible. And of those which we understand some are ungrammatical, others coarse; and his whole stile is so pester'd with Figurative expressions, that it is as affected as it is obscure. 'Tis true, that in his later Plays he had worn off somewhat of the rust; but the Tragedy which I have undertaken to correct, was, in all probability, one of his first endeavours on the Stage [. . .] (Dryden 1679: no sig.)

Equally influential, Thomas Rymer's *A short view of tragedy its original, excellency and corruption: with some reflections on Shakespear and other practitioners for the stage* (1693) became a source of ongoing debate for decades to come. Rymer devoted much time and space to lamentations over the shortcomings of Shakespeare's and his contemporaries' dramatic art in terms of anachronism, discontinuity, illogical plotting, implausible chronologies – in short, failures to satisfy the expectations of neo-classical dramaturgy. In the next generation, Alexander Pope among many others would feel compelled to defend Shakespeare against persisting complaints concerning his 'want of learning' and the 'irregularities' of his dramatic narratives. Pope mostly countered such accusations with fulsome praise, 'The Poetry of Shakespear was Inspiration indeed: he is not so much an Imitator, as an Instrument of Nature; and 'tis not so just to say that he speaks from her, as that she speaks thro' him' (Pope 1986: 13).

More generally in the eighteenth century, the growth in the reading and scholarship surrounding Shakespeare was enormously assisted by the publication of his complete works in such editions as those of Nicholas Rowe (1709), Alexander Pope (1725), Lewis Theobald (1733), Samuel Johnson (1765), George Steevens (1773) and Edmond Malone (1790). In the case of an edition such as Johnson's, the publication not only constituted a formidable resource for those who were able to afford it: Johnson supplemented the edited play-texts with his own appraisal of each of the plays which have continued to stimulate critical debate into the modern period – 'He sacrifices virtue to convenience and is so much more careful to please than to instruct that he seems to write without any moral purpose' (Johnson 1977: 307). In addition to the appearance of these grand tomes, there were others like those by Zachary Grey entitled *Critical, historical and explanatory notes on Shakespeare, with emendations of the text and metre* (1754), and William Kenrick's *Introduction to the school of Shakespeare; held, on Wednesday evenings, in the Apollo, at the Devil Tavern, Temple Bar* (1774) – all designed to facilitate the journey of the would-be student through the corpus of the bard's works.

The debate surrounding Shakespeare's achievement continued in a host of different places and was often framed by the interventions of leading literary figures (mostly of changeable opinions). Damning the bard with faint praise in a piece for the journal *The Champion* in 1740, Henry Fielding asserted that 'Sir *John Falstaff* and his whole Gang must have given much more Entertainment to the Spectators of Queen *Elizabeth*'s Days, than to a modern Audience' (Fielding 1974: 395); and Oliver Goldsmith wrote in a similar vein for *The Critical Review* in 1759 that Shakespeare was a man 'whose beauties seem rather the result of chance than design; who, while he laboured to satisfy his audience with monsters and mummery, seemed to throw in his inimitable beauties as trifles into the bargain'. The enormously popular novelist Samuel

Richardson was not as widely read as either Fielding or Goldsmith in the literatures of the past, but he did subscribe to Theobald's 1733 edition of Shakespeare's works, and maintained a reverence for him despite finding him 'less useful' than Addison (Eaves and Kimpel 1971: 572–73). The celebrity status of major actors, such as Thomas Betterton (c. 1635–1710), David Garrick (1717–79) and Sarah Siddons (1755–1831), clearly enhanced even further the adulation devoted to works of Shakespeare: indeed, in 1769, the actor-impresario David Garrick organized a Jubilee event celebrating Shakespeare's achievement. These figures were able to shape for large theatre-going audiences of the age the ways in which they engaged with the texts, and thus their performances became critical and affective encounters in themselves, as we see from Fanny Burney's account of Garrick's Richard III in 1772:

> Garrick was sublimely horrible! – 'Good Heaven' – how he made me shudder whenever he appeared! It is inconceivable, how terribly great he is in this Character. I will never see him so disfigured again – he seemed so truly the monster he performed, that I felt myself glow with indignation every time I saw him. The Applause he met with exceeds all belief [. . .] I thought, at the End, they would have torn the House down: Our seats shook under us. (Burney 1988: 225)

Moreover, the growing popularity of the bard was acknowledged in a succession of detailed critical engagements with the plays, such as Elizabeth Montagu's *An Essay on the Writings and Genius of Shakespeare, compared with the Greek and French Dramatic Poets* (1769), Elizabeth Griffith's *The morality of Shakespeare's drama* (1775), and William Whiter's *A Specimen of a Commentary on Shakespeare* (1794).

The Nineteenth Century

By the end of the eighteenth century, a well-established cultural awareness of and veneration for the bard had become common currency in all kinds of writing surviving from the period: Mary Wollstonecraft wrote to her lover Gilbert Imlay from Paris in 1794 that 'The world appears an "unweeded garden" where "things rank and vile" flourish best' (Wollstonecraft 1979: 242); Shelley contended in his *Discourse on the Manners of the Ancient Greeks Relative to the Subject of Love* (1818) that 'Perhaps Shakespeare, from the variety and comprehension of his genius, is to be considered on the whole as the greatest individual mind of which we have specimens remaining' (Shelley 1954: 217–18); and Sir Walter Scott confided in his journal of 1826, 'The blockheads talk of my being like Shakespeare – not fit to tie his brogues' (Scott 1972: 252). Such ongoing referencing of Shakespeare exists in addition to the major contributions of Shakespearean criticism of the period to be found, for example, in Charles Lamb's *Specimens of Dramatic Poets who lived about the time of Shakespeare* (1808) and 'On the tragedies of Shakespeare' (1811); William Hazlitt's *Characters of Shakespeare's Plays* (1817); and Coleridge's voluminous notes throughout his career as a prose writer on the dramatist's achievements.

In the nineteenth century, the works of Shakespeare continued to be printed for audiences anxious to obtain his words of wisdom for their libraries and to invest in the growing cult of 'bardolatry'. In *On Heroes, Hero-Worship and the Heroic in History* (1840), Thomas Carlyle hailed Shakespeare as 'the greatest intellect who, in our recorded world, has left record of himself in the way of Literature' (Carlyle 1840: 96). However, as may be witnessed in Keats's celebrated poem 'On Sitting Down to Read *King Lear* Once Again', as the nineteenth century wore on, Shakespeare was more often than not being associated with a reading, rather than a theatrical, experience. Indeed, he was now becoming firmly ensconced in the reading programme of anyone who wished to consider him or herself educated. Charlotte Brontë wrote to her friend Ellen Nussey in 1834:

> You ask me to recommend some books for your perusal [. . .] If you like poetry let it be first rate, Milton, Shakespeare, Thomson, Goldsmith, Pope (if you will though I don't admire him), Scott, Byron, Campbell, Wordsworth and Southey [. . .] don't be startled at the names of Shakespeare and Byron. Both these were great Men and their works are like themselves [. . .] Omit the Comedies of Shakespeare [. . .] (Brontë 1995: 130)

The nineteenth century witnessed an enormous growth in Shakespeare societies across Europe, North America and around the globe. The Sheffield Shakespeare Club, for example, was established as early as 1819, and the Stratford Shakespeare Club in 1824. In 1852, the Shakspere Society of Philadelphia began life with regular meetings, whereas F. J. Furnivall founded the New Shakspere Society in Britain in 1873 whose membership included both sexes. In 1884, the Melbourne Shakespeare Society was established and so the story went on. Furthermore, readers were now able to access critical debate and appreciations of Shakespeare's writing in periodicals of the period, such as *The Edinburgh Review, The Athenaeum, The Westminster Review* and *The Nineteenth Century*. The learning programme was intense for some, as may be witnessed from George Eliot's diary entry for 14 December 1854: 'Bad headache. A regularly wet morning. Read the Athenaeum and Leader and finished Iphigenia. In the evening finished Hermann and Dorothea. Read Henry IV 2nd part. Still headachy' (Eliot 1998: 38). However, her fellow novelist Anthony Trollope appears to have adopted a more relaxed engagement with this reading matter, as he explained in a letter of 1875 to Eliot's partner,

George Henry Lewes: 'I have always fancied that Shakespeare intended Hamlet to be, not mad, but erratic in the brain, "on & off" – first a little ajar, & then right again, & then again astray' (Trollope 1951: 343).

Actors such as Edmund Kean and Henry Irving continued a distinguished tradition inherited from the previous century, devoting much time and energy enhancing their celebrity status through the interpretation of major Shakespearean roles; however, by the final decades of the century, critics such as George Bernard Shaw would pour ridicule upon the remorseless adulation offered up by 'bardolaters' and upon the creaking productions which were staged by companies more attentive to costuming and finely-painted sets than to matters of dramatic narrative. It is in this second half of the nineteenth century that a generation of Shakespeare scholars emerged as the study of 'English Literature' began to be part of the bill of fayre offered at a whole of host of learning establishments, from the working men's institutes to universities. Edward Dowden's *Shakespere. A Critical Study of His Mind and Art* (1876), Edmund Gosse's *From Shakespeare to Pope* (1885) and Sir Walter Alexander Raleigh's *Shakespeare* (1907), all indicate the beginnings of what we might now term the practice of 'Shakespeare Studies' responding to audiences within academe and beyond. Responding to the increasing demands of a growing audience, a facsimile of the 1623 *First Folio* of Shakespeare's works was reproduced in publication for readers in the 1860s, and at the end of the following decade in 1879, the Shakespeare Memorial Theatre was opened in Stratford-upon-Avon. Trollope had his own views on the matter of fundraising which had supported the venture as he explained to a friend in 1878: 'I don't care two pence for the Shakespeare Memorial [. . .] If there be any one who does not want more memorials than have been already given, it is Shakespeare!' (Trollope 1951: 392).

The Twentieth Century: the Growth in Professional Criticism

The twentieth century was the first time in history that Shakespeare Studies became predominantly the preserve of professional, full-time scholars and critics. That statement demands an immediate caveat: that the twentieth century also saw the most critically-influential stagings of Shakespeare in history. For the vast majority of the time between the deaths of Shakespeare (1616) and Henry Irving (1905), it was impossible to see a Shakespeare play on the English stage with a text resembling an early printing of it. Notwithstanding the increasingly more fastidious work of Shakespearean editors, what worked on stage was a *Lear* in which Cordelia survived and married Edgar, where *Richard III* pulled in Richard's best lines from the *Henry VI* plays (along with others specially written to enhance the part, in best 'actor-manager' style), or where performances of *A Midsummer Night's Dream* had to fit in Mendelssohn's famous early-nineteenth-century music, usually by adding dancing and other forms of spectacle.

However, the twentieth century saw the increasing influence of the director-dramaturg, a theatrical intellectual attempting to change the way audiences saw and responded to Shakespeare. John Dover Wilson, editor of *The Cambridge Shakespeare*, knew his Shakespeare backwards, and often claimed that the kind of close reading demanded of editors produced some of the best criticism. His response to Tyrone Guthrie's 1936 Old Vic production of *Love's Labour's Lost* makes it clear that some Shakespeare productions are 'Shakespeare criticism of the best kind':

> For Mr. Guthrie not only gave me a new play, the existence of which I had never suspected, which indeed had been veiled from men's eyes for three centuries, but he set me at a fresh standpoint of understanding and appreciation from which the whole of Shakespearean comedy might be reviewed in a new light. (Wilson 1962: 64)

Of course, the twentieth century (or, to be exact, the period from 1899, when a twelve-minute version of *King John* was filmed) also gave us an entirely new kind of Shakespeare – Shakespeare on film, which won its first Oscars as long ago as 1936, for the Warner Brothers' version of *A Midsummer Night's Dream* co-directed by the great Austrian theatrical director Max Reinhardt and his protégé, William Dieterle. This version of the play, though it features Hollywood stars such as Mickey Rooney and James Cagney, also has a great deal of non-Shakespearean material in the form of Mendelssohn's music, and special fairy dances put together by the Russian choreographer Bronislawa Nijinska. For theatrical geniuses like Reinhardt or Laurence Olivier (whose Shakespeare films won him two Oscars), film could be informed by theatrical traditions while bringing the medium's incomparably superior visual resources to the feast. Olivier's own Shakespeare films are often seen as 'stagey', but his opening of *Henry V* with an imagined performance of the first scenes at the Globe raises questions of just what 'truth to the original' might be in terms of film adaptations.

Bradley and Character Criticism

Despite the fact that Shakespeare Studies was still in its infancy, the first great scholarly work in this field is generally regarded as an immensely successful summing-up, and consummation, of much of the preceding century's work. A. C. Bradley's *Shakespearean Tragedy* (1904) is probably the all-time best-selling English-language work of Shakespeare criticism, and is generally regarded as the 'classic' statement of the 'character' approach to Shakespeare's plays. Bradley's work was influenced by the character-oriented work of

Romantic-era critics such as Schlegel, Coleridge and Hazlitt, though it is never simply about 'character' in the narrow sense. It would be a mistake to take *Shakespearean Tragedy* for Bradley's last word on the peaks of Shakespearean characterization: of the four characters he finds 'most wonderful', only two – Hamlet and Iago, who gets a chapter to himself in the two devoted to *Othello* – are covered. The other two – Cleopatra and Falstaff – are included in his later *Oxford Lectures on Poetry* (1909).

Bradley's earlier work sets himself the task of 'dramatic appreciation' of the tragedies: 'to learn to apprehend the action and some of the personages of each with a somewhat greater truth and intensity, so that they may assume in our imaginations a shape a little less unlike the shape they wore in the imagination of their creator' (Bradley 1904: xxv). The correct way for 'lovers of Shakespeare' to approach the tragedies is to 'read a play more or less as if they were actors who had to study all the parts. They do not need, of course, to imagine where the persons are to stand, or what gestures they ought to use; but they want to realize fully and exactly the inner movements which produced these words and no other, these deeds and no other, at each particular moment' (Bradley 1904: xxv).

Tragedies, of course, are particular kinds of plays, and Bradley's engagement with them took him away from the more general focus on the relations between characters which the above suggests, and towards a deeper concern with one, or at most two, hyper-significant (and hyper-signifying) individuals, usually the figure(s) after whom the tragedy is named. Furthermore, in Bradley's opinion the plot of a tragedy cannot be full of accidents or supernaturally-caused events, for we would then have a story of bad luck, or of unavoidable fate: 'the calamities of tragedy do not simply happen, nor are they sent; they proceed mainly from actions, and those the actions of men' (Bradley 1904: 6). These actions, in turn, are 'acts or omissions thoroughly expressive of the doer – characteristic deeds' so that 'the centre of the tragedy, therefore, may be said with equal truth to lie in action issuing from character, or in character issuing in action' (1904: 7). In other words, tragedies do not work simply either by virtue of the sad things that happen or by virtue of the interesting or affecting 'character' they happen to. The point of 'Shakespearean tragedy' (and Bradley's qualifications indicate that he is seeking to define it as different in kind to, for example, 'Greek tragedy') is how people's deeds are rooted in, and expressive of, their characters.

Bradley points out that the plot of *Hamlet*, if recounted with no reference to the main character, is both sensationalist and inexplicable, for if the ghost's command had been obeyed straight away seven of the play's eight deaths would have been avoided: 'The whole story turns upon the peculiar character of the hero', he claims (1904: 70). Hamlet's difficulty in dispatching Claudius is not 'external' (it would be easy to kill him) but 'internal', and Bradley duly considers three views of his character before dispatching them with unprincely speed because 'they isolate one element in his character and situation and treat it as a whole' (1904: 76). These are the 'conscience' view – that Hamlet had conscientious objections to vengeance; the 'sentimental' view – that Hamlet was too otherworldly and sensitive to respond to the Ghost's demands; and the 'reflective' view – that Hamlet delays because he is unable to make up his mind. Bradley, on the other hand, proposes Hamlet as a victim of 'melancholy' whose tragedy is simply that at the one time his character is tested it is hardly his own. The liveliness and pleasure with which Hamlet sometimes speaks and acts are his 'true' character for Bradley; what we would now call his mood swings between passivity and action, his 'bursts of transitory, almost hysterical, and quite fruitless emotion' are symptoms of a condition rather than the man himself (1904: 99). So too are his lethargy or apathy, and his inability to understand why he is subject to them. Bradley then tests this theory to see if it will produce a more persuasive account of the play than those proposed by rival theories. Bradley is fairly sure that the question of Hamlet's and Ophelia's 'real' relationship, for example, has an answer, because Shakespeare knew what it was. However he concedes that the only way such knowledge could be transmitted is via a production where the actors' interpretations were informed by the intentions of the writer – that is to say, a performance during Shakespeare's own lifetime: 'The actor, instructed by the author, would make it clear to us by looks, tones, gestures and byplay how far Hamlet's feigned harshness to Ophelia was mingled with real bitterness, and again how far his melancholy had deadened his love' (1904: 128).

Though Bradley's chapters on the play are Hamlet-heavy (he is of the opinion that 'all the persons in *Hamlet* except the hero are minor characters, who fail to rise to the tragic level'), his remarks on other tragedies are not concentrated solely on the tragic hero. His discussion of *Othello* begins with the blunt statement that 'the character of Othello is comparatively simple' (1904: 151); he is far more interested in Othello's deceiver and downfall, Iago. The overwhelming question to be asked of this character is simply 'why?' Bradley denies Iago's own explanations – hatred for Othello, and ambition – as springing from passions nowhere else displayed by him in the play. Instead, he attends to three elements of Iago's plot which explain its attraction for him: it confirms his own pride in his superiority, it exerts his own superior abilities, and involves danger. Here, Bradley extrapolates the origins of the plot:

Othello's eminence, Othello's goodness, and his own dependence on Othello, must have been a perpetual annoyance to him. At *any* time he would have enjoyed befooling and tormenting Othello. Under ordinary circumstances he was restrained, chiefly by self-interest, in some slight degree perhaps by the faintest pulsations of conscience or humanity. But disappointment at the loss of the lieutenancy supplied the touch of lively resentment that was required to overcome these obstacles; and the prospect of satisfying the sense of power by mastering Othello through an intricate and hazardous intrigue now became irresistible. (Bradley 1904: 187)

Here, notwithstanding its very 'modern' focus on the psychopathology of everyday murder, Bradley's ability to piece together a 'character' from some-times slight scraps topples into an example of the very fault he chastises in others. For if Bradley objects to believing Iago to be motivated by hatred of Othello because this is mentioned only in the first act, how can he then base his final verdict on Iago's motivation on things which are not part of the play at all? This misapplication of the Bradleyan method appears in a more con-centrated form in some of the notes to the book, which investigate such ques-tions as 'Did Lady Macbeth really faint?' (Bradley doesn't know, and thinks it's not likely to show in performance either way), 'Did Emilia [Iago's wife] suspect Iago?' (Bradley is in no doubt the answer is no) and 'Where was Hamlet at the time of his father's death?' (in a peculiar interpretation of the references to returning to Wittenberg early in the play, Bradley thinks Hamlet had been living at court for some years before his father's death).

Notions of what 'we' approve of in a character are notoriously the products of particular times and places, and Bradley's are no exception. Much of what he finds moving in Desdemona is linked to his perception of her as 'passive and defenceless', possessing a 'frank childlike boldness and persistency', 'a child of nature' who in her marriage 'appeared again as the sweet and sub-missive being of her girlhood' (Bradley 1904: 166, 167). He thinks that his vision of *Othello*'s artistic power entails its unstageability, for 'perhaps if we saw Othello coal-black with the bodily eye [as opposed to simply imagining him], the aversion of our blood, an aversion which comes as near to being merely physical as anything human can, would overpower our imagination and sink us below not Shakespeare only but the audiences of the seventeenth and eighteenth centuries' (1904: 165).

After publishing *Shakespearean Tragedy*, Bradley continued to work on Shakespeare, and in his *Oxford Lectures on Poetry* (1909) he tackles a problem that 'character' approaches to tragedy, by their very nature, are unable to handle: the character developed across more than one play, and the comic character, at that. In his essay on 'The Rejection of Falstaff' (which occurs when Hal becomes king at the end of 2 *Henry IV*), he develops a kind of parallel to the catharsis he traced operating in tragedy, by focusing on how we respond to the rejection of Falstaff, and what this feeling implies about the characters of both Falstaff and the King. Here, he admits a division in responses to this celebrated scene between theatre-goers (who are likely to appreciate Falstaff) and readers (who he thinks are more judgemental).

Shakespeare, Bradley thinks, could have engineered Falstaff's rejection without inclining us against king Henry; the imprisonment of Falstaff, and Henry's 'sermon' to him, are signs of the 'ungenerous' and 'insincere' individual later memorably characterized by W. H. Auden, in 'Under Which Lyre' as 'the prig Prince Hal'. He concludes that Shakespeare included Henry's rejection as part of his realistic portrayal of an effective king, but that 'in the Falstaff scenes he overshot his mark. He created so extraordinary a being, and fixed him so firmly on his intellectual throne, that when he sought to dethrone him he could not . . . The moment comes when we are to look at Falstaff in a serious light, and the comic hero is to figure as the baffled schemer; but we cannot make the required change, either in our attitude or in our sympathies' (Bradley 1909: 259–60). Falstaff, Bradley concludes, is 'immortal' as 'a character almost purely humorous, and therefore no subject for moral judgements' (1909: 260). This means, in practice, a character whose essence is a contagious enjoyment of life, offering 'the bliss of freedom gained in humour' (1909: 262). Nonetheless, he is enough of a character for Bradley to feel bounden to follow the eighteenth-century critic Morgann in defending him against accusations of cowardice, which he does by his usual method of close textual reading.

In direct comparison with all his character studies, Bradley's assessment of Falstaff is formulated by abstracting him from the dramatic structure (and in particular the dramatic sequence) in which he is typically encountered by readers and audiences. In other words, for Bradley, the rejection of Falstaff at the end of the second *Henry IV* play was counterbalanced by his representation elsewhere, just as for Morgann, Falstaff's cowardice at Gad's Hill was read in the light of the later, more valiant, Falstaff. John Dover Wilson, writing during the Second World War, rejected Bradley's vigorous interest in the 'bliss of freedom' as a late-Victorian historical curiosity, much as E. M. W. Tillyard, writing at the same time, was to oppose romantic readings of the 'disorder' of the historical plays more generally. It is not much of an exaggeration to say that the Shakespeare criticism in English produced in the first half of the twentieth century is a response to Bradleyan character study. Objections to Bradley tended to coalesce around two of his governing assumptions. The first is that the characters' thoughts and motivations were far more interesting than the words they used, and the second is that the 'human nature' on display in Shakespeare's plays is accessible to readers with no specialist knowledge about his life, times, or theatre.

Shakespeare and the Anti-Bradleyan Reaction

The pendulum started to swing against Bradley in the 1920s. Significantly, this decade saw the first major stirrings of the 'practical criticism' critical method which focused initially on poetry, and whose inventor and chief proselytiser was the Cambridge academic I. A. Richards. Practical criticism, as befitted Richards's background in linguistics and psychology, presented itself as the antidote to the subjective, feelings-validated if not feelings-driven, methods of the Romantics, and of Bradley, the last great Romantic critic. One of the most famous anti-Bradleyan responses focusing on Shakespeare's language was L. C. Knights's cheekily titled 'How many children had Lady Macbeth?', first published in 1933. Knights claimed that a Shakespeare play, far from being essentially about characters and their interrelations, was 'a dramatic poem', and it is the critic's business to examine 'the words on the page' (Knights 1946: 6). For Knights, the growth of character study in the post-Shakespearean period was symptomatic of an increasing lack of understanding of Shakespeare's English, and a concomitant inability to appreciate 'Shakespeare's plays as poetry'. Just as Bradley had criticized Coleridge's discussion of *Hamlet* for telling us more about Coleridge than about Hamlet, Knights claimed that the character of the critic was always present in 'character study'. Against this kind of subjectivism, Knights proposed a method of reading Shakespeare which insisted on the private reading experience (as opposed to Bradley's recommendation that critics should read *as if they were actors playing parts*), and which it is useful to excerpt at length:

> We start with so many lines of verse on a printed page which we read as we should read any other poem. We have to elucidate the meaning (using Dr Richards' fourfold definition) and to unravel ambiguities; we have to estimate the kind and quality of the imagery and determine the precise degree of evocation of particular figures; we have to allow full weight to each word, exploring its 'tentacular roots', and to determine how it controls and is controlled by the rhythmic movement of the passage in which it occurs. In short, we have to decide exactly why the lines 'are so and not otherwise'.
>
> As we read other factors come into play. The lines have a cumulative effect. 'Plot', aspects of 'character' and recurrent 'themes' – all 'precipitates from the memory' – help to determine our reaction at a given point. There is a constant reference backwards and forwards. But the work of detailed analysis continues to the last line of the last act. If the razor-edge of sensibility is blunted at any point we cannot claim to have read what Shakespeare wrote, however often our eyes may have travelled over the page. A play of Shakespeare's is a precise particular experience – and precision and particularity are exactly what is lacking in the greater part of Shakespeare criticism, criticism that deals with *Hamlet* or *Othello* in terms of abstractions that have nothing to do with the unique arrangement of words that constitutes these plays. (Knights 1946: 16–17)

To illustrate his remarks, Knights self-consciously proposed a 'non-dramatic' reading of *Macbeth* as 'a statement of evil' with two main themes: 'the reversal of values and of unnatural disorder' (1946: 18). Using a great deal of quotation, and attending in particular to elements such as images, symbols, values, themes, and seemingly 'irrelevant' scenes, Knights argued for a coherent work of art which was much more than an exploration of our relation to one or two 'great terrible figures'. Essentially the same approach can be found in G. Wilson Knight's *The Wheel of Fire* (1930). Knight argued for the artistic unity of the plays, which he thought was obscured by a focus on plot and character, the experience of both of which became more intense towards the end of the play. Knight, on the other hand, thinks that

> A Shakespearian tragedy is set spatially as well as temporally in the mind. By this I mean that there are throughout the play a set of correspondences which relate to each other independently of the time-sequence which is the story: such are the intuition-intelligence opposition active within and across *Troilus and Cressida*, the death-theme in *Hamlet*, the nightmare evil of *Macbeth*. This I have sometimes called the play's 'atmosphere'. (Knight 1930: 3)

There were other works which attended to the poetry of Shakespeare's plays in terms of practical criticism, such as Caroline Spurgeon's *Shakespeare's Imagery and What it Tells Us* (1935), W. H. Clemen's *Shakespeares Bilder* (1935; translated into English as *The Development of Shakespeare's Imagery*, 1951), and M. M. Mahood's *Shakespeare's Wordplay* (1957). Spurgeon's work followed the idea that particular works had distinctive sets, or 'clusters', of verbal imagery prompted by and helping to constitute its unique atmosphere; Clemen was more interested in relating imagery to specific characters and situations. A couple of examples will help to clarify how this works. Clemen pointed out that in Shakespeare's early histories, some of his earliest plays, public speeches tended to be full of self-consciously 'ornamental' illustrative proverbial images. Solo speeches or monologues in plays like *Richard II* or *Hamlet*, on the other hand, were full of imagery directly springing from Richard's or Hamlet's character.

The growing interest in close reading which accompanied scholarship on Shakespeare's poetry at this time naturally enough produced some breakthroughs in the understanding of his poems, particularly the sonnets. Even before the early days of practical criticism, Sir Sidney Lee in his 1898 biography of Shakespeare had drawn attention to the ways in which the sonnets are conventional, working and reworking others' tropes and ideas, and therefore do not offer us access to the 'real' Shakespeare. Bradley's response to Lee was to claim that the 'story' of the sonnets, taken together, is 'very odd and unattractive', and that this must be because it is essentially true, as 'no capable poet, much less a Shakespeare, intending to produce a merely "dramatic" series of poems, would dream of inventing a story like that of these sonnets' (Bradley 1909: 331). The antithesis to Bradley's focus on the sonnets' 'story' was provided by the poets Robert Graves and Laura Riding, who produced in the 1920s a bravura reading of Sonnet 129, focusing on its first printing in 1609. They show how the commonly anthologized 'edited' version of the twentieth century altered the number of syllables ('murdrous' becomes 'murderous', for example), obscured some original sound patterns (because as our pronunciation has changed, so has our spelling, and we regularize Shakespeare to fit this), and re-punctuated the poem, removing ambiguities and drastically slowing down and over-clarifying its ambiguities (the 1609 version has twenty commas and two full stops; the modernized version has eighteen commas, two full stops, one colon and nine semi-colons) (Jones 1977: 63–70). In addition, Shakespeare's plays as well as the sonnets formed a major point of reference in Richards's student William Empson's *Seven Types of Ambiguity* (1930), which insisted that 'resolving' ambiguities (as Bradley typically attempted to in his discussions of the plays) ignored the precise form of their expression *as* ambiguities.

Historicising Shakespeare

The second major development in Shakespeare studies in the first half of the twentieth century, and one much more obviously enabled by the growing 'professionalization' of it, especially in the United States, was historicism. The bedrock of any attempt to understand a work 'in its own time' is scholarship, and the first two-thirds of the century, in particular, saw major advances in archivally based scholarship. The latter in its detail and comprehensiveness surpassed anything which had been produced before: E. K. Chambers's four volumes on *The Elizabethan Stage* (1923), and W. W. Greg's four-volume *A Bibliography of Printed Drama to the Restoration* (1939–59) were complemented by many other contributions to textual and editorial study: A. W. Pollard's many works on Shakespeare's quarto and folio texts; G. E. Bentley's seven volumes on *The Jacobean and Caroline Stage* (1941–68); Chambers's two volumes on *William Shakespeare: A Study of Facts and Problems* (1930); T. W. Baldwin's *The Organization and Personnel of the Shakespeare Company* (1927); Baldwin's two-volume study of Shakespeare's education and reading in *William Shakspere's Small Latine and Lesse Greeke* (1944); Harbage's *Shakespeare's Audience* (1941).

One of the earliest major critical projects to benefit from this increase in knowledge was Harley Granville-Barker's series of *Prefaces to Shakespeare*. Granville-Barker had worked with William Poel, who from 1895 had produced in London a range of Shakespeare performances using at least some 'original' stage conditions – bare stage, minimal or no scenery, an ensemble rather than 'star' system, minimal alterations to the text and rapid scene changes. Granville-Barker produced several Poel-like 'original' stagings of Shakespeare plays in the years preceding the First World War. His *Prefaces* (1927–47) combine Bradleyan character analysis with a strong architectural sense (Barker was a successful actor and dramatist as well as producer and director), the latter informed by an awareness of current textual and staging scholarship. His long *Preface to Hamlet*, for example, devotes more space to 'the nature of the play', its 'action', its 'movements', its verse and prose and its relationship to the first quarto than it does to the characters. As a man of the theatre, Barker's advice was to 'gain Shakespeare's effects by Shakespeare's means when you can; for, plainly, this will be the better way. But gain Shakespeare's effects; and it is your business to discern them' (Granville-Barker 1930: 23). The Romantic separation of the transcendent genius of Shakespeare from the theatrical and intellectual milieu of his time was decisively challenged by the work of critics such as M. C. Bradbrook. Her *Themes and Conventions of Elizabethan Tragedy* (1935) provided plenty of material for showing the continuity between Shakespeare and other writers in such matters as speech conventions or stock characterization. John Dover Wilson similarly challenged the Bradleyan view of Falstaff in his *The Fortunes of Falstaff* (1943) by using both stage history and intellectual history to indicate that, whatever his attractions for an audience, he would originally have been seen as something to be overcome by Hal on his way to the crown. The Elizabethans, with long memories of the civil war of the preceding century, were not as keen on Falstaff as late-Victorian critics in the midst of a Pax Britannica. Falstaff, in other words, cannot be abstracted from the plays in which he appears with Hal, whose development is their structural centre; the fat knight's rejection may not be pleasant, but it is just.

Writing at the same time as Wilson, E. M. W. Tillyard agreed that Bradley's values were of an age, not for all time:

> The school of criticism that furnished him with a tender heart and condemned the Prince for brutality in turning him away was deluded. Its delusion will probably be accounted for, in later years, through the facts of history. The sense of security created in nineteenth-century England by the predominance of the British navy induced men to rate that very security too cheaply and to exalt the instinct of rebellion above its legitimate station. They forgot the threat of disorder which was ever present with the Elizabethans. Schooled by recent events we should have no difficulty now in taking Falstaff as the Elizabethans took him. (Tillyard 1944: 296)

Tillyard's book *Shakespeare's History Plays*, from which the above quotation is taken, can be taken as the high-water mark of early- to mid-century historicism. Tillyard, like Wilson and others, sought to situate Shakespeare as a conventional thinker, at one with the political and cosmological truths of his age, and seeking to exemplify in his histories the political principles embodied in the pre-history of his own, Elizabethan, state. These principles were, broadly, that the story of English history from Richard II to the Tudors was of a crime against nature (Richard's deposition) destroying the political equilibrium for several generations until Elizabeth's grandfather came to the throne. But Tillyard is not seeking to cut Shakespeare down to the size of the commonplaces of his age. In his sequence of history plays, Tillyard finds Shakespeare creating the first 'English epic' worthy to stand next to those of Homer or Virgil; and in the *Henry IV* plays he finds – in a way Bradley could not have recognized – the whole to be definitely greater than the sum of its parts:

I have used the word epic to describe *Henry IV* but I do not mean that this epithet is merited simply through the English local colour. It is only the intense, the tragic, the agelong that can give the temporary and the local the necessary dignity. Without the eternal character of Achilles the mere life as lived in the *Iliad* would not be raised to epic height. In *Henry IV*, as I have remarked, there is nothing tragic, nothing to correspond to the greatest things in the *Iliad*; but there are other things that serve. First, there are the agelong types, the fool, the adventurer, the 'unofficial self', assembled in the character of Falstaff. Secondly, there is the great contrast . . . between the theme of civil war, the terrible vicissitudes of high politics, and the theme of the perennial cycles of ordinary life and their persistent rhythms: the cycles of birth and death; and of the seasons with their appropriate tasks, without which man simply cannot exist. Thus it is that the great variety of *Henry IV*, unequalled in Shakespeare, is given a coherence very different indeed from the coherence of Shakespearean tragedy but in its own way not inferior. (Tillyard 1944: 309)

Tillyard's vision of Shakespeare's vision was to become to the second half of the century what Bradley's had been to the first: almost continually in print, dominant for a generation, derided, defended, resurrected, but rarely ignored. It would not be until the 1980s that a 'new' historicism emerged from under his shadow. Elsewhere, pioneering work by C. L. Barber and Northrop Frye, in particular, changed the way in which critics thought about the comedies, and Jan Kott's Samuel Beckett-inspired readings of Shakespeare's plays, conceived under Eastern European communism, provided a distinctively European, post-atomic, post-Holocaust perspective for the 1960s. Work in disciplines such as philosophy, anthropology, linguistics and theatre studies helped produce new approaches. Most obviously, a new interest in social and political change, produced a range of self-consciously politically engaged critics – whose interest in early modern tragedy was stirred not because it was 'Shakespearean' but because, in Jonathan Dollimore's resounding title of one of the most influential critical books of the 1980s, it was *radical tragedy*.

Shakespearean Timeline

Peter Sillitoe

Date	Historical/Political	Literary/Cultural
1290	Edict expelling Jews from England issued by Edward I	
1517	Martin Luther's *Ninety-Five Theses on the Power of Indulgences*	
1527	Holy Roman Emperor, Charles V, invades and sacks Rome	
1534	England breaks with Catholic Church; Act of Supremacy; Subsidy Act	
1534	Archbishop Cranmer's *First Book of Homilies* being written	
1536	Act of the Ten Articles	
1536	Dissolution of monasteries begins	
1540	Monasticism at an end in England	
1547	Death of Henry VIII, accession of Edward VI	
1547	*First Book of Homilies* issued	
1547	Lord Protector Somerset invades Scotland	
1549	Book of Common Prayer introduced	
1551	Company of Merchant Adventurers founded	
1553	Death of Edward VI, names Lady Jane Grey as successor	
1553	Accession of Mary Tudor	
1555	Muscovy Company founded	

1558–1603 Reign of Elizabeth I
Dates for composition of Shakespeare's works are approximate unless otherwise indicated.

Date	Historical/Political	Literary/Cultural
1558	Charter of the Company of Stationers confirmed by Queen Elizabeth	
1559	Mary, Queen of Scots, asserts her right to the English throne	
1560	Stationers' Company petitions successfully for livery	
1560	Elizabeth's visit to Hampshire: the first of her recorded Progresses	
1562	Elizabeth contracts smallpox	
1564		Birth of Shakespeare
1565	Elizabeth resumes marriage negotiations with Charles, Archduke of Austria	
1572	St Bartholomew's Day Massacre in Paris	

Date	Historical/Political	Literary/Cultural
1574		Royal licence for theatre company granted to Robert Dudley, Earl of Leicester
1576		James Burbage secures lease in Shoreditch for construction of The Theatre
1578	Elizabeth's Progress through East Anglia	
1579	Elizabeth commences marriage arrangements with the Duke of Alençon	
1581	Laws and fines directed at those refusing to conform to the modes of worship of the Elizabethan Church, especially recusant Catholics Ralegh returns from Ireland Levant Company chartered	
1582		Shakespeare marries Anne Hathaway on 28 November
1583	Venice Company chartered	Birth of Susanna Shakespeare, daughter to William and Anne
1585	Elizabeth allows 'volunteers' to fight in the Netherlands against the imperial forces of Catholic Spain	Birth of Hamnet and Judith Shakespeare, twins to William and Anne
1585–92		The 'lost years' in the Shakespearean biography: little surviving archival evidence available
1587	Execution of Mary Queen of Scots Francis Drake raids Spanish port of Cadiz	Leicester's theatre company tours England with a stop in Stratford-upon-Avon
1588	Spanish Armada defeated	Thomas Hariot's *True Report of the New Found Land of Virginia* published
1589	Elizabeth continues to incur huge military expenses in the conflict with Spain	*Henry VI, Part 1* Richard Hakluyt's *Principall Navigations . . . of the English Nation* published
1590		*Henry VI, Parts 2 and 3, Edward III* (Shakespeare's involvement in this play debated; may date from as late as 1595) *The Two Gentleman of Verona* (possibly 1591) John White's engravings to Hariot's *True Report* published by Theodore de Bry
1591		*The Taming of the Shrew* (possibly 1592), *The Comedy of Errors, Richard III, Titus Andronicus* (with George Peele)
1592	Plague in London, intermittent outbreaks for the next two years	Closure of the London playhouses, owing to severe outbreak of plague (until 1594) Shakespeare almost certainly working on *Venus and Adonis* and *The Rape of Lucrece* in this period Playwright Robert Greene attacks Shakespeare in *Groatsworth of Wit* as an 'upstart crow' Shakespeare mentioned in ledgers of a London theatre company

Date	Historical/Political	Literary/Cultural
1593	Richard Hooker's *Laws of Ecclesiastical Politie* in four books (Book V in 1597)	Printing of Q1 of *Venus and Adonis*
1594	Rodrigo Lopes executed for trying to poison Queen Elizabeth	*Love's Labour's Lost* (possibly 1595) Q1 of *Henry VI, Part 2* printed as *The First Part of the Contention of the Two Famous Houses of York and Lancaster* Printing of Q1 for *Titus Andronicus* Printing of *The Rape of Lucrece* in Quarto form
1595	1000 apprentices march toward Tower Hill Martial law enforced Hugh O'Neill, Earl of Tyrone, in open rebellion against English rule in Ireland	*Richard II, Romeo and Juliet, A Midsummer Night's Dream* Printing of *Henry VI, Part 3* as the octavo *The True Tragedy of Richard Duke of York and the Good King Henry the Sixth* Philip Sidney's *The Defence of Poesie* published
1596		*King John, The Merchant of Venice* Printing of Q1 of *Edward III* Death of Hamnet Shakespeare
1597		*Henry IV, Parts 1 and 2, The Merry Wives of Windsor* (possibly 1598) Printing of Q1 of *Richard II*, Q1 of *Richard III* and Q1 of *Romeo and Juliet* Shakespeare purchases New Place in Stratford
1598		*Much Ado about Nothing* (possibly 1599) Possible date for first performance of the now lost *Love's Labour's Won* Printing of Q2 of *Love's Labour's Lost* (Q1 now lost) Printing of Q1 and Q2 of *Henry IV, Part 1* Shakespeare performs in Jonson's *Every Man in His Humour*
1599	Robert Devereux, Second Earl of Essex, lands in Ireland with 16,000 men	*Henry V, Julius Caesar, As You Like It* (possibly as early as 1598, or as late as 1600) Printing of Q2 of *Romeo and Juliet* (a more reliable text than Q1) Building of the Globe Theatre
1600	East India Company chartered	*Hamlet* (possibly later, c. 1601) Printing of Q1 of *A Midsummer Night's Dream*, Q1 of *The Merchant of Venice*, Q1 of *Henry IV, Part 2*, Q1 of *Much Ado About Nothing* and Q1 for *Henry V*
1601	Men knighted in the field by Essex account for half of all English knights Failed uprising by the Earl of Essex. Conspirators witness a performance of *Richard II*, almost certainly the play by Shakespeare Execution of Essex Elizabeth addresses her last Parliament	*Twelfth Night* Death of John Shakespeare, father to William

Date	Historical/Political	Literary/Cultural
1602		*Troilus and Cressida* (possibly 1601) Printing of Q1 of *The Merry Wives of Windsor* Shakespeare buys land in Stratford (107 acres)
1603–25 Reign of James I		
1603	Death of Elizabeth I and end of the Tudor dynasty Accession of James VI of Scotland to the English throne and the beginning of the Stuart dynasty in England	*Measure for Measure* Shakespeare's playing company (the Chamberlain's Men) becomes the King's Men Printing of Q1 of *Hamlet* Shakespeare probably at work on the collaborative *Sir Thomas More* (possibly in 1604) Shakespeare performs in Jonson's *Sejanus*
1604	Hampton Court Conference in January	*Othello* (possibly as early as 1603), *All's Well that Ends Well* Printing of Q2 of *Hamlet*
1604	England at peace with Spain	
1604–07	Ongoing talks over the union of England and Scotland	
1605	The Gunpowder Treason / Plot	*King Lear, Timon of Athens* (with Thomas Middleton) Francis Bacon's *The Advancement of Learning*
1606		*Macbeth, Antony and Cleopatra* (possibly 1607)
1607		*Pericles* (possibly 1608) Susanna Shakespeare marries John Hall
1608		*Coriolanus* Printing of First Quarto of *King Lear* Shakespeare sues John Addenbrooke for £6.00 Death of Shakespeare's mother, Mary Shakespeare
1609	Virginia Company chartered Robert Cecil garners £7000 for the fiscal year	*The Winter's Tale*, publication of *The Sonnets*, including 'A Lover's Complaint' Printing of Q1 of *Troilus and Cressida* and Q1 of *Pericles*
1610		*Cymbeline*
1611	Publication of the King James Bible	*The Tempest*
1612	Death of Prince Henry	Shakespeare involved in a legal dispute (Belott v Mountjoy)
1613	Princess Elizabeth marries Frederick, Elector Palatine	*King Henry VIII / All is Well, The Two Noble Kinsmen* (both with John Fletcher; *Kinsmen* possibly as late as 1614) The Globe burns down Shakespeare purchases property in Blackfriars, London
1614		Walter Ralegh's *History of the World*

Date	Historical/Political	Literary/Cultural
1615–16		Between January 1615 and January 1616 Shakespeare completes his will
1616		Death of Shakespeare Publication of the *Workes* of both Ben Jonson and King James Judith Shakespeare marries Thomas Quiney
1619	Death of Queen Anna of Denmark Dulwich College founded by Edward Alleyn	
1620	*Mayflower* leaves England for the New World	
1622		Printing of Q1 of *Othello*
1623		Death of Anne Shakespeare (Anne Hathaway) Publication of the First Folio (the first attempt at a collected works of Shakespeare)
1625	Death of James I; accession of King Charles I	
1625–49 Reign of Charles I		
1634		Printing of Q1 of *The Two Noble Kinsmen*

2 Historical Contexts for the Age of Shakespeare

William E. Engel

Chapter Overview

Telling History, Then and Now

Ten 'Histories' are listed in the 'Catalogue' of plays attributed to Shakespeare in the First Folio of 1623 (see Glossary). Like many of the sources he consulted, the Tudor royal line is shown in a favourable light. This is not surprising when we consider that the first of these plays, *King John*, was first performed at a time of heightened national pride, a few years after the defeat of the Spanish Armada. Each presents cautionary lessons about the political evils of factional dissension and the virtues of civic peace.

History and theatre were closely linked in the minds of Shakespeare's audience. Contemporary writers and statesmen, such as Walter Ralegh in his *History of the World* (1614), referred to people as 'tragicall actors' in a 'Great Theatre' overseen by God's Providence. This allegorical view of history builds on the earlier medieval notion of there being three domains of knowledge: Philosophy, with the corresponding human faculty of Reason; Poetry, whose faculty is Imagination; and History, corresponding to Memory. Philip Sidney discussed these branches of knowledge in precisely these terms in *The Defence of Poesie* (1595), as did Francis Bacon in *The Advancement of Learning* (1605). Philosophy concerned the wise words of the ancients expressed as *sententiae* (see Glossary); poetry brought forth precepts of ethical conduct using similes and allegories; and history concerned *exempla* (see Glossary), or the exemplary deeds of eminent men and women – the good to be imitated and the bad to be shunned. This moral dimension of history was not lost on Shakespeare. For example, Prince Hal wrestles to break free from the roguish charm of Falstaff, goes on to promise his father 'for the time will come / That I shall make this northern youth [Hotspur] exchange / His glorious deeds for my indignities', and ends up saving the Crown and redeeming his own reputation (*1 Henry IV*, 3. 2. 144–46, p. 1198).

Unlike the expectations, Shakespeare's audience had about the value of history as a moral mirror, the aim of this survey is to identify the pressures of the day – mainly religious, political, economic and social – that provide insight into the increasingly urban world in which Shakespeare found himself. This approach can be compared to using barometric readings to explain changes in weather patterns. And yet, as Ernst Cassirer cautioned, it is 'the rules of semantics, not the laws of nature, that are the general principles of historical thought. History is included in the field of hermeneutics, not that of natural science' for 'facts themselves are not immediately given to the historian. They are not observable like physical or chemical facts; they must be reconstructed' (Cassirer 1992: 195). Indeed, such facts are impregnated with interpretation, and so we must constantly be alert to what kinds of facts tend to come forward in any historical account.

Behind every 'fact' resides a series of decisions that the historian has assumed will best tell the story he or she would relate. What informs such decisions? In the case of Shakespeare, rather than tell the story of 'the life and times of a great man', I have elected to present a survey of what current historians have found to be at once typical and remarkable about the cultural conditions contributing to the rhythm of life in the state and communities within which Shakespeare lived and about which he wrote. 'Religious Change' is discussed first because these changes had consequences for economics, foreign policy, domestic and court politics, and even marriage negotiations. This is not to say definitively that the one caused the other, but rather to invite readers to consider the extent to which each of these considerations can be seen as mutually influencing or reinforcing the effects of the other in a dynamic manner that has left retrievable traces for us to follow and use.

Religious Change

Religion exerted a decisive and powerful pressure on daily life throughout the sixteenth century. The century into which Shakespeare was born saw a decisive split within Western European Christianity into opposing 'churches', with 'Protestant' Christians, mainly from northern Europe, breaking from the mostly more southern 'Catholic' Christian communities who accepted the spiritual authority of the Pope. At times the rivalry between Catholics and Protestants reached violent proportions: however, more often than not in Continental Europe, these conflicts owed more to political motives, ancestral rivalries and dynastic factions than to deeply felt religious convictions. Doctrinal disputes became more a part of the social equation in England and Scotland as radical Protestant ideas gained strength among those who believed that the Reformation had not gone far enough to eliminate doctrinal and ceremonial aspects of Catholicism ('the Old Faith') – such as the veneration of saints, the adoration of Mary, and singing masses for the dead to ease their way from Purgatory (see Glossary) to Heaven.

Many of Shakespeare's plays are implicated in these conflicts and negotiations. In 1517 one of the leading reformers on the continent, Martin Luther, had published his *Ninety-Five Theses on the Power of Indulgences* which attacked, among other abuses of the Church, the selling of pardons for the remission of sins and for the release of souls from punishment in Purgatory. This document was posted on the doors of the Castle Church in Wittenberg on 31 October 1517 where the Saxon ruler Frederick III had accumulated Europe's largest collections of holy relics of the saints, which were believed to have miraculous powers. That Hamlet is returning from his studies in Wittenberg for his father's funeral subtly links him to Protestant views on Purgatory. If there is no Purgatory, Hamlet rightly must question, from where did his father's ghost come to warn him about the treachery and treason of his usurping uncle?: 'What may this mean, / That thou, dead corpse, again in complete steel, / Revisits thus the glimpses of the moon, / Making night hideous, and we fools of nature / So horridly to shake our disposition / With thoughts beyond the reaches of our souls?' (*Hamlet*, 1. 4. 32–37, p. 1683). This crisis of knowledge has deep political implications in the play, and dramatically refracts the wider negotiations of faith at the time.

Roots of the Reformation in England

Long before Shakespeare's time there had been religious controversies surrounding those who urged Christians to return to the Bible as a source for beliefs and practices. For instance of these we may return to Chaucer's day with John Wycliffe's English version of the Bible, and the biblical focus of the teachings of the Lollards, whose strongest support was in London and East Anglia, Bristol and the Midlands. With this cultural context of repeated appeals for religious reform, and with the growth of Christian humanism (see Glossary), inspired by Erasmus and others, England was being exposed to calls for religious change from a host of difference directions (see Streete, this volume, Chapter 7). It is noteworthy that only one bishop, John Fisher of Rochester, opposed Henry VIII's break with the Catholic Church. The progress of religious change across the country was nevertheless slow and hesitant, despite expressions of official support and injunctions. The beliefs and piety associated with Roman Catholicism remained a powerful cultural influence among ordinary people, the gentry and aristocracy (Duffy 2005: 401–7).

Henry VIII and the Church of England

England's break with the Catholic Church took place in 1534. Henry VIII had petitioned the pope for an 'annulment' of his marriage to Catherine of Aragon (who originally had been married to his older brother, Arthur – see Genealogy). Notwithstanding detailed religious arguments and biblical precedents justifying this action, Pope Clement VII could hardly sanction the divorce (as Catherine was the maternal aunt of Charles V, the powerful head of the Holy Roman Empire, who in 1527 had sacked Rome and made the Pope his prisoner). With the help of Thomas Cromwell, who took over the cause after the fall of his former master Cardinal Wolsey, Henry had himself declared Head of the Church of England by the English Parliament.

Henry asserted his control over the church as well as the country by having Parliament pass the Act of Supremacy in December 1534. When he encountered resistance, the ageing and increasingly irascible king did not hesitate to execute dissenters, such as Bishop Fisher and the renowned humanist and statesman Thomas More; and, in 1536, to issue the Act of the Ten Articles. This was the first set of doctrinal mandates of the new church in which, of the seven sacraments, only baptism, penance and communion were retained. Cromwell was made 'vice-regent', empowered to issue injunctions to the bishops. He required that clergymen in their sermons defend the royal supremacy and condemn pilgrimages to holy sites, a Catholic practice associated with the gaining of 'merit' in the search for salvation. His second set of injunctions two years later went further by prohibiting rituals and beliefs not justified by Scripture and by placing a Bible in English in every church. The most notable of these changes called for the stripping of images of veneration from the churches and forbade the burning of candles for saints and the dead. Not every parish was quick to comply, but periodic visits by church officials sought to establish a widespread conformity. Still, we must reflect that 'conformity in itself implies nothing about the beliefs of clergy, wardens, or laity in the parishes' (Duffy 2005: 481).

Religious Change in Stratford-upon-Avon

At least by 1564, the year of Shakespeare's birth, the wall painting in the Guild Chapel at Stratford-upon-Avon depicting the story of St Helena

---

and the True Cross had been plastered over. Shakespeare's father, John, a glover and dealer in related commodities who had been prominent in local affairs, eventually becoming bailiff and justice of the peace, served as the chamberlain acting on behalf of the town corporation's decision to cover up this image.

When the Dissolution of the Monasteries began in 1536, lands and revenues formerly belonging to the Church went to the Crown. Estimates put this transfer as high as one-fifth to one-third of all the land in England. It was only in the North that these policies met with armed resistance, most notably in Lincolnshire, and later in Yorkshire with the so-called 'Pilgrimage of Grace'. However, these rebellions were not simply a matter of religion, for they came after two years of dearth, bad weather and poor harvests, as well as in the wake of the added tax burden associated with the Subsidy Act of 1534 (Fletcher & MacCulloch 1997: 35–36). At all events by 1540 monasticism was over in England, and the Crown realized a profit of about £1.3 million (Elton 1991: 143). Nonetheless, it should be stressed that at the time of Henry's death in 1547 the Church did not yet look Protestant, and few 'would have noticed many changes in the day-to-day practice of their religion' (Newcombe 1995: 2).

The Protectorate: Edward VI

It was not until the reign of Henry's only son, Edward VI, just nine years old on his accession, that the Church of England became noticeably Protestant with the introduction of Thomas Cranmer's Book of Common Prayer in 1549. The latter substituted English for the Latin of the Mass and expressed a theology based on justification by faith, the central tenet of Protestantism. The first *Book of Homilies* was issued in 1547, some of its contents having been composed as early as 1534 by Archbishop Cranmer, one of Edward's godfathers. Edward's political affairs were in large measure directed by Edward Seymour (brother of Henry VIII's third wife), the Earl of Hertford and later Duke of Somerset. At Henry's death, Seymour had been named the 'Protector and Governor' of Edward's person. When the boy-king died in 1553 his 'Device for the Succession' named as heir his Protestant cousin Lady Jane Grey rather than his Catholic half-sister Mary. This had been prompted by the then acting Protector, John Dudley, Earl of Warwick and later Duke of Northumberland, who ruled the country in the last years of Edward VI's reign. His son, Guildford Dudley, was married to Jane Grey. The dissolution and sale of chantry chapels (chapels set up as a place to pray for the souls of the founders) enriched many of the landed class, including those closest to the king.

Mary Tudor: 'Bloody Mary'

When Mary, the daughter of Catherine of Aragon, came to the throne in 1553, it was expected she would maintain the religion of Edward VI (Guy 1988: 226). Her succession was the result of allegiance to the Crown and its hereditary heirs on the part of both the English people and the principal state policy-makers.

Mary's restoration of Catholicism and the repeal of anti-papal laws were guided in part by her marriage to Philip II of Spain – a union not accepted by Parliament. The burning of bishops Cranmer, Ridley and Latimer at Oxford after their condemnation as heretics understandably won many over to the Protestant cause who otherwise might have tolerated the return to the 'Old Religion'. Though later Protestant chroniclers would label her 'Bloody Mary' for her persecution of Protestants, fewer than three hundred people were burned at the stake for religious non-conformity during her reign. This number pales in comparison to the death toll of Protestants and Catholics during the French Wars of Religion (1562–98). Religious persecution continued under Elizabeth I. Over two hundred Catholics were executed by Elizabeth's government, ostensibly for treason as they were mostly priests charged with being loyal to a foreign ruler, the Pope, rather than to the queen.

Elizabeth's Middle Way

Soon after her accession in 1558, Elizabeth, by action of Parliament, restored the Royal Supremacy over the English Church, appointed Protestants as bishops, and reintroduced the English Prayer Book. Eventually, she authorized Protestant teachings with the Thirty-Nine Articles. This period also saw a more pronounced split among Protestants with the rise of a movement seeking to purify the English Church. The Puritans, as they were known, maintained that the break with Rome was not enough: they wanted to get rid of the bishops and to simplify the liturgy. Maintaining that worldly glitter detracted from proper worship, they wanted to remove the outward trappings of worship not mentioned in the Bible, such as vestments and religious decorations of all kinds.

Gradually, after the papal excommunication of Elizabeth in 1570 and the introduction of undercover Catholic missionary priests into England, fines and other penalties were imposed on those who continued to practise Roman Catholicism. However, Catholics, especially families long confirmed in their faith, still risked hearing the mass sung in secret, whether in chapels in remote parts of their estates or hidden at the heart of their ancestral homes. Some, such as the Arundels and Treshams, regularly paid the heavy fines levied for not showing up at the parish where they had been assigned to hear state-sanctioned services of religious worship. Those who thus absented themselves came to be known as 'recusant Catholics'. Portable communion sets still survive which were carried by itinerant priests, many of the Jesuit order who had been sent to England expressly for the purpose of nurturing the faithful. Many English Catholics willingly risked death to embrace martyrdom for their faith.

The relatively benign treatment of the Catholics in the opening years of Elizabeth's reign changed in response to the Revolt of the Northern Earls (1569) led by Charles Neville, 6th Earl of Westmorland, and Thomas Percy, 7th Earl of Northumberland. This uprising sought the deposition of Elizabeth and the cause was further assisted in 1570 with Pius V's bull, or official pronouncement, calling for Elizabeth's excommunication and deposition. An Act of Parliament of 1581 'equated the activities of priests with treason and imposed the monthly fine of £20, directed against the leading Catholic laity, on those refusing to attend their parish church (Sheils 2004: 255). Still, Elizabeth, who preferred not to make windows into another's soul, and who had both crucifix and candles in her own private chapel, sought a middle way between the extremes.

Richard Hooker's *Laws of Ecclesiastical Politie* (1593, 1597) clarified just such a path. Not only did he set the terms of future discussions of Anglican theology but he also articulated how it should proceed. His rhythmic prose moves gracefully from arguments grounded in Greek philosophy to the simple faith of the primitive Christians, all in the hope of uniting English Christians in a state Church that did not reject Catholic forms simply because they had been used in the medieval Church and that held to a reformed faith that all Protestants, including Puritans, could embrace.

Still there were some factions at court who feared Catholic plots. Mary, Queen of Scots, under English house arrest for nearly twenty years, was executed on 8 February 1587 for her involvement in a plot to depose Elizabeth and place herself on the throne. Much of the credit for presenting Elizabeth with the evidence she required to sign the death warrant of her cousin and a queen goes to Francis Walsingham's well-developed intelligence and counter-espionage operations, which included cracking the code of Mary's clandestine correspondence (Hayes 1992: 70). And yet, for all the 'myths about its intelligence service, the greatest weakness of the Elizabethan government in formulating foreign policy was its failure to appreciate the divisions within the Catholic world' (Adams 2002: 201). Though English Protestant paranoia about Catholic plots was often intense, the Catholic world was also divided amongst itself, something appreciated more fully by Elizabeth's successor, James.

Although Jews officially were expelled from England in 1290 – except for those allowed by the Crown to reside in the *Domus Conversorum* (House of Conversion) in London – by the mid-sixteenth century there were, by most estimates, several hundred, who had settled around the country in various trades. Some Jews even found employment within the households of the nobility, though never attaining high rank or status. One such man was Rodrigo Lopes, a 'morrano' (see Glossary). Lopes was a forced convert under the Portuguese Inquisition who came to London because of its ostensible toleration. He served as physician to Robert Dudley (first Earl of Leicester and Elizabeth's long-time favourite at court), Francis Walsingham (head of Elizabeth's Intelligence service and master of counter-espionage), and eventually Queen Elizabeth herself. Despite, or perhaps because of, his high connections at court, in 1594 he was tried and executed for trying to poison the Queen, a victim of anti-Spanish sentiment as much as of the anti-Semitism of the day.

Jews at the Elizabethan Court and Theatres

Rodrigo Lopes, a Jewish convert to Christianity who had fled the Inquisition and settled in England, eventually became the English court physician. He was tried and executed in 1594 allegedly for trying to poison the Queen. Capitalizing on the nationalist public sentiment in and around London, The Lord Admiral's Men revived Christopher Marlowe's play *The Jew of Malta* with the pre-eminent tragedian Edward Alleyn in the lead role. Sometime after 1596 Shakespeare's company had a new play with a Jew as the antagonist, *The Merchant of Venice*.

King James and the Bible

Elizabeth's successor, James Stuart, the son of Mary, Queen of Scots, was raised as a Protestant in Presbyterian Scotland and took matters of religion seriously (Patterson 2000: 38–39).[1] As an indirect consequence of James having called a conference at Hampton Court in 1604 to see what needed to be done to ensure the smooth operations of the Church, a council of divines and scholars was convened to oversee an 'Authorised' translation of the English Bible. This enormously influential work owed a large debt to William Tyndale's 1524 translation of the New Testament, the first time any part of the Bible had been printed in English. 'If any individual is to be credited with the perfection of the English used by Shakespeare, then he was Tyndale' (Collinson 2002: 223). Although Tyndale repeatedly petitioned the king to license a version of the Bible in the vernacular and was close to reaching an agreement brokered by Cromwell, his efforts came to a halt when he was burned as a heretic in Antwerp (Lockyer 2005: 65).

Defenders of the Faith

William Tyndale completed his translation of the New Testament in voluntary exile in Germany. Along with other Lutheran books, it was burned in public bonfires shortly after Henry VIII had been acclaimed 'Fidei Defensor' (Defender of the Faith) by Pope Leo X. This title is still claimed by the reigning English monarch, though it now refers, of course, to Anglicanism.

The resulting 'King James Bible' of 1611 was free of the polemical marginal notes of the Geneva Bible, and thus was decidedly less militant (see Longstaffe, this volume, Chapter 3). The Geneva Bible, translated in the safety of Continental Europe by refugees from Mary's regime, reflected the rigorous theological views of austere reformers, most notably the Geneva-based John Calvin. The Geneva version was favoured by Englishmen with Puritan leanings, especially the separatist 'Pilgrims' who fled to Leyden and then made their way to the American colonies on the *Mayflower* in 1620.

Commercial and Military Exchanges

Monopolies

The colonies were established with commercial rather than religious ambitions in mind. They were part of a larger, though by no means systematic, programme of economic development. For Elizabeth's administration, this programme also involved reaping the benefits of selling monopolies, or exclusive trading rights and the fixing of prices, both as a way of enriching her coffers and of keeping her courtiers in line. Following his return from Ireland in 1581, Sir Walter Ralegh, an advocate of the anti-Spanish foreign policies of Leicester and Walsingham, was greatly enriched by being named 'Lord Warden of the Stanneries' which placed him in receipt of revenue from all of the mining towns of Dartmoor. This gave him absolute control over the trade in tin and related metals and ores. Shortly thereafter he was entrusted to go to Dartmouth to divide the spoils of the seven-decked Spanish ship, *Madre de Deos*, captured by Sir John Borough with an estimated haul of £500,000. There was another side to monopoly rights as well. After Essex's negotiations with the Irish rebel leader Tyrone became known, his fall from grace was assured; and when in 1600 his 'short-term debts alone exceeded £5,000, the final blow came with Elizabeth's pointed refusal to renew the earl's monopoly of sweet wines, [which had been] over the past decade the key to his solvency' (Nicholls 1999: 300).

There were repeated calls for abolishing this practice, for, in effect, it amounted to taxation without the consent of Parliament. Towards the end of Elizabeth's reign a dozen monopolies were not renewed, but these concessionary reforms were superficial. But monopoly patents were not just granted to peers. For example, Thomas Smith and William Cecil, in seeking to promote new projects that would make small but essential items, such as pins and nails, accessible to all but the very poor, also gave project entrepreneurs sole rights of manufacture for a given period (Lockyer 2005: 49–50).

Companies and Compacts

The logic and laws of such companies applied to the world of entertainment as well. Theatres required a royal licence. The first was granted to Robert Dudley, Earl of Leicester in 1574. Among the leaders of Leicester's company of actors was James Burbage, an actor and entrepreneur who in 1576 secured the lease of land at Shoreditch for the construction of the first playhouse, called simply The Theatre. About a decade later, in 1587, Leicester's company acted, among other places, at Stratford-upon-Avon, where Shakespeare, mentioned in connection with a lawsuit at the time, is presumed to have been residing. Since we have no surviving record of what Shakespeare was doing after 1587 until he shows up in ledgers as an actor and dramatist in London in 1592, some have conjectured that he took part in the plays of the theatrical companies known to have visited Stratford-upon-Avon in 1586–87 or at least that he saw the possibilities of making a living in this trade. After he had retired to Stratford-upon-Avon, his will shows that by the time Shakespeare died in 1616 he had accumulated a considerable estate (Schoenbaum 1975: 246). By the same token, the great tragedian Edward Alleyn, who went on to marry the step-daughter of the pre-eminent theatre manager and entrepreneur Philip Henslowe, was able to pay £5000 for a manor and, in 1619, obtained a royal charter to found Dulwich College.

The chartering of the Company of Stationers of the City of London, established originally by Queen Mary to serve as a 'suitable remedy' against the rise of Protestant publications, was confirmed by Elizabeth in 1558. However, her intention was to confer on its members 'privileges and practices common to the older guilds (see Glossary): rights of property ownership, self-regulation, keeping apprentices and engaging in searches to protect the trade from "foreigners" (non-members) and poor workmanship' (Clegg 2001: 24). The Stationers were successful in their petition in 1560 for livery (a costume to be worn by its members). This now meant that they had voting rights in both London and parliamentary elections, participation in the city's governance, and status among the leading livery companies.

Similar in kind, there were also agreements for the speculative trading of products from abroad. Most were modelled in part on the Company of

Merchant Adventurers, dating back to the beginning of the fifteenth century, which had been formed to compete with the Hanseatic League, an alliance of trading guilds operating out of Northern Germany. The Elizabethan 'Mystery and Company of Merchant Adventurers for the Discovery of Regions, Dominions, Islands, and Places unknown', as it was formally recognized, was founded in London in 1551 initially to search for a Northwest Passage (a Western trade route to China and the East). Although not succeeding in this objective, it did give rise to the Muscovy Company in 1555, which enabled the intrepid diplomat Anthony Jenkinson to open trade routes as far away as Persia. Because the Company of Merchant Adventurers maintained permanent agents – known as 'factors' – abroad, they could wait for the right market conditions to sell their stock, most prominently unfinished woollen goods (Loades 1997: 234).

In effect they acted as bankers for the Crown, and so their commercial priorities had to be taken seriously. For example, Robert Cecil received nearly £7000 alone in the fiscal year 1608–09 (Loades 1987: 146). The monarchy encouraged but did not actually fund the creation of the Levant Company (1581), The Venice Company (1583), the East India Company (1600) and Ralegh's Virginia Company (1609).

Colonial Ventures Abroad

Ralegh's expedition to the outer banks of the Atlantic seaboard and establishment of an English colony on Roanoke Island led directly to Thomas Hariot's ethnographic and economic survey of the Algonquin people, *Briefe and True Report of the New Found Land of Virginia*, first published in 1588 (see Greenblatt discussions in Robson, Chapter 5; Hopkins, Chapter 8, this volume). It was reprinted the following year in Richard Hakluyt's compendious *Principall Navigations, Voiages, and Discoveries of the English Nation*, and continued to capture the public imagination. This collection may well have influenced Shakespeare's *The Tempest*, in part because of the engravings made from drawings by John White and published by Theodore de Bry in 1590. All the same, 'English maritime expansion during the century was characterized less by mercantile considerations than by the complex growth of piracy and privateering' (Adams 2002: 210). Whilst the state papers from Elizabeth's reign contain hundreds of complaints about acts of piracy, little was done unless a significant English merchant suffered losses or there was risk of a major incident with foreign powers. Indeed, the queen herself loaned ships and resources for some of these ventures, and invariably expected a substantial return for her 'investments'.

Relations with Other Nations in the British Isles

England was about a century behind the Spanish and Portuguese in the scramble for trading posts and colonies. Mary Tudor's husband, Philip II of

Spain, cherished the dream of a pan-Catholic world order, with himself as the head, but at Elizabeth's court there was no unifying vision or policy motivating English expansion. The main colonial push during Elizabeth's reign concerned subduing the Irish and replacing the existing tenants and lords with those of English stock or with locals who were willing to accept English rule. By January 1595 Hugh O'Neill, the Earl of Tyrone, was in open rebellion against the establishment of English government in Ireland. He was able to unite many chiefs of previously divisive *'septs'* (ancestral Irish clans) who wanted to retain power in their own districts or who objected to Protestantism supplanting Catholicism. The conflict reached its most fevered pitch in 1599 when Elizabeth's one-time favourite, Robert Devereux, 2nd Earl of Essex, in an effort to consolidate his power at court and accomplish once and for all what had been so severely depleting the country's revenues, landed in Ireland with 16,000 English troops.

Essex did little to endear himself to his sovereign during this campaign. The decision to knight men in the field (an honour which Elizabeth was exceptionally careful to bestow only sparingly) meant that it has been estimated that half of the total of all English knights were now engaged in this Irish venture. Misguided military tactics, the decimation of his forces by disease, and his decision finally to strike a truce with Tyrone could only lead to further condemnation. Before he could be recalled and chastised by Elizabeth, he left his post without royal permission and led what amounted to a failed political rebellion in London.

There was already much anxiety over Elizabeth's refusal to name an heir, and the day before 'Essex's Rebellion', his followers paid for a production of Shakespeare's *Richard II* at the Globe. Elizabeth is reported to have snapped at a councillor: 'I am Richard II, know ye not that?' according to the antiquarian William Lambarde. After a trial, Essex was beheaded on 25 February 1601 on Tower Green, and Shakespeare's acting company, the Lord Chamberlain's Men, while subject to an enquiry, was found not culpable of anything related to the would-be coup d'état.

England had also been encroaching on Wales for centuries before the Wars of the Roses. The main figure associated with Welsh nationalism, Owain Glyndwr, rose against the English occupying forces at the beginning of the fifteenth century. Even now, there remains a great deal of critical speculation about this popular leader who, in Shakespeare's history, describes himself as: 'extraordinary, / And all the courses of my life do show / I am not in the roll of common men' (*1 Henry IV*, 3. 1. 39–41, p. 1190).

Conflict with Scotland was much more pronounced in the sixteenth century. The dismal relations with Scotland that Elizabeth inherited stemmed from Protector Somerset's near-obsessive objective of conquering Scotland, which he saw as the principal means of consolidating his family's power over the

Crown. Initially, he sought a marriage between his ward, Edward VI, and the infant queen Mary Stuart (later to become Mary, Queen of Scots). He built up garrisons in the north along the border and, in 1547, invaded Scotland. Unfortunately, he grossly underestimated Franco-Scottish amity and failed to secure a blockade on the strategic Firth of Forth. France sent six thousand troops with artillery to Leith. Military expenditures against Scotland totalled nearly £600,000 as 7434 mercenaries were hired from Italy, Spain, Germany, Hungary and even Ireland (Guy 1988: 202). Much of the war effort was paid for from funds obtained from the dissolution of chantries and colleges, as well as the sale of Crown lands.

Nonetheless, when her turn came, Elizabeth did not underestimate the age-old alliance of France and Scotland – especially when her cousin, Mary, Queen of Scots, married King Francis II and in 1559 declared herself the rightful Queen of England. Mary's mother, Marie de Guise, maintained armed garrisons to keep England in its place, but Elizabeth found allies in a group of Scottish lords who forced the acceptance of the Treaty of Edinburgh calling for all French troops to withdraw. This was consistent with Elizabeth's overall policy to limit her costs, as she had high expenditures on the continent. The resolution to the ongoing conflict involving England, Scotland and France only came to an end with Elizabeth's death, as the most powerful faction at court led by Robert Cecil manoeuvred to secure her cousin, James VI of Scotland, as her successor. When James came to the English throne in 1603, his personal union of the English and Scottish crowns meant that the new Great Britain 'would occupy a potentially far stronger position in Europe than England alone had ever done' (Adams 2002: 214).

Relations with the Continent: Martial and Marital

Elizabeth's foreign policy involved maintaining a delicate balance between the Catholic powers of France and Spain, either of which could intervene in England, while supporting the Protestant Dutch in their struggle to win independence from Spain. After 1585 this led to a long struggle with Spain at sea which, most famously, involved the defeat of the Armada, the vast Spanish fleet of invading warships sent by Philip II. Between 1589 and 1591, Elizabeth spent £144,786 on military operations in France, £100,000 per year for troops in the Netherlands, £1000 per month for Channel guards of seven frigates, and another £5000 per month for additional summer garrisons in Ireland (Guy 1988: 347). But the demoralizing cost in human lives was even more disastrous to Elizabeth's reign: owing to disease and insufficient supplies, eleven thousand English soldiers died in France, of these only about eleven hundred having fallen in battle. The nature of some of the responses at the time to such costly wars may be witnessed in Shakespeare's scenes depicting the hardships endured by soldiers: see Falstaff's poignant soliloquy about the rag-tag bunch of men he has pressed into military service in the king's name (*1 Henry IV*, 4. 2. 11–42, pp. 1206–7).

The Netherlands, France and Spain

If Elizabeth would not allow herself to be manipulated by her councillors in matters of religion, she remained equally reluctant to commit troops in the field to assist the Dutch Revolt. However, she did value the advice of William Cecil, Lord Burghley, who impressed upon her the importance for England that the Low Countries 'should continue in their ancient government, without either subduing it to the Spanish nation or joining it to the Crown of France' (Guy 1988: 282). This was a fine line to walk indeed. While Elizabeth tried to avoid intervening directly in the Netherlands, from 1585 on she did allow 'volunteers', most famously the courtier and poet Philip Sidney, to assist the Protestant Dutch in their struggle for independence from Catholic Spain.

On his part, Philip II had been encouraging the Irish rebellion against English control, and for years had been contemplating how to add England to his empire. Initially, upon the death of his wife Mary, Philip asked Princess Elizabeth for her hand in marriage rather than that of her potential rival Mary, Queen of Scots, who had married Francis, the heir to the French throne, a few months before Mary Tudor had died. But France's fortunes had waned owing to its own internal conflicts between Catholics and French Calvinist Protestants (known as Huguenots), culminating in the St Bartholomew's Day Massacre of 1572. The latter saw the slaughter of thousands of Protestants who had gathered in Paris to celebrate the marriage of Marguerite de Valois to the Protestant prince, Henry of Navarre (the future French King Henry IV).

Philip stepped up plans for an invasion, deploying his 'Invincible Armada' of over 130 oversized ships. Sailing from Spain, it was to meet up with a huge army raised by the Duke of Parma, then Governor of the Spanish Netherlands, and sail up the English Channel. Spain's hopes foundered, however, owing to storms, shifting winds, and the smaller, more mobile assault ships commanded by able seaman such as Sir Francis Drake. Drake's bold raid on the port of Cadiz in 1587 had already delayed the mobilization of the Armada for a year. Despite the remarkable victory over the Armada, in the last decade of Elizabeth's reign 'England was involved in fighting on the high seas, in the Low Countries, in France and, most costly of all, in Ireland. Together these campaigns cost £3,500,000' (Sharpe 1997: 13–14).

Marriage Negotiations

Nonetheless, lulls in such fighting and temporary treaties were frequent, especially when Elizabeth allowed princes to compete for her hand in marriage. This has been considered one of her most successful methods of diplomacy. The disadvantage to this policy, of course, was that no marriage meant no uncontested heir, and the question of succession dogged Elizabeth throughout her forty-five-year reign. As has already been noted, Mary Tudor died without issue and this led to the voicing of a number of rival claims to the English throne. From the very beginning of her reign, Elizabeth prudently feared that once she named an heir she would find herself back in the Tower and that court factions would take control of the government as they had during her brother Edward's reign.

This issue was brought to a crisis in October 1562 when Elizabeth contracted smallpox and nearly died. She consented to reopen previous marriage negotiations in 1565 with Archduke Charles of Austria (brother of the Holy Roman Emperor, Maximilian II), a match favoured by Cecil and Norfolk as a way to end England's isolation and to keep France and Scotland at bay.

The most protracted of such negotiations, and the only suitor to court her in person rather than by ambassadorial proxy, was the Duke of Alençon, the youngest son of Henry II of France. Arrangements for the marriage began in 1579, though the Privy Council debated it for more than a month, 'with Burghley and Sussex acting as the main spokesmen on one side and Walsingham and Mildmay on the other' (Doran 1996: 157). Him being twenty years Elizabeth's junior, she seemed to enjoy his presence despite his having been scarred by smallpox. She even gave him a jewelled velvet cap with a small crown to wear at court. Although the match was supported by Elizabeth's most trusted and long-standing advisor, William Cecil, then Lord Burghley, the match was unthinkable to most of her Privy Council given that Alençon was Catholic, French and the son of Catherine de Medici who had orchestrated the Massacre of 1572. Nonetheless, if nothing else came of these negotiations, it did send a message to Philip II of Spain that she was prepared to ally herself in a way that would thwart his imperial designs. Moreover, the image of Elizabeth that emerges from these matrimonial negotiations is that of a highly intelligent actress and an expert strategist: 'Like all successful heads of state she had a highly developed instinct for survival: a sensitivity to public opinion and an awareness of what was politically acceptable. [. . .] Aware of her own limitations, therefore, she listened to counsel, rejected controversial matches and in the event remained single' (Doran 1996: 217–18).

Her eventual heir, King James VI of Scotland and later James I of England, the son of Mary, Queen of Scots, was cautiously allied by marriage to the Lutheran Princess Anne of Denmark. However, Anne had converted to Catholicism in the decade before James's accession to the English throne and caused some embarrassment by refusing to take communion at James's coronation. She was a patron of the arts, especially the court entertainment known as the masque, in which on occasions she would take a non-speaking role. Perhaps the most celebrated of her involvements in this art form was the occasion of the court performance of Ben Jonson's *The Masque of Blackness*.

Celebrations for a Winter Bride

On St Valentine's Day 1613, just three months after the death of the accomplished and promising heir to the throne Prince Henry, King James's daughter, Princess Elizabeth, was married to the Protestant Frederick V, Elector Palatine of the Holy Roman Empire and briefly King of Bohemia (see genealogy). Shakespeare's *The Tempest*, with the masque inserted in 4.1, was among the many winter entertainments staged in celebration of the forthcoming marriage. His company alone, The King's Men, performed twenty different plays, many of them at court. This provided steady income at a time when the city theatre season was sluggish owing to adverse weather conditions.

Urban Growth in the Capital

By the time *Hamlet* and *Twelfth Night* were in repertoire, London had become one of the most populous urban centres in Europe, just behind Paris and Naples (deVries 1984: 140). At the beginning of the reign of Henry VIII, London was still within its ancient walls on the north bank of the Thames; Westminster, the seat of the emerging national government, was west of the city, and Southwark, the southern approach to London Bridge, was beyond the City's jurisdiction on the south bank. Crossing the bridge into the city, you would have been within earshot of the bells of more than one hundred churches from both sides of the river, and you would in all likelihood have seen heads of traitors and criminals on spikes, reminiscent of Pericles's entrance into Antioch where 'dead cheeks advise thee to desist' (*Pericles*, 1. 82, p. 2720). By the end of Elizabeth's reign there was extensive development outside the walls: greater London had about 50,000 people at the beginning of the sixteenth century and 200,000 by the end (Ward 2004: 347). This contrasted sharply to Shakespeare's market town of Stratford-upon-Avon, with only eight or nine streets, two hundred and fifty households and fifteen hundred inhabitants. His town was still guided by seasonal rhythms, market days, sheep festivals and lamb ales – much like Perdita's green world idealized in *The Winter's Tale*.

The increase in the number of people (like Shakespeare himself) seeking jobs in the city was paralleled by a large number of gentlemen seeking legal training at the Inns of Court. This resulted in a need for more taverns, shops and theatres, and led to expanded commercial networks of all kinds. However, with the added congestion came periodic epidemics – most devastatingly the bubonic plague of 1592–94, which led to the closing of the theatres and places of public gathering. As might be expected, all forms of urban life, including 'the old theatrical companies and alignments', were radically disrupted at such times (Frye 1967: 28). It was during this extended period of theatrical inactivity that Shakespeare wrote his two narrative poems *Venus and Adonis* and *The Rape of Lucrece* in an effort to secure patronage and preferment.

In addition to people from the countryside coming to London, in the last quarter of the sixteenth century about six thousand foreigners arrived per year and thus fuelled Tudor London's growth (Ward 2004: 353). French and Dutch Protestants found religious asylum in the city, and brought with them their connections to trading, artistic and humanist networks from the continent. Between 40,000 and 50,000 'strangers' (the Elizabethan term for people coming from abroad) migrated to London between 1550 and 1585, some with special talents and letters of introduction.

London had become a thriving cultural centre owing to the influx of broader European influences in the visual and performing arts (Ward 2004: 357). 'Alien' churches and institutions assisted in helping immigrants to find places to live and work, yet for the most part these communities were 'separate from the rest of London' (Ward 2004: 353). The 1590s were an especially tense time in London, not because of the resident 'aliens' or the religious changes of the day, but owing to riots over the high prices of fish and butter. In 1595, for example, the city was placed under martial law after one thousand apprentices marched towards Tower Hill. The price of flour had tripled between 1593 and 1597, owing to poor harvests and demands of the military; real wages declined by 29 per cent during this inflationary surge (Ward 2004: 354).

Court Culture and Centres of Power

Although Elizabeth's court was based in palaces around London, most notably Whitehall, Richmond and Greenwich, she embarked on summer 'progresses' with her household – followed by ambitious courtiers. This was an ideal way for her to be seen in resplendent glory by her subjects, to keep an eye on nobles who had estates outside of London, and to pass on the cost of maintaining her royal retinue. Leading nobility and gentry were counted among her train; and it is evident from documents preserved from the period that these visits were rich in political symbolism: 'On these occasions the host's house and grounds became allegorical terrain abounding in gods, nymphs, and wild-men, who eulogized the queen in prose or verse' (Guy 1988: 427).

Writers frequently dedicated their productions to high and mighty within society in the hope of gaining protection, social advancement and revenue from such patrons. More generally in the sixteenth century, it is clear that the potential benefits of royal favour, if not permission to proceed with an economic scheme or martial enterprise, were sufficient to 'consolidate the position of the court as the heart and focus of the patronage network' (Loades 1987: 146). Royal service was the most viable career option for an ambitious gentleman irrespective of his family ties. Nonetheless, there were some families who continued to prosper under each successive monarch, most notably the Cecil family.

The Cecils and Royal Service

The grandfather of William Cecil, Lord Burghley – Elizabeth's chief confidant, secretary of state and later lord treasurer – had secured the favour of Henry VII, most probably by serving in the yeoman of the guard, and later as sergeant-at-arms to Henry VIII. His father was yeoman of the wardrobe. William and his son, Robert, 1st Earl of Salisbury, held the two highest civic offices in the land during the reigns of Elizabeth and James. Bitter rivalry existed between Robert Cecil and Robert Devereux, Earl of Essex, for the favour of the Queen, most notably over who would become Master of the Court of Wards. This was an extremely lucrative post which Cecil eventually won.

Conclusion

What emerges from this survey is a sketch of a developing, multilateral notion of 'the state' in Shakespeare's lifetime (1564–1616), where 'state' and 'community' are not treated as opposites, but as 'points on a continuum of interest and identity'. The early modern state 'did not become more active at the expense of society; rather, it did so as a consequence of social need' (Hindle 2002: 16). The emerging state was characterized by a complex, functioning system of law and government, including a prominent representative institution, an awareness of its distinctive religion and culture, and an expanding and increasingly internationalized economy. The following historical tableau provides a way to understand Shakespeare's London and England, which, it is hoped, will inform and enrich your reading of his poems and plays.

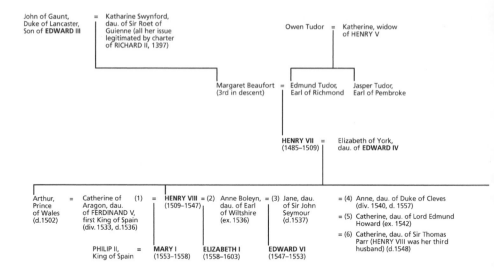

John of Gaunt, Duke of Lancaster, Son of **EDWARD III** = Katharine Swynford, dau. of Sir Roet of Guienne (all her issue legitimated by charter of RICHARD II, 1397)

Owen Tudor = Katherine, widow of HENRY V

Margaret Beaufort (3rd in descent) = Edmund Tudor, Earl of Richmond

Jasper Tudor, Earl of Pembroke

HENRY VII (1485–1509) = Elizabeth of York, dau. of **EDWARD IV**

Arthur, Prince of Wales (d.1502) = Catherine of Aragon, dau. of FERDINAND V, first King of Spain (div. 1533, d.1536) (1) = **HENRY VIII** (1509–1547) = (2) Anne Boleyn, dau. of Earl of Wiltshire (ex. 1536) = (3) Jane, dau. of Sir John Seymour (d.1537)

= (4) Anne, dau. of Duke of Cleves (div. 1540, d. 1557)

= (5) Catherine, dau. of Lord Edmund Howard (ex. 1542)

= (6) Catherine, dau. of Sir Thomas Parr (HENRY VIII was her third husband) (d.1548)

PHILIP II, King of Spain = **MARY I** (1553–1558)

ELIZABETH I (1558–1603)

EDWARD VI (1547–1553)

THE STUARTS 1603–1714

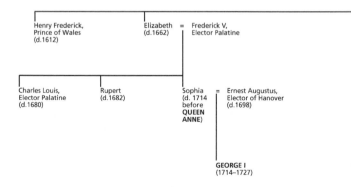

Henry Frederick, Prince of Wales (d.1612)

Elizabeth (d.1662) = Frederick V, Elector Palatine

Charles Louis, Elector Palatine (d.1680)

Rupert (d.1682)

Sophia (d. 1714 before **QUEEN ANNE**) = Ernest Augustus, Elector of Hanover (d.1698)

GEORGE I (1714–1727)

THE TUDORS
1485–1603

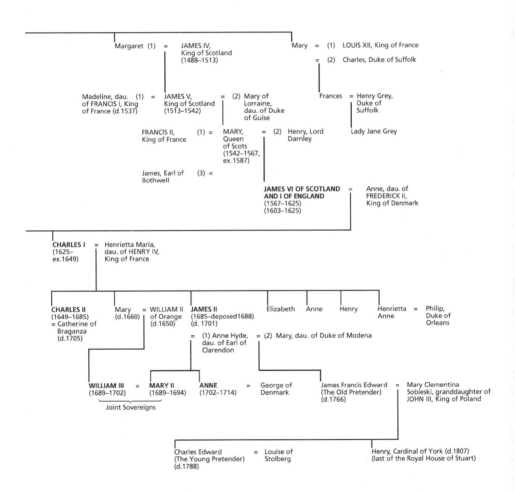

Margaret (1) = JAMES IV,
King of Scotland
(1488–1513)

Mary = (1) LOUIS XII, King of France
= (2) Charles, Duke of Suffolk

Madeline, dau. (1) = JAMES V,
of FRANCIS I, King   King of Scotland
of France (d.1537)   (1513–1542)

= (2) Mary of
Lorraine,
dau. of Duke
of Guise

Frances = Henry Grey,
Duke of
Suffolk

FRANCIS II, (1) = MARY,
King of France   Queen
of Scots
(1542–1567,
ex.1587)

= (2) Henry, Lord
Darnley

Lady Jane Grey

James, Earl of (3) =
Bothwell

JAMES VI OF SCOTLAND = Anne, dau. of
AND I OF ENGLAND   FREDERICK II,
(1567–1625)   King of Denmark
(1603–1625)

CHARLES I = Henrietta Maria,
(1625–   dau. of HENRY IV,
ex.1649)   King of France

CHARLES II   Mary   = WILLIAM II   JAMES II   Elizabeth   Anne   Henry   Henrietta = Philip,
(1649–1685)   (d.1660) of Orange   (1685–deposed1688)   Anne   Duke of
= Catherine of   (d.1650)   (d. 1701)   Orleans
Braganza
(d.1705)   = (1) Anne Hyde,   = (2) Mary, dau. of Duke of Modena
                                          dau. of Earl of
                                          Clarendon

WILLIAM III   =   MARY II   ANNE   =   George of   James Francis Edward   =   Mary Clementina
(1689–1702)   (1689–1694)   (1702–1714)   Denmark   (The Old Pretender)   Sobieski, granddaughter of
                                                                      (d.1766)   JOHN III, King of Poland

        Joint Sovereigns

Charles Edward   = Louise of   Henry, Cardinal of York (d.1807)
(The Young Pretender) Stolberg   (last of the Royal House of Stuart)
(d.1788)

3 Shakespeare's Literary and Cultural Contexts

Stephen Longstaffe

Chapter Overview

This reference chapter focuses on the key elements of Shakespeare's cultural contexts. It is intended to help you place Shakespeare's work in its broader context, and, along with the Glossary, to support your reading of other chapters.

Acting

The professional framework within which Elizabethan and Jacobean actors worked was very different to that usually operating today. Under the repertory system, when the theatres were open a different play would usually be put on each day. This meant that rehearsal time was of necessity limited; actors worked on their 'part' alone, sometimes taking instruction from the writer. 'Part' here really does mean the actor's part; as companies bought a single manuscript from their writers, actors were not given the whole play. Rather, they were given their lines, and part of the preceding cue line (see *A Midsummer Night's Dream* which has some comic business about cues being mixed up).

Given the demands of the repertory system, it is likely that actors specialized in playing particular types of character. The best example of this is the clown – in Shakespeare's time a clown was a comical character, often with a 'country' origin. The earliest printed versions of Shakespeare's plays sometimes have the 'type' name rather than the character name for speech headings; indeed, some 'characters' have no names at all ('Fool' in *King Lear*, for example). Because time for 'blocking' (working out where actors would stand and how they would move onstage) was limited, it is likely that actors worked by convention, so that a king would stand in a certain way, and in a certain relation to other onstage characters.

In addition, the acoustics of open-air theatres, and the distance of some audience members from the stage, would have demanded a 'large' style of acting, making use of stock gestures and positions to communicate (so that, for example, there might be a 'stock' way to indicate grief, surprise, anger and so on). This in turn means that the acting of Shakespeare's time was not striving for 'realism' in the modern sense so much as 'communication', particularly of emotions. Actors, particularly comic actors, are likely to have addressed audiences directly in places, particularly in solo set speeches or soliloquies. A range of standard devices could draw the audience outside the frame of the story, amongst them asides (where actors speak but are not heard by some or all of those on stage), prologues and epilogues (speeches introducing or wrapping up plays), choruses (linking speeches during plays), dumb shows (where actors mime events), soliloquies and songs and dances.

Authorship

The typical play of Shakespeare's time was written not by a single author, but by a team, much as successful contemporary TV shows are, and for much the same reason. We have records of as many as four or five writers working on a single play. Companies, especially early in Shakespeare's career, needed a lot of plays in order to offer something different to their audiences every day, and needed to update and revise old ones for revival. Since editors began looking closely at Shakespeare's plays, they have often supposed that plays published under Shakespeare's name are collaborations. In earlier centuries, this tends to have been motivated by the belief that those elements of the plays not meeting current critical standards were written by someone else; recently, computers have provided much more systematic knowledge of the linguistic structures of Shakespeare's plays, and have led to a range of theories about Shakespeare's work with others on, for example, *Henry VIII, Pericles* or *1 Henry VI*.

Blackfriars Playhouse

An indoor theatre which became the regular playing place for Shakespeare's company, along with the Globe, from 1608. This was on the site of a Dominican monastery dissolved during the Reformation. In 1576, boy companies began to perform plays in a room within the complex. In 1596, James Burbage, who had built the first permanent theatre in London in 1576 called 'the Theatre', and whose son Richard was the star tragic actor with Shakespeare's company, bought the property for use by the Lord Chamberlain's Men, as the ground lease at the Theatre was due to expire in 1597 and leave them without a permanent base. However, the plan was blocked by local residents' objections, and the Lord Chamberlain's Men used the wood from the Theatre to build the Globe on the other side of the Thames. The Blackfriars Theatre was leased back to a boy company. In 1608 the resident boy company offended the king with one of its plays, and was disbanded. By now the Lord Chamberlain's

Men had become the King's Men, and this may have helped them take over the theatre which they had sought ten years earlier. The audience capacity was roughly one-quarter of the Globe's. Though admission was more expensive at the Blackfriars, the King's Men presented the same plays here as at the Globe. The Blackfriars, like all theatres, was closed at the start of the civil war in 1642.

The stage at the Blackfriars was a different shape to that at the Globe, occupying one of the short walls of the rectangular building. Whereas with the Globe the cheapest place to be was standing next to the stage, in the Blackfriars the cheapest seats were furthest away from the stage. The different spatial arrangements in this indoor theatre are likely to have affected acting style. As the theatre was smaller than the Globe, a quieter and (perhaps) less physical acting could be developed and, as the sight lines were better than those at the Globe, there was perhaps less need for movement in order to ensure everybody got a good view. At the end of each act there was an interval in which the candles, which were the only source of light, were trimmed to ensure safety, and music was played. One of the advantages of the smaller space was that different, quieter, musical instruments could be used, and this may again have impacted upon the company's production values.

Blazon

This word comes from the French for 'coat of arms', and refers to a literary convention ultimately derived from Greek and Latin poets. A blazon characteristically dwells on or lists parts of the body. It was often used in love poetry, typically comparing parts of a woman's body to naturally beautiful things (lips to cherries, for example). Shakespeare's Sonnet 130 both wittily plays on the convention and uses it to attack the insincerity of writing of love using tired conventions:

> My mistress' eyes are nothing like the sun;
> Coral is far more red than her lips' red.
> If snow be white, why then her breasts are dun;
> If hairs be wires, black wires grow on her head.
> I have seen roses damasked, red and white,
> But no such roses see I in her cheeks;
> And in some perfumes is there more delight
> Than in the breath that from my mistress reeks.
> I love to hear her speak, yet well I know
> That music hath a far more pleasing sound.
> I grant I never saw a goddess go:
> My mistress when she walks treads on the ground.

> And yet, by heaven, I think my love as rare
> As any she belied with false compare.

Boy Players

Up until the reopening of the theatres in 1660, women's parts on the public stage were played by boys. The reasons for this are complex. Patriarchal morality preferred women to be chaste, silent and obedient, and anti-theatrical writers suggested that public theatrical performance posed especial moral dangers to performers and audience alike. However, this objection naturally was very dangerous to raise in relation to court theatricals or masquing: the Stuart royal family was particularly fond of such entertainments. Dressing boys as women was also thought by some to be dangerous, but most of the evidence we have suggests that boys were convincingly able to present women and femininity. For example, we have an approving reference to the moving nature of a boy's performance of Desdemona in *Othello*. Henry Jackson wrote of a performance in Oxford in 1610 that 'although she always acted her whole part supremely well, yet when she was killed she was even more moving, for when she fell back upon the bed she implored the pity of the spectators by her very face'.

Of course, boys also played boys (in plays like *The Winter's Tale* or *Macbeth*), and adults (in the boy companies in which boys took all the parts). The songs given to women in plays like *1 Henry IV* (where the action stops while 'the lady sings a Welsh song'), *Hamlet* and *Othello* show that boys could bring particular musical skills to the company, perhaps because they had attended one of London's choir schools. Some boy players went on to make a living as adult performers.

Critics have recently begun to explore more fully the theatrical experience of watching boy players, prompted by the development of feminist and psychoanalytic theory, and have been particularly interested in the way young women disguising themselves as boys seem to 'play' with gender. For example, in *Twelfth Night* a boy playing a woman (Olivia) falls in love with a boy playing a woman (Viola) playing a boy (Cesario).

Censorship

Shakespeare's plays were printed and performed under a system of censorship which licensed performance and printing of a script separately. Performance in London was controlled by a court official known as the 'Master of the Revels' whose function initially was to make sure that plays offered for performance at court were suitable. However, by Shakespeare's time the Master judged all plays put on in London, whether they were to be performed at court or not. The Master saw a manuscript of the play and either 'licensed' it or returned it to the theatrical company with suggested alterations (usually cuts). In the most extreme case on record, after Shakespeare's time, the Master of the Revels burnt the script 'for the ribaldry (obscenity, rudeness or debauchery) that was in it', and fined the writer. There are still a few of these original manuscripts in existence with the Master's comments on them. Revivals of old plays were similarly scrutinized, though sometimes the Master watched a private performance rather than read a script. From existing evidence, we know that at different times the Master was likely to object to personal satire of influential people, mockery or criticism of friendly foreign powers, and critical comment on the government or religious controversy.

Books had a separate system of licensing, which changed throughout Shakespeare's lifetime. They were licensed by the Church (technically, by the Archbishop of Canterbury); in practice this work was done by independent agents working on behalf of the authorities. This work was not necessarily done in a systematic or conscientious way. We only have evidence that one of Shakespeare's three published volumes of poetry (*Venus and Adonis*) was scrutinized by censors.

Shakespeare's work was produced under a variety of other, less direct cultural constraints. In 1606, an Act to Restrain Abuses of Players was passed which forbade actors from 'jestingly or profanely speak or use the holy Name of God or of Christ Jesus, or of the Holy Ghost or of the Trinity'. This is one of the reasons why Shakespeare's characters so often refer to, or swear by, non-Christian gods. Revivals of plays first published before 1606 had to be altered to conform to the new law (the latter did not apply to print). It was also risky to refer to powerful people, whether by direct reference or insinuation. Several London theatre companies were simply closed down because they had offended a person with some political influence; offending writers might be imprisoned, or called in for questioning at the highest level. The character 'Falstaff' in 1 *Henry IV* was originally called 'Oldcastle', the name of a real person who was executed for heresy under Henry V (the 'Hal' of 1 *Henry IV*). Sir John Oldcastle had been hailed as a religious martyr (rather than a heretic) in John Foxe's great reformist work, the *Acts and Monuments*. However, the change of name from Oldcastle to Falstaff in Shakespeare's play for the presentation of a fat, old, lecherous criminal was probably linked to pressure being brought to bear by some of his descendants. In the second part of *Henry IV*, Shakespeare even has Falstaff come on at the end of the play to say that he is not Oldcastle, 'for Oldcastle died a martyr, and this is not the man'.

Classical Heritage

'Classical' means produced by the civilizations of Greece and Rome over a thousand years before Shakespeare was born. The Western discovery of print in the fifteenth century contributed to a 'renaissance' (rebirth) of interest in these great pre-Christian cultures as print made them more generally available. In literary terms, the classics supplied conventions and models in a range of genres – epic, comedy, tragedy, lyric, satire, epigram, elegy and romance. Shakespeare's education (see below) equipped him to read the Latin classics; he read Greek works – such as Plutarch's *Lives*, a major source for his Roman plays – in translation.

Comedy

A play with a predominantly light-hearted tone, representing characters below a certain social rank, with a happy ending. Elizabethan theorists of comedy tended to emphasize its functions; typically, to instruct and delight. Most Renaissance thinkers accepted the idea that true art had to have a moral purpose. For us, comedy means laughter; but for some Renaissance thinkers, laughter in itself was deeply suspect. Laughter can, after all, be provoked by nothing more than tickling, and yet in other circumstance it may signify a dismissive response. That said, in his *Apology for Poetry* (1595), Sir Philip Sidney does allow laughter, so long as it is subordinated to a moral, corrective purpose: the displaying of vices to ridicule, the roles 'which we play naturally' (that is, easily, but also foolishly, as a 'natural' was somebody born foolish, like Sir Andrew Aguecheek in *Twelfth Night*).

'Correction' is the territory of satire, and Ben Jonson, in the preface to *Every Man In His Humour* (1599), explains that in this satirical comedy he offers 'deeds, and language, such as men do use / And persons, such as Comedy would choose, / When she would show an Image of the times, / And sport with human follies, not with crimes'. The purpose is corrective; by laughing at follies on stage, an audience is drawn to consider the ridiculousness of its own greed, envy or lust. Jonson believes that the most effective way of doing this as by maintaining the dramatic illusion. In the prologue to *Every Man In*, he criticizes the use of choruses (in the same year that Shakespeare used one, very self-consciously, in *Henry V*), people growing old during the play, a couple of paid hands representing whole armies, conventional sound effects or descents of gods from the sky.

All of these devices, and more, were adopted at one time or another, by Shakespeare, who was much less concerned with such questions of representational decorum. Shakespeare's comedies frequently do have a satiric point, but satire is not their dominant mode. Broadly speaking, they are concerned with periods of time, or with places, in which the normal rules of behaviour do not apply, where normal cultural pressures are forgotten, or weaken and, as a result, human appetites are expressed without restraint. If Jonson's satiric comedy shows the negative side of breaking society's rules, Shakespeare's romantic comedy demonstrates the positive necessity of doing so, on both an individual and a social level. Energy is liberated; laughter is created, broken families are put back together, lovers meet. Characters 'lose' their identity, but the movement is from winter to spring; from death to rebirth. Gonzalo's words at the end of *The Tempest* sum it up nicely:

> O, rejoice
> Beyond a common joy! and set it down
> With gold on lasting pillars: in one voyage
> Did Claribel her husband find at Tunis,
> And Ferdinand her brother found a wife
> Where he himself was lost; Prospero his dukedom
> In a poor isle; and all of us ourselves,
> When no man was his own. (5. 1. 209–16, p. 3103)

Costumes

In Shakespeare's day clothes in general were expensive items, and it was quite usual for the costumes for a production to be the most expensive of the company's properties (much more valuable than the script). It has even been suggested that the Globe was designed so as to keep the expensive clothing of both performers and audience out of direct sunlight, thus avoiding damage by ultraviolet light. Costumes themselves gave a range of information about a character, then as now – what they did for a living, what their social level was. So in *Hamlet*, for example, costume would differentiate a relatively minor (but high-status) role like an ambassador from a lower-status servant. In fact, as most of Shakespeare's plays include far more speaking roles than actors, the ambassador and the servant might be played by the same person, who would 'double' the role (doubling, strictly speaking, is playing more than one role – one actor could take five or six very small parts). The change of role would be signalled by an offstage change of costume, and sometimes plays are structured so as to make these possible. Sub-plots are very useful in this respect, as are clown scenes. One of the consequences of doubling is that characters relatively infrequently change costume *in character*, to minimize potential confusion about which character is which. The main exception to this was disguise; by convention, a simple change of clothing was a completely impenetrable camouflage. Often when characters disguise themselves, they either prepare the audience beforehand (like Viola in *Twelfth Night*), or identify themselves in some other way (as Kent does in *King Lear*). Occasionally, much more elaborate costumes were commissioned. For example, the prologue to the second part of *Henry IV*, Rumour, has a costume 'painted full of tongues'.

Court

The English court was the network of people in physical proximity to the monarch rather than an actual place (see Engel, this volume, Chapter 2). There were several royal residences/palaces around London – St James's, Greenwich, Hampton Court, Richmond – and the monarch would also go on 'progress', often to visit particular nobles. Wherever the monarch was, the court was. Personal advisers and servants had direct access to the monarch, but the court was full of others seeking to gain in other ways – honours, military appointments, protection, fact-finding missions, lobbying for a particular cause, the right to collect customs duties on an item, or a monopoly on manufacturing and so on. It was the most influential (and potentially financially rewarding) institution in the country, and much depended on the monarch's opinion. For that reason, the stakes were high, and it was common to think of the court itself as volatile, full of flattery and corruption.

However, the English court was not merely a seat of political power; as the gathering place for the most influential and powerful people in the nation, it was also a source of cultural patronage for creative artists of all kinds. Festivals and holidays of all kinds involved the London-based players taking their plays out of their own theatres and into the court, where temporary stages would be put up in a variety of rooms, from the very large to the quite small. That they might be called upon to play 'by royal appointment' was at times an important part of the players' defence of their profession against attempts by the city of London authorities to regulate, or even suppress, their activities. As one of the 'King's Men', Shakespeare was technically a royal servant, and thus entitled to wear the royal livery (uniform). Though Shakespeare's company by no means was the only company to perform at court, we do know that James's court saw at least *The Merry Wives of Windsor*, *The Comedy of Errors*, *Henry V*, *The Merchant of Venice*, *King Lear*, *The Tempest*, and *The Winter's Tale*. At the celebrations to mark the wedding of James's daughter Princess Elizabeth in the winter of 1612 we know that Shakespeare's company performed, amongst others, *Much Ado About Nothing*, *1 Henry IV*, *The Winter's Tale*, *Othello*, *Julius Caesar*, and *The Tempest*. Court performances were extremely helpful to the players, both financially and politically. However, the companies' main focus, in both artistic and business terms, remained the varied audiences at the London playhouses (and, to a lesser extent, to the audiences they might find on tour around the country). This relative independence from the court has often been seen as enabling Shakespeare's plays (and, indeed, the Elizabethan and Jacobean theatre more generally) to adopt a wider range of styles, attitudes, subjects, and stories than might otherwise have been the case.

Education

Shakespeare did not go to university. He did, however, receive an education at Stratford's school. In Shakespeare's time education was almost entirely based around Latin, the universal language of learning in Europe at this time, and rhetoric, which is the use of language for particular effects, especially to persuade. Shakespeare is likely to have spent ten or eleven years reading and writing Latin texts of all kinds, including philosophy, literature and history, and composing poems and other writing exercises. By the time he left school, Shakespeare would have been familiar with another, non-Christian, European culture, and would have read at least as much Latin as an undergraduate studying classics would today. Latin was not at this time a 'dead' language; it was the main European language of scholarship and science (or natural philosophy, as it was called at the time).

In the school and university classroom, the pupils might frequently be called upon to *disputatio in utramque partem*. This Latin phrase means 'arguing on both sides of the question'. In order to improve their persuasive skills, pupils would be required to, for example, write for and against a particular position, or for and against a historical personage. Many people see this as good training for dramatic writers and audiences alike, as it enabled them imaginatively to create characters with whom they are not necessarily personally in sympathy. The arguments of the disputation would use as building blocks literally hundreds of 'figures of speech'. Today, we recognize only a few of these – metaphor, onomatopoeia, metonymy, hyperbole (all Greek words, as the ancient Greeks invented rhetoric), but there are many more to be found in Shakespeare's writings. Though Shakespeare was a particularly creative exponent of it, anyone receiving a rhetorical education would have been faced with the challenge of coming up with their own examples of rhetorical 'figures' – for example, the particular kind of wordplay to be found in Falstaff's words 'were it not here apparent that thou art heir apparent'.

As paper and ink were very expensive, children also were required to memorize hundreds of lines of quotations, and also individual Psalms from the Bible. It would have been a very common experience in this society to listen to someone reading aloud. Indeed, at a time when only a fraction of the population was literate, this was necessarily the case. The Bible had become legally available in English in the 1530s, three decades before Shakespeare was born; its earliest translators into English were concerned that it should be *memorable*. A phrase such as 'Ask, and it shall be given you;

seek, and ye shall find; knock, and it shall be opened unto you' (Matthew 7:7) is skilfully constructed so as to stick in the memory. Shakespeare's education as a child and young man also lay in his gaining an understanding of the main principles of Christianity: he would have listened to preaching, prayers and scriptural readings during his church attendance on Sundays and holy days. However, study of Shakespeare's biblical references shows that he was well acquainted with scripture through his private reading – for example, he clearly knows the last book of the Bible, Revelation, even though most of it was never read in church.

Globe Theatre

An outdoor theatre built for and owned by members of Shakespeare's company, and their regular base from 1599. This theatre was the first theatre owned by Shakespeare's company; the company had previously played in theatres and locations belonging to other people. It was Shakespeare's financial share in the Globe and other assets of his theatrical company which made him his fortune (although his plays contributed to the company's success, he would have been paid very little for delivering the script itself). The Globe was built in 1599 on the south bank of the Thames, and was the main base for the King's Men until 1608, when they acquired the Blackfriars Playhouse. After that year, it was used in the summertime. The Globe burned down in 1613, during a performance of Shakespeare's *Henry VIII*, when a spark from a cannon set the thatched roof alight. It was rebuilt, this time with a tiled roof. When it was full, the Globe could hold up to three thousand spectators at once (a proportion of the population which nowadays would be at least equivalent to the capacity of the modern Wembley football stadium).

The Globe was a cylindrical structure with twenty sides and three levels of seating. It did not have a roof, and so plays took place during the day in natural light. The stage was thrust out into a yard so that the audience was on three sides. There were two doors at the back of the stage into the building through which actors' exits and entrances were made. The stage had a trap-door (this is used in *Hamlet* for the gravedigger scene; Hamlet's reference to the ghost of his father as 'old mole' in the same play indicates that this scene is likely to have featured an actor beneath the stage). Above the stage was a gallery, which was used by musicians, and sometimes by actors (the most famous usage is probably the 'balcony scene' in *Romeo and Juliet*).

History Play

The 'First Folio' (see Glossary) was divided into comedies, tragedies and histories. Though Shakespeare wrote many other plays set in the past, the 'histories' focus specifically upon medieval English history, beginning with *King John* and ending with *Henry VIII*. There are many non-Shakespearean tragedies and comedies, but relatively few non-Shakespearean histories. The 'genre' of the English history play (defined as plays on post-Norman conquest English history using similar dramaturgy to Shakespeare) includes only about forty examples. It is thus not as established a genre as comedy and tragedy in this period. Though history plays by Shakespeare and others remained very popular, there were few new ones written after the middle of the first decade of the seventeenth century.

King James Bible

This English translation, published in 1611, became the 'authorized version' of the Bible for centuries to come, but it was not read or used by Shakespeare himself (see Engel, this volume, Chapter 2). Indeed, close study of Shakespeare's biblical language has established that he seems to have been very familiar with one translation, the 'Geneva' Bible. Shakespeare also clearly knew other translations, such as the 'Bishops' Bible' (1568). The Geneva Bible was extremely popular, in part because of the quality of the translation, but also because of its size (many Bibles were published in the large Folio format, but the Geneva Bible was published in quarto) (see Glossary). The Geneva Bible was first published in full in England in 1560. Shakespeare was also very familiar with the separate publication of the biblical book of the Psalms (known as the Psalter) which differs from the Geneva Bible's translation of them. Shakespeare's plays refer most frequently to Matthew's Gospel, and then to the Psalms.

However, as the King James Bible was built on earlier translations (see Engel, this volume, Chapter 2), and often therefore 'quoted' them, reading it will give you a good idea of the kind of scriptural language to which Shakespeare and his contemporaries were accustomed.

London

London was a centre of commerce, trade and manufacture as well as the political hub of the nation, and continually attracted migrants from all over the country as well as Protestant refugees from persecutions abroad (see Engel, this volume, Chapter 2). Nonetheless, it should be stressed that the death rate in the city was high, in part because of plague. Recent studies estimate that no more than thirty per cent of those living in London in the sixteenth or early seventeenth centuries had been born there. The Reformation made many buildings and much land available for non-religious use; the Blackfriars Theatre was built on land formerly belonging to a religious order, and the area in which the Globe was situated was under the authority of the Bishop of Winchester rather than that of the city itself. In addition, the social mix in London was extremely diverse. High mortality rates meant a relatively high proportion of households were headed by women; there was a high concentration of gentry; the court was nearby. The unique social conditions of London, a city always in flux and at the forefront of social change, greatly helped the development of the unique theatrical conditions of Shakespeare's day. The city was governed by members of the trade guilds. These were associations governing crafts and industries, such as goldsmithing. Members of the guilds, like the servants of aristocrats, were entitled to wear 'livery', a distinctive uniform, and were involved in government on a local level, often on a voluntary basis.

The relation between the city of London and the theatre was often antagonistic. The city authorities sometimes objected to theatres on the grounds that they took people (especially young people) away from their workplaces or from more respectable pursuits, such as sermons. Theatres, as gathering places for crowds, often presented a public order (or, in times of sickness, public health) problem. However, professional playing was able to survive through a combination of factors: royal and aristocratic protection; the siting of many playing places outside the city's jurisdiction (for example, the south bank of the Thames); flexibility in touring when theatres were closed and (most obviously) the ability to keep paying customers coming through the doors.

Masque

A lavish aristocratic or royal entertainment. In the Early Stuart period, the court actively sought and commissioned such theatrical performances. James VI/I's consort, Anne of Denmark and her ladies-in-waiting are known to have taken non-speaking roles for some masque productions. Those who commissioned these spectacles often demanded the very best that money could buy in terms of dramatic text, music, dance, costume and stage effects. The principal subject of the masque at court was praise of the royal family, particularly the monarch. Masques usually worked allegorically, and employed classical mythology. Structurally, the idealized elements might be offset by those of the 'anti-masque', which featured elements of disorder, evil or ugliness soon challenged and defeated by the masque proper. The fourth act of *The Tempest* features a 'wedding masque' for Ferdinand and Miranda at which the classical goddesses Ceres and Juno appear.

Earl of Oxford

Edward de Vere (1550–1604) proposed as the true author of Shakespeare's plays by 'Oxfordians' or 'anti-Stratfordians' (an alternative anti-Stratfordian candidate is Francis Bacon, who did at least outlive Shakespeare). The basic anti-Stratfordian argument is that Shakespeare's plays are so perceptive about court life and politics that they must have been written by a true insider, a courtier; equally, such an insider could never allow his name to be attached to anything as low-status as plays, so William Shakespeare of Stratford was chosen as the 'front man'. The main arguments against de Vere are that Shakespeare's later plays depend on sources which were not printed until after de Vere's death, and that the assumption that you have to be a full-time member of a particular court in order to write about courts in general is in itself unsustainable.

Pastoral

The word 'pastoral' comes from the Latin for shepherd, and is a literary convention identifying the often idealized portrayal of shepherds and shepherdesses in particular, and country life in general. Greek and Latin pastoral is predominantly a poetic convention. The convention is based on the idea that shepherds do very little work (as opposed to, say, plough-men), and consequently have a great deal of time on their hands in which to 'sing' (create poems), enjoy the beauties of nature and fall in and out of love. Greek and Roman culture was polytheistic, believing in many gods and other powerful non-human beings. In the world of pastoral, this means that an encounter with a local spirit, or perhaps even a god, cannot be ruled out.

However, Greek and Roman pastoral poetry did not assume that this was how real country people lived. Rather, it was a nostalgic recreation of a lost 'golden age' of perpetual spring in which nobody had to work – the natural world provided everything which was needed, and peace and social harmony prevailed. Writing about this lost world was not necessarily simple escapism; it could sometimes be a way of indirectly criticizing the much worse world in which writer or reader lived. Because the relationship between shepherd and flock had such obvious political parallels, pastoral writing could have satirical or religious meanings. Equally, writing of the joys of a rural estate, or the simplicity of country life, could be by way of implicit contrast to the anxieties, corruption or dangers of court or city life. The European encounter with other cultures (especially across the Atlantic Ocean) gathered momentum during the sixteenth century, and gave pastoral new possibilities of meaning. How close were these native inhabitants to Golden Age shepherds? Were they ignorant or innocent? Did it matter that they too, like Greek and Roman shepherds, were pagan rather than Christian?

Understanding the expectations surrounding pastoral writing can help bring into focus some elements of Shakespeare's plays. *A Midsummer Night's Dream* associates the woods with supernatural beings (fairies), magic, getting lost, fulfilling (and misplacing) desire; in other words, it is an imagined space where the normal rules do not apply. The second part of *Henry IV* presents the English countryside as a kind of mellow and benevolent environment and, as such, presents a clear contrast to the harshness of the court, high politics and war. *As You Like It* features a court decamping to the forest of Arden, and the range of freedoms and discoveries this enables. *The Tempest*, as several chapters of this book consider, grafts the centuries-old genre of pastoral onto a very contemporary situation.

Patronage

Patronage is a system of reciprocal obligations between parties of different economic or social status or power. Apart from the richest and most powerful members of Shakespeare's society, advancement (and sometimes survival) depended on cultivating relationships with those in a better position. This was particularly true of writers. There was no copyright system, and it was virtually impossible for a writer to survive by selling manuscripts to publishers for a one-off fee.

Shakespeare was enmeshed in the patronage system as poet, dramatist and actor. As a poet, he sought the patronage of Henry Wriothesley, Earl of Southampton, to whom he dedicated *Venus and Adonis* and *The Rape of Lucrece* (1593) and William Herbert, Earl of Pembroke, to whom he dedicated the *Sonnets* (1609). It has been suggested that Pembroke was influential in securing King James's patronage for Shakespeare's company in 1603. As an actor and dramatist, he was under the patronage of (at first) the Lord Chamberlain and (later) King James himself, but for theatre companies patronage was a legal necessity. Effectively, the patron provided a 'passport' guaranteeing the respectability, at the least, of the group, and could provide protection against anti-theatrical elements within London and society more generally.

Plague

An extremely deadly disease which broke out epidemically between the fourteenth and seventeenth centuries. It was transmitted by flea bites. In the year Shakespeare was born, a quarter of the inhabitants of Stratford-upon-Avon died; the vast majority of these deaths were the result of plague. In London, the plague epidemic of 1593 led to the death of some ten per cent of the population, and the closure of the theatres for about twenty months. The epidemic of 1603, combined with the funeral of Queen Elizabeth, led to a closure of the theatres for over a year, and another led to a closure for eighteen months beginning in July 1608. There were other closures in the summer and early autumn of 1596 and the autumn of 1605 as well as several smaller closures. In the period 1603–11, the theatres were closed for roughly half the time, with plague being the leading cause. In any case, companies often toured outside London in the summer months (which were the worst for plague), and relied on touring economically (with the odd commissioned performance at a noble's house, and under James's patronage, the occasional cash gift) during times of plague. During the 1593 closure, Shakespeare wrote his long poems *Venus and Adonis* and *The Rape of Lucrece*, and some think he collected and revised his sonnets during the 1603–4 closure (though they were not printed until 1609). It has been suggested, however, that one of the reasons we have fewer plays from Shakespeare from the second half of his career than from the first is that for much of the time there was nowhere to perform them in London. By the opening years of the seventeenth century, the capital (rather than court performances) had become the main base for the company.

Playing Company

A full-time and durable troupe of actors, usually under the patronage of a member of the aristocracy or the royal family. The patronage of companies had grown up in the days before the permanent London theatres to distinguish groups of players from vagabonds. The names of the companies generally indicated the identity of their patron; Shakespeare, for example, was a member of the Lord Chamberlain's Men, the first company with which we can definitely associate him. When King James came to the throne, the monarch took over the role as patron, and so the company was renamed 'The King's Men'. Boy companies were known either by their patron's name, or by the venue in which they performed ('Blackfriars Boys', [St.] 'Paul's Boys').

There were two kinds of theatre company. The first was dependent upon one dominant figure, as organizer or financier. This was the model for the boy companies which flourished fitfully on the London scene, and for some other adult companies. For example, the theatrical impresario, Philip Henslowe, rented out theatres to companies, bought plays for them and provided them with costumes and props during the 1590s. We still have part of Henslowe's 'diary' which includes lists of props and expenses laid out on costumes and scripts, and money received at performances of particular plays. The other kind of company, luckily for Shakespeare, was much more democratic. It consisted of an average of ten actors, and was based on group management of the day-to-day business, and an income derived from profit sharing.

Shakespeare was a 'sharer' (we would now say 'share-holder') in the Lord Chamberlain's Men and the King's Men, and also in the Globe Theatre, which was built as a dedicated space for his company in 1599. It is this 'sharing' which made Shakespeare enough money to buy his properties in Stratford.

Props

These are conventionally divided into those the actors can bring on with them ('handheld' or 'hand props') and larger props, such as beds or thrones, which might interrupt or distract from the stage action while they were transported on- and off-stage. Before Shakespeare's company acquired the indoor Black-friars Playhouse in 1608 its usual practice was to play straight through with no breaks (this was particularly necessary in the winter, as plays did not start until 2 o'clock in the afternoon and there was no artificial lighting). One reason for the relatively few references to large props is thus the need to keep the play flowing. In addition, owing to the fact that the players might have to leave the purpose-built theatres to play elsewhere (for example, because of plague), it made sense not to have elaborate props requirements built into the action.

Some hand props acquire significance as the action unfolds: the hand-kerchief in *Othello*, for example. Others have in themselves all kinds of cultural significance. For example, Yorick's skull does not merely contrast with the fondly remembered earlier encounters with the clown; the skull itself was a conventional sign of mortality, the certainty that everyone will die and be held to account in the final Day of Judgement. For that reason, it was a common motif on funeral monuments and sometimes personal jewel-lery. So Hamlet's holding this prop is the focus for all kinds of cultural meanings.

Publishing

The script of a play belonged to the theatre company or impresario, who paid its writer or writers a one-off fee. The writer's involvement in the publication of his plays might end at this point. Shakespeare, as a company sharer, was unusual in the level of input he could have over publishing decisions; still, the market for plays (and the money to be made from putting them into print) was limited, and half of Shakespeare's plays were not published during his lifetime. Plays which appeared for the first time after his death in the First Folio include *Twelfth Night, Macbeth, The Tempest* and many others. Poetry had higher status, and Shakespeare appears to have cared more about the publica-tion of his poetry than his plays, particularly the sonnets. His long poem *Venus and Adonis* (1593) is his most popular *book* in the period up to 1660.

Poems, like plays, would have been sold to a publisher and a single payment (a couple of pounds usually) would have been made to the seller.

The publication history of Shakespeare's plays is complicated. Counting the posthumous First Folio (see Glossary), which presents itself as a 'collected' dramatic works, there were three substantially different versions of *Hamlet*, two of *King Lear*, two of *Romeo and Juliet* and two of *Richard III*, to name only a few. Some of these differences are relatively small, but not all. For example, the earliest printed version of *Hamlet* has 'To be or not to be, aye there's the point / To die, to sleep, is that all? Aye, all', instead of 'To be or not to be; that is the question / Whether 'tis nobler in the mind . . .' As living theatrical creations, it is likely that plays were revised for a variety of reasons (touring, personnel changes, creative second thoughts); it is also likely that the manuscripts received by some publishers had to be 'mended', 'improved' or added to. It may be that actors who had been in the plays were consulted: their memories appear to have been extremely well developed, even by the standards of modern actors. It is also possible that scribes made changes to the manuscripts they copied, and that those involved in printing manuscripts changed texts in less significant ways. Just which sections of which texts we can attribute authoritatively to 'Shakespeare' is a source of continuing debate, not least because Shakespeare may have changed his mind about his own plays during the course of their lives on the stage.

Repertoire

The range of plays a company offered depended on whether they were in London or on tour. Touring companies were constrained in terms of props and costumes and they would offer a limited choice of plays at each venue. In London, competition between companies for audiences mostly led to them offering a different play every day. This was certainly the situation in the 1590s. If a play was reasonably successful it would be revived again, some weeks later, so that the 'run' of a successful play might take in twenty performances over a number of years. If old plays were revived after their initial run, they were often revised. So *The Merry Wives of Windsor* (a play putting Falstaff in a contemporary rather than historical setting) was revised to alter allusions to the now-dead Queen Elizabeth. A play written for a public, 'outdoor' theatre like the Globe might be revised to take advantage of the scenic or other possibilities of an indoor theatre like the Blackfriars. Shakespeare also probably revised his plays for structural reasons, making major changes to *Hamlet* and *King Lear* which are visible in the differences between quarto and folio publications of the plays.

One consequence of the repertory system was that companies put on competing versions of the same tragic or historical story – so there were several plays about Henry V. Shakespeare worked very closely with earlier plays on King John and Henry V when he was producing his own, to the extent of even lifting lines from them. The evidence is very patchy, but it appears that comedies were the most popular offerings; one analysis of a company backed by the impresario Henslowe in the period 1595–96 counts thirty-seven plays, seventeen of which were new and seventeen of which appear to have been comedies.

Rhetoric

This is the name given to the use of language, written or spoken, to persuade, and was a major part of the Elizabethan school syllabus. Its aim was to help its practitioners achieve success by breaking down a particular language use into its component parts, which could then be addressed in detail. For example, rhetorical theory broke down a public speech into identifying its arguments, arranging them in the right order, employing the right style, memorizing them and delivering them. Each of these elements was then broken down further into figures of speech, or 'tropes'. There are relatively few 'set-piece' public speeches in Shakespeare's plays – Mark Antony's oration over the dead Julius Caesar is one example. However, Shakespeare and the educated members of his audience (and, by definition, his readers) approached literary language, particularly its style and structure, with the knowledge that there was an incredible range of different rhetorical figures at their disposal.

Romance

The defining feature of romance as a literary genre is its unlikeliness, and the sub-category of 'romance' is now a generally accepted term referring to Shakespeare's last plays – *Pericles, Cymbeline, The Winter's Tale, The Tempest, Henry VIII* and *The Two Noble Kinsmen* – which feature a variety of unlikely happenings and situations. These include heavenly visions, gods descending to earth, omnipotent magicians and a statue 'coming to life'. Shakespeare's romances are comedies (and were so identified in the First Folio) in the sense that they end happily, but they lack comedy's consistent lightness of tone and typically also represent some of the negative extremes of human experience. In this, and their blurring the boundaries between the world we know and other realities, they resemble folk tales.

Scenery

The theatrical traditions Shakespeare inherited were many and various. The location of a scene, if one were noted at all, would frequently be noted or implied in the speech of the characters. The permanent theatres in London employed some very large props, amounting to scenic items. Henslowe's diary records a mouth of hell, for example. One exception to this in theatres like the Globe or the Blackfriars was the use of the balcony: the physical fabric of the theatre could thus function to indicate, for example, the walls of a city or (as in *Hamlet*) a castle. In cases like this, however, there is no evidence that there was any effort made to 'disguise' the balcony as something else, though 'hangings' (painted cloths or curtains) were used on occasions to decorate the inside of the theatre, and sometimes stages.

Stage Directions

These are instructions to be found in a printed text of plays indicating actions, gestures or speaking tones. Many nineteenth- and twentieth-century plays provide very full instructions about where and when actors should move, perform an action, enter or exit. Some of them even specify how actors should speak their lines, using brackets – for example '(angrily)'. Good modern editions of Shakespeare's plays never specify how actors should speak their lines, but they do often elaborate upon the directions present in early plays and also 'invent' stage directions of their own. They do this to make what they think is happening clearer to the modern reader, but as what is happening (and, often, where it is happening) is not authoritatively stated in the text, such 'editorial' stage directions do not so much describe a reality as create it. In addition, both actors and editors look for 'stage directions' to the actual words spoken in characters' speeches to give them clues on how a scene might be played. If Ariel says 'I go', it is pretty clear from his words alone that s/he is moving towards a stage exit. If a character says 'my lord' it is immediately clear who they are speaking to. This kind of stage direction is often known as an 'embedded' stage direction, because it is embedded in characters' lines rather than clearly stated in the original text. Even 'original' stage directions are not necessarily from the author; as the manuscript given to a printer could be a 'working' version, stage directions could have been written by different people at different times, and could even have been inserted by a scribe making a 'fair copy' of the manuscript to give to the printer.

Stages

When thinking of how Shakespeare's plays were performed, it is better to think of 'stages' rather than theatres, because we have records of many occasions when Shakespeare's company performed outside purpose-built London theatres – town halls, the Inns of Court, the yards of London inns, aristocratic houses inside and outside London and the court itself to name but a few. Shakespeare's company did eventually come to operate out of two purpose-built London theatres (the Globe and the Blackfriars). Despite this variety of playing places, theatres and halls shared a basic stage structure. At the back of the stage, however it was shaped, were two doors visible to the audience. The vast majority of exits and entrances were made through these. Stages themselves could be 'thrust' out into the audience, who were thus on three sides of the action and could see each other, or set more closely against a wall of the building or at one edge of the space.

Sumptuary Laws

These were a series of laws beginning well before the sixteenth century and subsequently extended which attempted to restrict certain expensive or high-status clothes to particular orders of society. For example, a 1562 proclamation attempted to regulate 'monstrous and outrageous greatness of hose' [ridiculously baggy trousers, then in fashion] by stating how much cloth tailors were allowed to use in making them, and forbidding anyone below the rank of knight from gilding metal accessories like spurs or daggers. If sumptuary laws had worked, it would have been possible to tell somebody's social status with some accuracy simply by looking at them. However, as there are many proclamations attempting to tighten up on this particular branch of law enforcement, it is sensible to conclude that sumptuary laws were not respected, and that many seized the opportunity to dress like their social superiors when their purses allowed.

Tragedy

A play with a predominantly sombre tone representing characters principally from a social elite and ending unhappily with a death. Theories of tragedy in Shakespeare's time emphasized its function as a true representation of the negative aspects of human experience (in Sir Philip Sidney's words, it shows 'the ulcers that are covered with tissue'). The most compelling representation of this was taken to be the death (and, more importantly, the downfall) of someone of high social status in whom the audience had a strong emotional investment.

Just as comedy had a variety of stock characters – like the stupid yokel – so tragedy soon developed a range of recognizable figures. Examples include the revenger and the Machiavel. Machiavels (named after the supposedly immoral Italian historian and political theorist Machiavelli) were, effectively, psychopaths, villains with no concern for moral codes who wreak havoc before themselves dying. 'Revenge tragedies' (such as *Hamlet*) typically feature a clash between individual honour and social and cosmic government, where it becomes increasingly clear that the revenger cannot survive.

Where comedy focuses on society as a whole, and its capacity to renew itself, tragedy typically zooms in on one or two impressive but flawed individuals and their inability to escape their fate. The experience of tragedy is typically one of increasing tension as this fate draws to its conclusion, a tension which in some theories is 'discharged' at the tragic death of the protagonist (Aristotle termed this 'catharsis'). The tragic world is without mercy or justice, without second chances and without laughter. Tragedy unveils the possibility that human knowledge and understanding may grow in certain extraordinary individuals (such as protagonists) during times of intense suffering but conventionally it places rigorous limits on human autonomy. We frequently discover the tragic hero or heroine caught between mutually exclusive codes of behaviour and subsequently destroyed spiritually and physically by the consequences of their actions.

Part II
How to Read Shakespeare

Case Studies in Reading I: Reading the Texts

Kirk Melnikoff

Chapter Overview

In this chapter, we will examine the various dimensions of Shakespeare's verbal art. Shakespeare was, after all, a poet as well as a dramatist, interested as much in the finer details of language – its sound, its rhythm, its grammar, its ambiguities etc. – as he was in action, character and plot. Throughout his dramatic career, however, Shakespeare never tired of mocking those who over-read or thoughtlessly obsess about language. In the plays that we have taken as our objects, Malvolio and Polonius are most guilty of these respective sins, but literally dozens of similarly flawed characters exist in the full body of Shakespeare's dramatic work. As we explore his English, his craft in poetic composition and his word-play, we will bear this in mind, remembering always that Shakespeare's language is a part of a larger artistic whole.

Shakespeare's English

To say that Shakespeare's England was a nation in transition is not, on the face of it, a startling observation. Transition, of course, could be said to be the inevitable condition of all nations, modern or early modern. But when Shakespeare was born in 1564, England was in the midst of unprecedented change (see Engel, this volume, Chapter 2). Accompanying these developments was a significant shift in the fortunes of the nation's vernacular, or native language. At the beginning of the sixteenth century, English was routinely maligned for its limited vocabulary and crude workings. French remained the preferred medium of the social elite, and Latin and Greek were still thought the only acceptable languages for scholars. Bolstered by the emergence of a native print industry and driven by Protestantism's focus on laity access to a vernacular Bible (see Engel, this volume, Chapter 2), however, English would quickly supplant French and rival Latin. By the later years of the century, not only would its vocabulary be greatly expanded by as many as 10,000 new words, but its ascent would be ensured by spectacular new works written in the vernacular like Spenser's *Faerie Queene* (1590) and the King James Bible (1611) (see Engel and Longstaffe chapters 1 and 2, this volume).

In fact, it was during Shakespeare's lifetime that written English was taking a number of important steps towards becoming the language that we recognize today. Nevertheless, Shakespeare's English can still seem unfamiliar to the modern ear and eye for a number of reasons. This is mainly because at the end of the sixteenth century, spelling and grammar had yet to be standardized, meaning that for Shakespeare and his contemporaries there was neither one *correct* spelling of a word nor the same restrictions over where one put words in a sentence. Our modern English editions of Shakespeare's plays have veiled the capricious spelling of a playwright who during his lifetime spelled his name in at least two different ways: 'Shakspere' and 'Shakspeare'. But Shakespeare's variable grammar, essential as we shall see in constructing the rhythmic flow of his verse and prose, still looms large. In composing questions, Shakespeare could choose between two basic patterns, either forming them with the more modern 'do' or through the now-obsolete method of inversion. Hamlet, for example, asks Horatio 'Stayed [the ghost] long?' (1. 2. 235). But he also could have asked, 'Did [the ghost] stay long?' Similarly, in forming negative statements, Shakespeare could choose between putting 'do not' before a verb or placing 'not' after the verb. In *The Tempest*'s epilogue, Prospero asks the audience to '*Let me not* [my emphasis] [. . .] dwell. In this bare island by your spell' (5–8); if metre were not an issue, he also could have asked, '*Do not let me* [my emphasis] [. . .] dwell / In this bare island by your spell'.

Shakespeare also had more options when it came to verb endings and pronouns. For his present-tense verbs in the third-person singular, either '-es' or '-eth' could be used. In the following two-line example from Sonnet 135, Shakespeare employs both options following the subject 'sea':

> The sea, all water, yet *receives* rain still,
> And in abundance *addeth* to his store. [my emphasis] (p. 1969)

Here, the sonnet's ten-syllable line explains why 'the sea' first 'receives rain still' and then 'addeth ["abundance"] to his store'. 'Receiveth' would have given the former line eleven syllables, while 'adds' would have given the latter nine syllables. In his plays, when the requirements of rhythm and metre were not at issue, Shakespeare generally seems to have favoured the ending '-eth' for his more formal scenes.

Formality was also at issue in Shakespeare's choosing to use the second-person pronouns 'thee', 'thou', 'thy' and 'thine' as opposed to 'you' and 'your'. During the sixteenth century, friends, family and acquaintances addressed one another using 'thou' and its various forms. 'You' and 'your' were reserved for more formal situations and when a social inferior was addressing his or her superior. The more informal 'thou' could conversely be used by a social superior or elder in respectively addressing an inferior or youth. Hamlet's past intimacy with Ophelia is suggested in his letter to her by his use of the more personal 'thee' and 'thine' in the closing: ' "But that I love thee best, O most best, believe it. Adieu. / Thine evermore, most dear lady, whilst this machine is to him, / Hamlet" ' (2. 2. 121–24, pp. 1693–4). In another example, Orsino's use of 'thou' and its forms in his first interaction with 'Cesario' (the disguised Viola) underscores his own sense of social superiority: 'Cesario, / Thou know'st no less but all. I have unclasped / To thee the book even of my secret soul. / Therefore, good youth, address thy gait unto her, / Be not denied access [. . .] / Till thou have audience' (1. 4. 12–17, p. 1774). Orsino's use of thou and thine at the same time, however, ironically invites Viola's own desire for more familiarity with him as his beloved.

Shakespeare's Verse

Along with its now archaic grammar, Shakespeare's dramatic language can also seem alien in other ways with its normative 'swell'. Like most of the sixteenth-century professional playwrights, Shakespeare wrote poetic drama, which means that taken together the majority of Shakespeare's dramatic language is written not in prose, but in some form of verse. Most of the lines in his plays, in other words, contain a set number of syllables and a regular rhythmic pattern. In reading Shakespeare's plays (as opposed to watching them), the difference between Shakespeare's verse and prose is usually apparent in the layout of the printed page. Given below is the opening of *Twelfth Night*'s first scene, a scene written entirely in verse. Underneath the emboldened Act and scene number ('1.1') and the opening stage direction for '*Music*' to be played and characters to '*Enter*' are the first eight lines of a speech to be spoken by Orsino, the Duke of Ilyria. This speech is in verse, and this is typographically indicated by the facts that: (1) Orsino's lines do not extend to the edge of the right margin and that: (2) each of them begins with a capitalized word (even though most of them do not begin a new sentence):

1.1

Music. Enter ORSINO *Duke of Illyria,* CURIO, *and other lords*

ORSINO   If music be the food of love, play on,
          Give me excess of it that, surfeiting,
          The appetite may sicken and so die.
          That strain again, it had a dying fall.
          O, it came o'er my ear like the sweet sound
          That breathes upon a bank of violets,
          Stealing and giving odour. Enough, no more,
          'Tis not so sweet now as it was before. (1. 1. 1–8, p. 1768)

Conversely, *Twelfth Night*'s third scene is written entirely in prose. Given below is the opening of this third scene, with the first speech beginning under the emboldened Act and scene number ('1.3') and the opening stage direction.

1.3

Enter SIR TOBY [*Belch*] *and* MARIA

SIR TOBY   What a plague means my niece to take the death of her brother thus? I am sure care's an enemy to life. (1. 3. 1–2, p. 1771)

Unlike the typographical appearance of the previous scene, here (1) Sir Toby's opening line extends to the right margin and (2) the beginning of his successive line is not capitalized.

Throughout his plays and poetry, Shakespeare's preferred metrical pattern is *iambic pentameter*. It is the rhythm in which Orsino sighs 'If music be the food of love, play on' in the lines quoted above, and it is the poetic metre in which Hamlet famously asks 'To be or not to be . . .'. *Iambic* is the adjectival form of *iamb* and refers to a two-syllable metrical unit (a *foot*) in which the first syllable is unstressed and the second syllable is stressed. There are many common words that are by themselves iambic in their stress patterns like *behold* (bĕ / hóld), *untie* (ŭn / tíe), and *against* (ă / gaínst). The most common metrical feet or units in early English poetry are, along with the iamb, the *trochee* (stressed/unstressed), the *dactyl* (stressed/unstressed/unstressed), the *anapaest* (unstressed / unstressed / stressed) and the *spondee* (stressed / stressed). *Pentameter* refers to a poetic line that contains five metrical units. In Shakespeare's day, the most commonly employed metres were *trimeter* (three metrical units), *tetrameter* (four metrical units), pentameter, *hexameter* (six metrical units) and *heptameter* (seven metrical units).

Shakespeare's liking for iambic pentameter had many roots. Immortalized in Chaucer's *Canterbury Tales* two centuries earlier, the metrical pattern had become a mainstay of English poetry by the end of the sixteenth century. It had helped to enliven the lyric poetry of Wyatt, Howard and Sidney; bolstered the ambitious intentions of Spenser in his epic *Faerie Queene* and underpinned the mighty lines of Shakespeare's ill-fated contemporary Christopher Marlowe in *Tamburlaine* and *Doctor Faustus*. But perhaps more importantly, it was also the rhythmic metre thought closest to everyday speech, both in its unstressed / stressed rhythm (reminiscent of the beat of a human heart – *de dum*, *de dum*, *de dum*) and in its length (similar to the span of a normal breath). Thus, in iambic pentameter, Shakespeare found an ideal vehicle for the extraordinary yet patently human personalities that he would create for his comedies, history plays, tragedies and romances.

In fashioning the rhythmic musings of Viola, Hamlet, Prince Hal, Prospero and others, Shakespeare was undoubtedly inspired by his extensive early work with the sonnet (see Glossary). In total, Shakespeare penned 154 of these short lyric love poems. First published together in 1609, these sonnets are famously idiosyncratic in their two addressees: the first 126 are dedicated to a 'young man'; while the last 28 are dedicated to a 'dark lady'. Following the poetic conventions of the time, almost all of them are composed using iambic pentameter, and together they document Shakespeare's changing poetic engagement with two very different beloveds. As such, they afford excellent examples of Shakespeare's methods of expression within his favourite rhythmic metre.

Analysing the Sonnet

Printed below is Shakespeare's twelfth sonnet. As a poem endorsing marriage and reproduction for the young man as a 'defence' against 'the wastes of time', this sonnet echoes a number of similarly-themed sonnets at the beginning of the 1609 collection. For our purposes, the poem affords a good starting place in that its iambic rhythm is relatively easy to recognize. As you read, note that the opening line is written with perfect – what is called 'regular' – iambic pentameter:

> When I do count the clock that tells the time,
> And see the brave day sunk in hideous night;

> When I behold the violet past prime,
> And sable curls ensilvered o'er with white;
> When lofty trees I see barren of leaves,
> Which erst from heat did canopy the herd,
> And summer's green all girded up in sheaves
> Borne on the bier with white and bristly beard:
> Then of thy beauty do I question make
> That thou among the wastes of time must go,
> Since sweets and beauties do themselves forsake,
> And die as fast as they see others grow;
>   And nothing 'gainst time's scythe can make defence
>   Save breed to brave him when he takes thee hence. (p. 1927)

Like a number of Shakespeare's poems and dramatic speeches, Sonnet 12 is composed with a remarkably consistent metrical beat. Even though thirteen of its fourteen lines are not entirely regular, close to three-quarters of the poem's feet are iambic. As such, the poem develops a mechanical rhythm, one difficult to ignore either when read or heard. This is the basic rhythm that underscores – in varying regularity and pacing – much of Shakespeare's dramatic verse. It is the rhythmic frame of Prince Hal's surprising declaration that 'I know you all' at the end of *1 Henry IV*'s second scene, the energetic beat underlying all of Hamlet's soliloquies, and the delicate cadence of Prospero's pained recognition that 'our little life / Is rounded with a sleep' in the fourth Act of *The Tempest*.

It is important to recognize, however, that here and in all of his iambic pentameter, Shakespeare rarely confines himself to the regular. Put bluntly, perfect rhythm tends towards sing-song, towards the artificial or pat. Shakespeare consistently avoided such regularity, fashioning his iambic rhythm to create particular effects and to reinforce his larger artistic designs. To continue with it as our exemplum, Sonnet 12 offers a good instance of such careful fashioning. It aptly begins with a regular line because such regularity well introduces the poem's principal theme of unceasing time. Monosyllabic and exactingly filled out with a completely regular iambic 'unstressed/ stressed' pattern, this line reads with the even pace of a clock's 'tic toc, tic toc, tic toc, tic toc, tic toc'. To this, line 2 adds the doubly stressed spondee rhythm of 'day sunk' to suggest the adjoining movement of the sun's inexorable 'sinking' in the sea of night. Shakespeare creates a similar double movement in the poem's second-to-last line when he joins the spondee of 'time's scythe' to the rest of the line's regular iambic metre, suggesting the quick sweep of the grim reaper within the constant current of time. Only in the sonnet's final line does Shakespeare essentially abandon iambic pentameter. Here, the line's only iambic foot 'to brave' precedes three final spondee rhythms: 'him when';

'he takes'; 'thee hence'. This six-stressed ending underscores the finality of 'time's scythe' taking the young man in death; it also signals the possibility of another place outside of regular time where there are no tic-tocs and, as Hamlet tells us before his death, '[t]he rest is silence' (5. 2. 300).

Language and Dramatic Communication

In direct comparison with his modes of composition in the sonnets, Shake-speare used an *irregularly regular* iambic pentameter in his plays for specific purposes: to help conjure the mood or energy of a particular scene; to delineate the characteristic movement of a particular speaker's mind and/or to help indicate a character's emotional state. Shakespeare's iambic rhythms would become more complicated and diverse as his dramatic career progressed, yielding the dynamic personalities of Hamlet, Lear, Macbeth and Cleopatra. His pentameter would follow a similar trajectory; it would become more and more extrametrical (having lines containing eleven syllables rather than just ten) and less and less end-stopped with punctuation. At the beginning of *Hamlet*, for example, Hamlet's distraught reaction to the death of his father and quick remarriage of his mother is well encapsulated by the irregular rhythms and lineation of his first soliloquy:

> HAMLET   O that this too too solid flesh would melt,
> Thaw, and resolve itself into a dew,
> Or that the Everlasting had not fixed
> His canon 'gainst self-slaughter! O God, O God,
> How weary, stale, flat, and unprofitable
> Seem to me all the uses of this world!
> Fie on't, ah fie, fie! 'Tis an unweeded garden
> That grows to seed; things rank and gross in nature
> Possess it merely. That it should come to this –
> But two months dead – nay, not so much, not two –
> So excellent a king, that was to this
> Hyperion to a satyr, so loving to my mother
> That he might not beteem the winds of heaven
> Visit her face too roughly! (1. 2. 129–42, pp. 1675–6)

Unlike those in Sonnet 12, Hamlet's lines here are anything but predominantly iambic. Instead, the rhythm of his language is fitful and unpredictable, broken up with a number of mid-line pauses (what we call 'caesuras') and spondee exclamations like 'O God, O God' and 'Fie on't, ah fie [. . .]!' At the same time, half of Hamlet's lines are not punctuated at their endings, creating unbroken bursts of sentiment such as 'Or that the Everlasting had not fixed /

His canon 'gainst self-slaughter!' Such sentiment literally bursts the bounds of regular pentameter in Hamlet's last quoted sentence, pushing both line 140 ('Hyperion to a satyr, so loving to my mother') and line 141 ('That he might not beteem the winds of heaven / Visit her face too roughly!') outside of their ten-syllable bounds with extra beats. In effect, Hamlet's early language aptly moves with the unpredictable energy of an unsettled and passionate mind.

As you may have noticed, besides being more irregular in pacing and length, this opening soliloquy is also very different from Sonnet 12 in that Hamlet's lines are all unrhymed. While patterns of rhyme like the 'Italian' (abbaabbacdcdee) and the 'English' (ababacdcdefefgg) rhyme schemes were the norm for sonnet writing, unrhymed iambic pentameter or 'blank verse' had been the standard dramatic idiom ever since Marlowe had reigned triumphant with it in his 1587 theatrical debut *Tamburlaine*. In the face of changing theatrical norms, Shakespeare would continue to employ rhyme for a number of dramatic purposes. It most obviously turns up in the many songs in plays like *Twelfth Night* and *The Tempest*. These songs can function in performance as important dramatic set-pieces, powerfully affecting atmospheres and moods. Rhyme also can commonly be found signalling transitions between scenes or speeches with an abrupt poetic flourish. Orsino, for example, closes his aforementioned opening appearance in *Twelfth Night* with such poetic emphasis. To Valentine, he optimistically declares, 'Away before me to sweet beds of flowers. / Love-thoughts lie rich when canopied with bowers' (1. 1. 39–40). Similarly, after saving Alonso from Antonio and Sebastian's usurping swords in *The Tempest*'s second Act, Ariel punctuates the scene with a rhymed iambic pentameter couplet: 'Prospero my lord shall know what I have done. / So, King, go safely on to seek thy son' (2. 1. 323–24).

Especially in his early plays, Shakespeare used rhyme to shift the mood of a moment or of an entire scene. In Viola's second disguised interaction with Orsino, the growing emotional bond between the two characters is marked by their both suddenly speaking in rhyme:

VIOLA	I think it well, my lord.
ORSINO	Then let thy love be younger than thyself,
	Or thy affection cannot hold the bent;
	For women are as roses, whose fair flower
	Being once displayed, doth fall that very hour.
VIOLA	And so they are. Alas that they are so:
	To die even when they to perfection grow.

(2. 4. 34–40, p. 1787)

A different kind of mood shift is effected through rhyme at the end of *1 Henry IV*. After having defeated Hotspur in battle, Prince Hal initially provides a moving blank-verse tribute to the fallen young warrior. Upon seeing Falstaff on the ground, however, Hal's mood and language changes:

PRINCE HARRY   [. . .] This earth that bears thee dead
                       Bears not alive so stout a gentleman.

....

                       Adieu, and take thy praise with thee to heaven.
                       Thy ignominy sleep with thee in the grave,
                       But not remembered in thy epitaph.
                           He spieth FALSTAFF *on the ground*
                       What, old acquaintance! Could not all this flesh
                       Keep in a little life? Poor Jack, farewell.
                       I could have better spared a better man.
                       O, I should have a heavy miss of thee,
                       If I were much in love with vanity.
                       Death hath not struck so fat a deer today,
                       Though many dearer in this bloody fray.
                       Embowelled will I see thee by and by.
                       Till then, in blood by noble Percy lie.   *Exit*
                                       (5. 4. 91–92, 98–109, p. 1220)

In addressing his seemingly-dead friend, not only is Hal's diction simpler and more informal – 'Could not all this flesh / Keep in a little life? Poor Jack, farewell' – but it also becomes lighter and more impish. With 'heavy miss', Hal cleverly suggests both that he will 'greatly lament' Falstaff's death and that Falstaff's fat body constitutes a 'heavy' object to be missed. He continues his focus on Falstaff's huge body in playing with the identical sounds but different meanings of 'deer' and 'dear'. Rhyme, in the form of three rhymed couplets, provides an ending frame for Hal's witty tribute. It is a fitting part of Hal's playful homage to the friend who mentored him in the possibilities of language and play.

Shakespeare's Prose

However, in at least one sense, Hal's homage is not entirely apt. Falstaff himself rarely speaks in 'numbers' ('metre'); his normal language is not verse but the 'everyday' language of prose. While prose may constitute the smaller portion of Shakespeare's dramatic language, it is a *significant* portion, functioning in a number of provocative ways. At the beginning of his career, Shakespeare subscribed to a conventional distinction between prose and

verse usage. Just as elite characters were thought to be the appropriate subjects of tragedy and should speak in the elevated language of verse, lower-
order characters were thought to be the appropriate subjects of comedy and
should speak in the everyday language of prose. Shakespeare's adherence to
this stylistic system can be recognized in the prose musings of Feste and
Malvolio in *Twelfth Night*, of the gravediggers in *Hamlet*, and of the tavern
goers in *1 Henry IV*. It also undergirds one of Shakespeare's most memorable
openings. Set at sea amidst the thunder and lightning of a powerful storm,
The Tempest's first scene energetically begins with the Master and the Boatswain's direct and command-laden prose:

MASTER	Boatswain!
BOATSWAIN	Here, Master. What cheer?
MASTER	Good, speak to th'mariners. Fall to't yarely, or we run ourselves aground. Bestir, bestir! *Exit*
	Enter MARINERS
BOATSWAIN	Heigh, my hearts! Cheerly, cheerly, my hearts! Yare, yare! Take in the topsail! Tend to th'Master's whistle! – Blow till thou burst thy wind, if room enough.' (1. 1. 1–7, p. 3055)

Prose also proves to be the idiom of the play's comic duo Trinculo and
Stefano, Alonso's jester and butler. Trinculo enters the play's second Act com-
plaining in prose that there is 'neither bush nor shrub to bear off any weather
at all' (2. 2. 18–19), while Stefano's clownish prose is only momentarily
delayed when he first enters singing a 'scurvy tune'. Ironically, prose is *not* the
idiom of their co-conspirator Caliban, and his preference for verse is continually in tension with Trinculo and Stefano's prose utterances. This underscores
not simply his different nature and motivation but also calls into question his
ubiquitous tag of 'monster'.

As we will see, Shakespeare would quickly develop his own brands of
division between prose and verse. What would not change, though, was his
unsurpassed ability to inscribe personality into his characters' language, not
just in verse but also in prose. In *Twelfth Night*, Olivia's steward Malvolio is
anything but subtle about his austerity, particularly in his derisive attitude
towards the domestic misrule of Feste and Sir Toby. Maria's scheme with the
forged letter shows us that Malvolio's austerity is in fact driven by his own
ambition and narcissism. Such overriding personality traits become amply
clear in both the content *and* form of Malvolio's prose response to this letter:

MALVOLIO Daylight and champaign discovers not more. This is open. I
will be proud, I will read politic authors, I will baffle Sir Toby, I will
wash off gross acquaintance, I will be point-device the very man. I do

> not now fool myself, to let imagination jade me; for every reason
> excites to this, that my lady loves me. (2. 5. 140–44, p. 1792)

In imagining what 'will' be his affair with Olivia, Malvolio can only think in terms of himself and what *he* will gain. Underscoring this self focus, 'I' is five times the subject of Malvolio's compound third sentence, and this sentence's bare-bone, repeated grammar subtly suggests its speaker's overly simplistic vision of action in the world. Malvolio imagines that he 'will' do everything he sets out to do, with no adverb to qualify the force of his actions. Not surprisingly, Malvolio's fourth quoted sentence begins and ends with Malvolio ('I' and 'me').

A much more attractive brand of narcissism defines the comic centre of *1 Henry IV*. As Prince Hal describes it at the beginning of the play, for the mountain of flesh that is Falstaff, nothing has any significance that is outside the bounds of his great appetite, even time. 'What a devil hast thou to do with the time of the day?' asks Hal, 'Unless hours were cups of sack, and minutes capons, and clocks the tongues of bawds, and dials the signs of leaping-houses, and the blessed sun himself a fair hot wench in flame-coloured taffeta' (1. 2. 5–9, p. 1160). Never one to concede anything, especially the last word, Falstaff responds quickly to Hal's playful accusation:

> FALSTAFF   Marry then, sweet wag, when thou art king let not us that are
> squires of the night's body be called thieves of the day's beauty. Let us
> be 'Diana's foresters', 'gentlemen of the shade', 'minions of the moon',
> and let men say we be men of good government, being governed, as
> the sea is, by our noble and chaste mistress the moon, under whose
> countenance we steal. (1. 2. 20–26, p. 1160)

Like Malvolio's language, Falstaff's prose reveals much. His vocabulary demonstrates his extensive knowledge. At the same time, his symmetrical phrasing – 'squires of the night's body' has the same amount of syllables as 'thieves of the day's beauty'; 'Diana's foresters'='gentlemen of the shade'='minions of the moon' – shows his impressive linguistic artistry. And perhaps most importantly, these evenly-weighed compound constructions underscore his expansive vision. He can equally imagine his crew as 'squires', as 'thieves', as 'foresters', as 'gentlemen', as 'minions' and as 'men of good government'.

Both of the examples well illustrate that Shakespeare's prose can itself be as artful as his verse. In the four plays that we have been considering, though, Shakespeare shows himself perhaps to be most interested in the dramatic potential of prose. Though it still functions as the defining idiom of his lower-order servants and clowns like Malvolio and Trinculo, it at the same time is frequently used by his elite characters. In these plays, *who* speaks prose is less important than *when* they speak it. Prose, in other words, tells us something about the dramatic situation of the play. It usually signals some kind of change, either within a scene or between one scene and the next, and it clearly also functioned as a performance prompt for actors, indicating less-formal modes of delivery. Ophelia's shift to prose in the fourth Act of *Hamlet* – 'Come, my coach! Good night, ladies, good night, sweet ladies, good night, good night' (4. 5. 69–70) – points to her own descent into madness. Similarly, Hamlet's own alteration from speaking verse at the end of Act One to speaking prose in the second scene of Act Two tells us not simply that he has lowered his language to the level of Polonius, but it also suggests the early chameleon-like trappings of Hamlet's promised 'antic disposition' (1. 5. 173).

The Movement between Poetry and Prose

Shifts in and out of prose can also indicate changes in characters' moods within a single scene. In Olivia's first interview with the disguised Viola in *Twelfth Night*, Viola's change from playful wit to serious wooer is signalled by her shift from prose to verse in speaking of 'beauty [being] truly blent' in Olivia's face. At the same time, Olivia's initial resistance to this poetical wooing is expressed clearly in her sarcastic prose responses:

VIOLA   Good madam, let me see your face.

OLIVIA   Have you any commission from your lord to negotiate with my face? You are now out of your text. But we will draw the curtain and show you the picture.
     [*She unveils*]
    Look you, sir, such a one I was this present. Is't not well done?

VIOLA   Excellently done, if God did all.

OLIVIA   'Tis in grain, sir, 'twill endure wind and weather.

VIOLA   'Tis beauty truly blent, whose red and white
      Nature's own sweet and cunning hand laid on.
      Lady, you are the cruell'st she alive
      If you will lead these graces to the grave
      And leave the world no copy.

OLIVIA   O sir, I will not be so hard-hearted. I will give out divers schedules of my beauty. It shall be inventoried and every particle and utensil labelled to my will, as, *item*, two lips, indifferent red; *item*, two grey eyes, with lids to them; *item*, one neck, one chin, and so forth. (1. 5. 202–18, p. 1779)

Cynical prose, however, quickly shifts to poignant verse after Viola speaks of Orsino's 'fertile tears' and 'groans that thunder love, with sighs of fire'

(224–25). To such fervent assurances of Orsino's passion, Olivia admits in blank verse that 'I suppose him virtuous, know him noble, / Of great estate, of fresh and stainless youth, / In voices well divulged, free, learned, and valiant, / And in dimension and the shape of nature / A gracious person; but yet I cannot love him' (227–31). Of course, the irony here is that Olivia *does* love, and her ardour for the disguised Viola is subtly suggested by the heightened language of this denial.

More generally, changes in a scene's overall mood can also be affected by shifts in and out of prose. At the beginning of *The Tempest*'s second Act, for example, for the first time we see Alonso and his party safely landed on Prospero's island. Predictably, the good-natured yet voluble Gonzalo opens the scene with a verse appeal to his king who is melancholy at the prospect of his son's death:

> GONZALO [*to* ALONSO] Beseech you, sir, be merry. You have cause,
> So have we all, of joy; for our escape
> Is much beyond our loss. Our hint of woe
> Is common; every day some sailor's wife,
> The masters of some merchant, and the merchant,
> Have just our theme of woe. But for the miracle,
> I mean our preservation, few in millions
> Can speak like us. (2. 1. 1–8, p. 3070)

Alonso, however, refuses to embrace Gonzalo's optimistic musings, responding only with the entreaty 'Prithee, peace'. Alonso's pat refusal quickly changes the scene's language and mood. For the next ninety lines, the contemptuous prose rejoinders of Antonio and Sebastian dominate the scene, undermining the positive efforts of both Gonzalo and Adrian to inspire hope – and leadership – in their distraught king. Gonzalo's own language quickly succumbs to the uncertain, qualifying prose of Antonio and Sebastian. It is only when Alonso finally engages with the situation that the scene's mood and language temporarily changes:

> GONZALO [*to* ALONSO] Is not, sir, my doublet as fresh as the first day I
> wore it? I mean in a sort.
> ANTONIO [*to* SEBASTIAN] That 'sort' was well fished for.
> GONZALO [*to* ALONSO] When I wore it at your daughter's marriage.
> ALONSO You cram these words into mine ears against
> The stomach of my sense. Would I had never
> Married my daughter there! For, coming thence,
> My son is lost; and, in my rate, she too,
> Who is so far from Italy removed

> I ne'er again shall see her. O thou mine heir
> Of Naples and of Milan, what strange fish
> Hath made his meal on thee? (2. 1. 101–13, p. 3072)

Alonso's verse outburst elevates the mood of the scene, reclaiming it from Gonzalo's bumbling reassurances and Antonio and Sebastian's acidic interjections and asides. Here heartfelt grief temporarily trumps cynicism, noble passion silences rebelliousness. In miniature, this scene's movements from verse to prose and prose to verse underscore the power of legitimate political authority. In doing so, it also subtly criticizes the present truant leader that is Alonso and the past truant leader that was Prospero.

Shakespeare's Imagery

Shakespeare's art is, of course, anything but limited to the rhythms and dramatic effects of his verse and prose. His artistic rendering of the world includes narratives taken from history and literature *and*, as we shall discuss in this section, imagery taken from nature, from his daily life, from the body and from the arts. In fact, as commentators from as early as the seventeenth century have acknowledged, Shakespeare's language is literally 'top full' of imagery. The term 'imagery' can mean a number of things, but for our purposes we will be using it to refer to language that either (1) plays directly to our five senses (i.e. sight, hearing, smell, taste and/or touch) or that (2) draws analogies that appeal to our senses, most often through the poetic vehicles of 'simile' (explicit comparisons using 'like' or 'as') and 'metaphor' (implicit comparisons). In *Hamlet*, Horatio's description of the Ghost's first appearances offers a relatively straightforward example of imagery in the first sense. To Hamlet, Horatio describes an entity that, 'Armed at all points exactly, cap-à-pie [head to foot], / Appears before them [Marcellus and Barnardo], and with solemn march / Goes slow and stately by them. Thrice he walked / By their oppressed and fear-surprisèd eyes / Within his truncheon's [staff's] length, [. . .]' (1. 2. 200–4, p. 1677). Appealing particularly to our sense of sight, Horatio's image is not simply one of a 'solemn' martial figure, but also one that outlines an eerily close encounter, one 'Within his truncheon's length'.

However, Shakespeare's images often function as tools of analogy. They are, in other words, used to describe something – be it an object, a person, a place or something more abstract like time or an idea – in a different, frequently unexpected way. Such comparative language is, as Russ McDonald has written, 'among the most valuable tools in the Shakespearean kit' (2001: 54), and learning to recognize *and* appreciate it is an essential part of closely engaging with Shakespeare's poetic art. Returning briefly to our Sonnet 12 example, we can see that it provides good examples of imagery in this vein.

The poem's images of 'lofty trees [. . .] barren of leaves' and the 'the violet past prime' offer simple pictures of natural decay while they at the same time subtly figure the necessary withering of both powerful men ('lofty trees') and beautiful women ('violet[s]'). As we shall see, in his plays Shakespeare uses imagery to add depth to his characters, to underscore moods and themes, and to provide, as he does in Sonnet 12, the simple pleasure that comes from recognizing similarity in difference.

For another example, we can return to *1 Henry IV* and look more closely at Prince Hal's surprising revelation that 'I know you all'. In this Act One speech, Hal essentially reveals his plan to reform his 'idle' behaviour, contending that this reformation will make him seem 'more goodly and attract more eyes' than if he had never had to reform at all. In the abstract, this is not a difficult idea to express. Hal, however, communicates it through a series of images, the most extended of which comes at the beginning of the speech:

PRINCE HARRY   I know you all, and will a while uphold
                    The unyoked humour of your idleness.
                    Yet herein will I imitate the sun,
                    Who doth permit the base contagious clouds
                    To smother up his beauty from the world,
                    That when he please again to be himself,
                    Being wanted he may be more wondered at
                    By breaking through the foul and ugly mists
                    Of vapours that did seem to strangle him.
                                    (1. 2. 173–81, p. 1164)

Referring to Falstaff and his cohorts with the impersonal second-person pronoun 'you', Hal offers an image wherein he compares the sun spectacularly 'breaking' through cloud cover to what he expects will be his own awe-inspiring emergence from the tavern world of Falstaff. This extended image not only intimates ego, even presumption in Hal's seeing himself as the mighty 'sun', but it, in its rendering of the clouds as 'base contagious' and 'foul and ugly', also reveals Hal's surprising disdain for his lower-order 'mist' companions. Such disdain is hinted at in the second line. There Hal paints an image of his lower-order companions as livestock in suggesting that their inclinations ('humours') are unbridled ('unyoked'). Together, these images complicate Hal's character by subtly unveiling his heavy investment in 'sun'-like status and social difference, an investment not immediately apparent in his first interactions with Falstaff and company. At the same time, they also pleasurably enmesh us in Hal's own creativeness and facility with language.

Not so long ago, the critical investigation of Shakespeare's imagery was informed by the contention that such imagery reveals the playwright's personal idiosyncrasies (see Hiscock/Longstaffe, this volume, Chapter 1). Shakespeare's various images were taken to suggest – among other things – the playwright's fondness for the countryside, for the feelings of animals, for the simple domestic life, even for particular types of food. At first blush, these conclusions are strained, even bizarre, but they are based upon sound observations, namely, upon the undeniable fact that patterns *do* exist among Shakespeare's images, particularly within his individual plays. What these patterns reveal, however, is not Shakespeare the man – at least not in any straightforward way – but rather Shakespeare's subtle methods of dramatic art.

As his dramatic career progressed, Shakespeare would rely more and more upon imagery as a vehicle for character development. In some instances – as we saw with Hal's emerging-sun metaphor – a single image can reveal as much or more about a character's persona as his/her actions or clear-cut expressions. In other instances, constellations of related images within a single speech can suggest the complex contours of a character's personality. Towards the end of *The Tempest*, to cite another example, Prospero's latent melancholy and his expansive creativity are revealed in the imagery of his well-known Act Four speech:

> PROSPERO Our revels now are ended. These our actors,
> As I foretold you, were all spirits, and
> Are melted into air, into thin air;
> And like the baseless fabric of this vision,
> The cloud-capped towers, the gorgeous palaces,
> The solemn temples, the great globe itself,
> Yea, all which it inherit, shall dissolve;
> And, this the insubstantial pageant faded,
> Leave not a rack behind. (4. 1. 148–56, p. 3095)

Moving from his wispy image of 'melting' 'spirits', Prospero quickly fashions the more profound image of our world and its social institutions – the political ('towers'), the economic and artistic ('gorgeous palaces') and the religious ('temples') – as 'dissolving' into nothingness. In the tension between the range and content of its images, this speech gives shape to the contradictions at the heart of Prospero's character.

Plays as Dramatic Poems

Patterns of imagery can not only be found in Shakespeare's speeches; they can also be found more broadly within many of his plays. (see Hiscock/Longstaffe, this volume, Chapter 1) Throughout *The Tempest*, imagery having to do with the sea, storms and the natural elements continually reminds us of the power of the natural world; these images also help to underscore the play's major theme of humanity's unavoidable confrontation with nature, both without *and* within. It is the latter sense of nature that Prospero invokes when, at the end of the play, he admits that 'This thing of darkness I / Acknowledge mine' (5. 1. 278–79). Most immediately, he is taking responsibility for his truant slave, but he is admitting as well that he himself is also guilty of all the 'dark' natural passions embodied in Caliban. In *Hamlet*, images relating to poisoning, sickness, and decay infuse the entire play. Such imagery establishes and reinforces the play's political themes concerning a corrupt and corrupting state, but it also contributes strongly to the play's dark moods and tones. Paying attention to both the play's action *and* imagery, it is hard to miss that '[s]omething', as Marcellus says at the end of the play's fourth scene, 'is rotten in the state of Denmark' (67).

Shakespeare's Word-play

It is also hard to miss that throughout Shakespeare's works, language can be, as Feste has it, a 'very rascal'. In his plays and in his poems, in his tragedies and in his comedies, in his prose and in his verse, words can often have double, triple, even quadruple meanings or connotations. Such 'word-play' colours Shakespeare's titles, his most passionate exchanges, and even his most heartrending speeches. It can fill a scene with dizzying pace and energy, and at the same time it can subtly reveal the hidden depths of a character's personality. That said, Shakespeare's undeniable fondness for the 'pun', 'quibble' or 'play on words' has also long been a sore point for some of his greatest admirers. In an oft-quoted passage from his *Preface to Shakespeare*, Samuel Johnson (or 'Dr Johnson' as he has been called since the eighteenth century) famously lamented that 'A quibble is to Shakespeare what luminous vapours are to the traveller: he follows it at all adventures; it is sure to lead him out of his way, and sure to engulf him in the mire' (Johnson 1968: 74). For early critics like Dr Johnson, puns – like that on 'rest' in Hamlet's last line 'the rest is silence' (5. 2. 300) – deform Shakespeare's best creations; they mar by frequently becoming ends in and of themselves.

More recent commentators on Shakespeare's fondness for the pun have been less judgmental. Instead, they have shown how this penchant reflected the playwright's own fascination with the permeability of language. At the start of his career, Shakespeare was clearly more interested in the more positive aspects of language's irrepressible ambiguity. In his early comedies, word-play is coupled with the latent transformability of all things – of society, of relationships and of individuals. Just as meaning is not static, people and places can be metamorphosed, most of the time for the better. Something of this optimism can still be seen in the happy ending of *Twelfth Night*. Here, situational ambiguities stimulate new possibilities of human experience and lead to love between Olivia and Sebastian, Orsino and Viola. As his career progressed, however, Shakespeare also increasingly explored the darker side of latent ambiguity. In his tragedies, multiplicity of meaning is associated with political and personal manipulation, with madness and with emptiness and death. Ophelia's initiation into a world of ambiguity and doubt is obviously anything but redemptive; instead, her inability to understand the changeability of Hamlet directly leads to her deterioration and death in Act Four.

Shakespeare's 'puns' are as varied in their workings as the dramatic scenarios in which they occur. They are also always meant to be a source of pleasure in and of themselves. All of his plays are densely packed with puns wherein one word suggests two or more different meanings. Shakespeare's favourites include playing upon the different meanings of 'light', 'lie', 'kind' and 'prick'. Another of Shakespeare's most frequent forms of word-play has to do with using words that sound alike but that have different meanings like 'hart' and 'heart' or 'tale' and 'tail'. As we have already seen, Hal, at the end of *1 Henry IV*, invokes the different meanings of the like-sounding words 'deer' and 'dear' in his fitting tribute to what he believes to be his dead friend Falstaff. Shakespeare also employs puns involving repetition, wherein a word or phrase is repeated to mean something different in its second instance. Falstaff employs such a figure when he responds to Hal's complaint that he has often used 'his credit' to pay Falstaff's debts. To this, Falstaff cynically responds, 'Yea, and so used it that were it not *here apparent* that thou art *heir apparent* [my emphasis]' (1. 2. 50–51). Words and their different possible meanings are also frequently bandied about between characters. Such competitive word-play is everywhere in the aforementioned exchanges between Hal and Falstaff and between Olivia and the disguised Viola; it also pervades such scenes as Hamlet's first interaction with Polonius (2. 2) and Feste's first exchange with Olivia (1. 5).

Throughout his plays and his poems, Shakespeare consistently turned to word-play as both entertainment and dramatic vehicle. Even the simple presence or absence of word-play can be meaningful. Especially in his comedies, Shakespeare uses exchanges of wit to indicate deep interpersonal connections. In *Twelfth Night*, for example, Olivia's fondness for Feste is well signified by her willingness to 'take delight' in the verbal machinations of the newly returned jester. At the same time, Olivia's passion for the disguised Viola is clearly sparked by their initial war of wit in Act 1, scene 5. Even Maria's ending engagement to Sir Toby can be explained by the two characters' frequent verbal sparring. Shared word-play, Shakespeare suggests again and again, requires intimacy, an intimacy that can ground true love and lasting friendship.

Conversely, the absence of shared verbal play often figures distance between Shakespeare's characters. When Hamlet first encounters Rosencrantz and Guildenstern in Act 2, scene 2, their exchanges quickly move from being playful – with shared jokes about the whorishness of dame Fortune (220–30) – to being stilted and uncomfortable:

> HAMLET   What's the news?
> ROSENCRANTZ   None, my Lord, but that the world's grown honest.
> HAMLET   Then is doomsday near. But your news is not true. Let me question more in particular. What have you, my good friends, deserved at the hand of Fortune that she sends you to prison hither?
> GUILDENSTERN   Prison, my lord?
> HAMLET   Denmark's a prison.
> ROSENCRANTZ   Then is the world one.
> HAMLET   A goodly one, in which there are many confines, wards, and dungeons, Denmark being one o' th' worst.
> ROSENCRANTZ   We think not so, my Lord. (2. 2. 231–43, p. 1696)

Unlike their initial verbal play, no witty rejoinder is offered to Hamlet's assertion that Denmark is a 'prison', only Guildenstern's incredulous 'Prison, my Lord?' Similarly, to Hamlet's subsequent riff on the world being a prison, Rosencrantz can only offer the verbal roadblock 'We think not so, my lord'. Rosencrantz and Guildenstern will admit that they were 'sent for', that they are more Claudius's lackeys than Hamlet's close friends, but this failure of verbal play has already made their distance from their school fellow very clear.

Language and the Lower Orders

Of course, word-play most obviously turns up in the language of Shakespeare's rustics, fools and servants. It not only endows their varying expressions with a pleasurable unpredictability, but it also serves as the primary means of what often proves to be their irreverent engagement with authority. When Shakespeare began his theatrical career in the late 1580s and early 1590s, the professional stage had for a decade been under the spell of the 'clown' performer (see Longstaffe, this volume, Chapter 3). A combination of country bumpkin, acrobatic entertainer and scallywag, the Elizabethan 'clown' headlined the plays in which he appeared, enthralling London's newly urbanized audiences with his ability to triumph in the face of his own rustic naiveté. Something of this character's energy and uncanny acumen is captured in the ambiguous language of *Hamlet*'s fifth-Act 'clown' gravediggers. Speaking in familiar prose to a social inferior, Hamlet's initial question to the first gravedigger sparks a short bout of word-play, one turning on the meanings and connotations of the words 'lie', 'quick', and 'man':

HAMLET   Whose grave's this, sirrah?
FIRST CLOWN   Mine, sir.
    (*Sings*)   O, a pit of clay for to be made
                For such a guest is meet.
HAMLET   I think it be thine indeed, for thou liest in't.
FIRST CLOWN   You lie out on't, sir, and therefore it is not yours. For my part, I do not lie in't, and yet it is mine.
HAMLET   Thou dost lie in't, to be in't and say 'tis thine. 'Tis for the dead, not for the quick; therefore thou liest.
FIRST CLOWN   'Tis a quick lie, sir, 'twill away again from me to you.
HAMLET   What man dost thou dig it for?
FIRST CLOWN   For no man, sir.
HAMLET   What woman, then?
FIRST CLOWN   For none, neither.
HAMLET   Who is to be buried in't?
FIRST CLOWN   One that was a woman, sir; but, rest her soul, she's dead.
    (5. 1. 107–25, p. 1743)

What begins with Hamlet's simple query about the grave's future occupant soon turns into a dizzying exchange driven by the possible meanings of 'lie in't': (1) to be located in the grave or (2) to tell untruths within the grave. When Hamlet finally insists that the grave cannot be the gravedigger's because it is not for the 'quick' (or 'living'), the gravedigger ironically agrees, admitting that his work in the grave will only be 'quick' (or 'short'). When Hamlet tries to reframe his question, the gravedigger again thwarts his investigation by recalling Hamlet's own previous insistence upon a distinction between the living and the dead. The gravedigger ends by also insisting that he does not dig a grave for a 'man' (or a 'living person') but for someone who is dead. In this exchange with the gravedigger, Hamlet's own words betray him, and he is forced to bow to the uncanny wisdom of the clown.

Shakespeare's Language Experts

When it comes to linguistic dexterity and irreverent wisdom, however, no character in Shakespeare's canon can overshadow *1 Henry IV*'s Falstaff. Falstaff's words and body together attest to his worldly, self-centred perspective. His ample girth bears witness to his bodily excess, and his tavern lifestyle is fashioned explicitly against work and responsibility. As we have already seen, Falstaff subjects all to his levelling energy. Nothing – not ideals, not language, not authority – proves secure from his probing wit. Wandering the battlefield of Shrewsbury at the end of the play, Falstaff directs much of his derision at notions of valour, honour and martial heroism. When he comes upon the body of the dead knight Sir Walter Blunt, Falstaff's response proves to be anything but sympathetic or reverent:

> FALSTAFF   Though I could scape shot-free at London, I fear the shot here. Here's no scoring but upon the pate. – Soft, who are you? – Sir Walter Blunt. There's honour for you. Here's no vanity. I am as hot as molten lead, and as heavy too. God keep lead out of me; I need no more weight than my own bowels. I have led my ragamuffins where they are peppered; there's not three of my hundred and fifty left alive, and they are for the town's end, to beg during life. (5. 3. 30–37, p. 1217)

Playing on the double meanings of 'shot' (as both a tavern bill and a bullet) and 'scoring' (as both a running debt 'scored' on a tavern wall and a wound), Falstaff playfully draws a distinction between the hazards of the tavern and the battlefield, the former being preferable to the latter. Seeing the dead Blunt before him, he then turns his attention to 'honour'. As Falstaff sees it, honour is for the dead and the elite. While it may ironically endow the knight's dead body with dignity, it has no place with the living, especially the under-privileged. Though *they* survived the battle, his 'three' poor soldiers will only end up 'beg[ging] during life'; they will reap no benefits from their mar-tial exploits. Irreverent word-play – along with an underpinning worldly wisdom – defines Falstaff as a character. Throughout *1 Henry IV*, Falstaff functions not simply as Hal's friend but as his mentor. From him, Hal not only becomes skilled at navigating the world of the dispossessed, but he also learns the value of being able to manipulate language and perspective, skills that will all come to define his successful kingship in *Henry V*.

Shakespeare again and again uses word-play to help him to distinguish his characters. More subtly, as we have seen with his imagery, he also employs it to help develop his plays' various themes. In *Hamlet*, this 'associative use of wordplay' (Mahood 1957) can be traced in the many puns that reveal an irreconcilable tension between expected conduct and necessary constraint in this world. Perhaps one of the most revealing of these puns occurs in Hamlet's famed 'To be or not to be' speech at the beginning of the third Act. Qualifying his initial optimism about a pleasant 'sleep' after '[taking] arms against a sea of troubles' (61) is, he realizes, the potential 'rub' (or impedi-ment) of unwelcome 'dreams':

> HAMLET   [. . .] To die, to sleep.
>   To sleep, perchance to dream. Ay, there's the rub,
>   For in that sleep of death what dreams may come
>   When we have shuffled off this mortal coil
>   Must give us pause. There's the respect
>   That makes calamity of so long life, [. . .] (3.1 66–71, p. 1705)

Central in this section of Hamlet's musings is a conflict between energy and confinement that is well expressed by his pun on 'coil', which in Shakespeare's day could mean either 'bustle or turmoil' or a 'length of rope gathered up into a number of concentric rings'. Hamlet himself, of course, is at this moment undecided about what to do in the future, and his inaction – a central theme in the play – is well signalled by his pun's irreconcilable meanings. Other examples of such theme-revealing word-play can also be found in Feste's play on 'patch' (conflating both repaired and made into a fool) in 'Anything that's mended is but patched' (1. 5. 40–41); or in Prospero's play on 'globe' (conflating both the world and Shakespeare's outdoor theatre, 'the Globe') in his aforementioned reference to 'the great globe itself' (4. 1. 153).

However, having said all of this, it bears remembering that Shakespeare was himself no island; he, like all of us, was moulded by the world in which he was born. His society – its norms and everyday practices – irrevocably shaped his writing, and its particular social logics can be traced within the less-obvious connotations of his ubiquitous word-play. Complicated associations having to do with status – specifically with the uncertain social position of the messenger or go-between – are continually bandied about in *1 Henry IV*'s numerous puns having to do with conveyance such as 'bear' and 'carry'. Insights into the social place of women can be inferred from *Hamlet*'s two-dozen occurrences of the word 'nothing', alluding both to a non-entity *and*, as Hamlet has it at the beginning of *The Mousetrap* scene, that which 'lie[s] between maids' legs' (3. 2. 107). And the violence of early modern colonial expansion is hinted at in Miranda's ironic charge against Caliban that he would not willingly take 'any print of goodness' (1. 2. 355) – 'print' suggesting both an impression *and* the mark of a foot.

5 Case Studies in Reading II: From Texts to Theory

Mark Robson

Chapter Overview

Shakespeare in Theory

Shakespeare has always attracted theories. Some of these theories are based on Shakespeare himself, that is, on the biographical status of the author of the poems and plays. They ask questions about whether Shakespeare *was* Shakespeare, or whether the writer was someone else, such as Francis Bacon, or Edward de Vere, Earl of Oxford, or Elizabeth I, or Christopher Marlowe. Equally, there are theories about the identity of the Dark Lady of the sonnets or that of 'Mr. W. H.', about the missing years between Shakespeare's departure from Stratford and his arrival in London, about his sexuality, his politics, his 'philosophy' (or whether he can be said to have had one), about his will, his retirement and so on (see Egan, this volume, Chapter 9). No answers to any of these questions will be given here.

More interestingly for our purposes, there are also theories about the works themselves. Either a critic tries to formulate some general principles on the basis of a reading of one or more texts, or else a critic will bring a set of assumptions (about language, or the essence of literature, or the history of the period in which the texts were first written, or about staging conditions, or the nature of being human, or sexuality, or politics and so on) against which the text or texts will be held up as a 'test case'. There are, then, two basic procedures that characterize these critical activities: to move from the specific to the general (what can *Hamlet* tell us about the human mind?) or to move from the general to the specific (what can psychoanalysis tell us about *Hamlet*?). Sometimes critics look for confirmation of the position from which they begin ('[. . .] and thus this proves in a new way that Shakespeare was a genius [. . .]' or '[. . .] and so we find further confirmation of the rightness of Judith Butler's ideas on gender performance [. . .]'), sometimes they wish to use a text to demonstrate that a theory is wrong ('Michel Foucault says x, Shakespeare says y, and since Shakespeare is a genius clearly Foucault is in error').

Every critical school or methodology has been tried out on Shakespeare's texts, and there are more books published on Shakespeare in a year than most people will read in a lifetime. Inevitably, this chapter will do little more than scratch the surface of the material available, and there is no substitute for immersing yourself in the original critical texts. One word of warning, however: the title of this chapter declares a movement from texts to theory, but this should not be thought of as leaving the texts behind. The best theoretical work seeks not only to tell us something 'new' about the text being read, it also reflects on the critical procedures that it employs in producing that reading, and this should not lead to replacing the texts with theory. In other words, theory can lead us both to think about a particular text differently and to rethink the broader category into which that text fits (literature, drama, the early modern period, tragedy and so on). Thus, rather than leaving the text behind, theory may be seen as a way of returning to the text anew.

There is another reason for avoiding the impression that theory and text might be in some way opposed, or that just sticking with the text is somehow 'better' or easier than engaging with theory. Central to the theoretical projects that have influenced the study of Shakespeare in recent decades – whatever the differences between them – has been a shared sense that there is *no* reading of a text which does not carry with it a set of assumptions. There is no neutral reading, and no critic can claim – in good faith – pure objectivity. This does not mean that all readings are simply subjective, or that a reader is free to say whatever he or she likes about a text. Language is a social medium – as is theatre, of course, or print culture – and thus reading is never simply a personal or private matter, since it must engage in and with practices of meaning-generation (however we wish to conceive it) that are themselves socially determined.

That there are limits to interpretation, is suggested by the need to provide evidence for a reading. Any theory about a text must be demonstrable to the satisfaction of a reader or hearer if it is to be persuasive. The reader of a critical essay has to be able to recognize and acknowledge something in the reading of the text that is shared, and which the reader can accept as agreeing with her or his own view of the text. A theory that is accepted by only one person is unlikely to have much lasting impact. Similarly, no theory that works for only a single literary example is of much use to anyone, even if the creation of a theory must always proceed from the singular nature of a given text and it must always be possible to test it against a specific case.

Reading Reading

In the rest of this chapter, I will be looking at the ways in which various theoretically-informed approaches have attempted to answer the question posed in the title of this section of this book: 'How to read Shakespeare?' But as Nicholas Royle has commented, in a book entitled *How to Read Shakespeare*: 'There is something laughable or even crazy about the phrase "how to read Shakespeare" ' (Royle 2005: 2). Royle is not simply saying that reading 'Shakespeare' is tricky, but noting that 'reading' is itself a far from transparent or innocent activity. Even discounting the fact that different texts may demand to be read in different ways (most obviously in terms of genres), there are different ways of reading, and people read for different reasons. For example, it seems obvious that in most cases reading a recipe is not the same activity as reading a poem; in the first case what the reader wants is primarily a set of instructions or information that will allow him or her to do something, that is, to cook a meal, while in the second, the reading may have a less explicit purpose. It may be 'for pleasure', that is, without a specific objective in mind beyond the experience of reading the text. Equally, however, readings of a poem can also differ depending on the circumstances in which it is read.

What a reader wants from a text impacts on the kind of reading that takes place. Coming to an unknown text, one might read it driven primarily by the desire to find out what happens. For a remembered text, 'what happens' is already known, and so the reader is looking primarily for something beyond the satisfaction provided by the narrative alone, perhaps taking pleasure less from what happens than from how it happens. In terms of thinking about Shakespeare this question of familiarity and unfamiliarity is a tricky one. A Shakespeare play may seem to be very familiar; *Hamlet*, for example, contains moments that are known on some level even to those who have never read it in full or seen it performed. Many people will be aware of lines such as 'To be or not to be', 'Alas, poor Yorick' and 'The rest is silence'. This is true to some extent of every Shakespeare text, and many phrases that are to be found in Shakespeare's works have passed into everyday speech, just as the plots and scenes from his works – few of which were original to him in the first place – have been reworked by other writers and artists to produce other plays and poems, novels, films, operas, paintings and so on. For any critic of Shakespeare there is always a challenge. After four hundred years of commentary, what more can be said? If the critic is not simply content to repeat whatever has been written in the past, it is necessary to find something 'new' to say while anchoring that newness in the best of that tradition.

New Historicism

In one of the most famous definitions of new historicism, Louis Montrose identifies a commitment to what he terms 'The Historicity of Texts and Textuality of History'. Explaining this comment, Montrose notes:

> The new orientation to history in Renaissance literary studies may be succinctly characterized, on the one hand, by its acknowledgment of the *historicity of texts*: the cultural specificity, the social embedment, of all modes of writing – not only those texts that critics study but also the texts in which they study them; and, on the other hand, by its acknowledgement of the *textuality of history*: the unavailability of a full and authentic past, a lived material existence, that has not already been mediated by the surviving texts of the society in question – those 'documents' that historians construe in their own texts, called 'histories', histories that necessarily but always incompletely construct the 'History' to which they offer access. (Montrose 1986: 8)

Montrose is suggesting two apparently opposed things here. First, texts are always produced in a specific historical context, and are thus not 'timeless' works of art. But, he warns, what we call history is itself the product of our readings of historical documents, in other words, texts. So, one of Shakespeare's plays comes from a particular point in history: the late sixteenth or early seventeenth century. But what we understand of that period is, in part, shaped by texts such as Shakespeare's plays. For the new historicist critic a change in our understanding of the culture from which Shakespeare's texts come should lead to a change in our readings of Shakespeare. Equally, a changed reading of Shakespeare might lead us to revise our ideas about early modern culture.

New historicism has changed the kinds of questions that are asked about Shakespeare's texts. It particularly attends to the 'marginalized' (that is, not central or dominant) aspects of a culture, and thus topics such as race and ethnicity, colonial and postcolonial experiences, non-standard sexualities and desires, and class and political power have come to characterize the field. But this emphasis on themes and issues that apparently lie 'outside' the texts has led some critics to wonder where exactly the plays and poems stand in all this concern for history. There is always the risk that the texts become historical documents, valued primarily for the information that they can give us about something other than themselves, depriving them of the capacity to create any of the effects that we associate with art.

Let us begin with one of the most famous uses of non-literary texts in new historicism, Stephen Greenblatt's treatment of *Henry IV, part 1* in 'Invisible Bullets', from his book *Shakespearean Negotiations* (1988). Greenblatt reads this play as part of a sequence that runs through both of the *Henry IV* plays, culminating in *Henry V* and which could be said to have started in *Richard II*, thus forming a sequence of four plays, or tetralogy. Greenblatt says little about *Richard II* in this essay, and this is largely because his focus is primarily on the character of Hal, who will go on to become Henry V. However, in the reading that Greenblatt produces, he goes beyond the usual sense of character-study to focus on the structural position of Hal as emblematic of a certain understanding of power.

In direct comparison with the quotation from Montrose that we studied a moment ago, Greenblatt draws together the world that the plays depict, the world in which they were produced, and modern critical attitudes towards both the text and the world:

> In literary criticism Renaissance artists function like Renaissance monarchs: at some level we know perfectly well that the power of the prince is largely a collective invention, the symbolic embodiment of the desire, pleasure, and violence of thousands of subjects, the instrumental expression of complex networks of dependency and fear, the agent rather than the maker of social will. Yet we can scarcely write of prince or poet without accepting the fiction that power directly emanates from him and that society draws upon this power. (Greenblatt 1988: 4)

Greenblatt is here giving voice to an understanding of power that stems from the work of the twentieth-century French thinker Michel Foucault. It is usual, perhaps, to think of power as something that is exercised from above: monarchs or dictators or governments have power over the people who inhabit the space over which they rule. Power is a kind of possession – some have it, some don't – and social hierarchy (wealth, status, property, influence and so on) reflects a hierarchy that runs from the powerful at the top to the powerless at the bottom. Foucault's thinking on power challenges this model. In a famous statement that is endorsed explicitly or implicitly by many new historicist critics, Foucault suggests that 'Power is everywhere; not because it embraces everything, but because it comes from everywhere' (Foucault 1990: 93). In other words, power is not the preserve of those who rule; rulers are able to rule in part because those who are ruled allow them to. Every member of a society either challenges or maintains the structure of that society, and most maintain it by acting in ways that conform to notions of law and order.

Greenblatt draws on Foucault's work partly because he believes that 'Shakespeare's plays are centrally, repeatedly concerned with the production and containment of subversion and disorder [. . .] above all in the plays that meditate on the consolidation of state power' (Greenblatt 1988: 40). From this perspective, Foucault's work reflects a preoccupation with power that seems to be at work within the plays themselves. But it is also a useful model of how power functions because it allows Greenblatt to examine the plays as part of the process by which power is consolidated: if all the elements of a culture either challenge or maintain the structures of society, then this includes the theatre. This political interpretation of theatre is not in itself new. Topics such as censorship or political allegory were well established long before new historicism. There is a different emphasis, however, in this sense that even in the absence of explicit engagement with the politics of the period in which the play is written and first performed, and even where there is no clear parallel or 'application' of the events or characters depicted, there is a political dimension to the structures of power that Shakespeare's texts present.

If we turn to the reading of the play itself we find Greenblatt quoting the following speech by the Earl of Warwick from *Henry IV, part 2*:

> The Prince but studies his companions,
> Like a strange tongue, wherein, to gain the language,
> 'Tis needful that the most immodest word
> Be looked upon and learnt, which once attained,
> Your highness knows, comes to no further use
> But to be known and hated; so, like gross terms,
> The Prince will in the perfectness of time
> Cast off his followers, and their memory
> Shall as a pattern or a measure live
> By which his grace must mete the lives of other,
> Turning past evils to advantages.   (4. 3. 68–78)

Warwick, as one of King Henry's loyal followers, is offering consolation to the sick king, although it is not immediately convincing. Warwick argues that Hal has been misjudged, and that the apparent wildness and folly of his youth has been a kind of training for his future kingship. In this way, the audience is prompted to rethink the Eastcheap scenes, creating at once both a more positive image of Hal as someone who has a strategy and a critical distance from the excesses, self-deception and criminality of Falstaff's world and a negative sense that Hal is cunning, insincere and deceiving his supposed friends. In the process of this rethinking, Hal becomes both more and less reassuring as a future king.

Warwick's assessment of him echoes Hal's own speech at the end of the first scene in which he appears. Left alone on the stage, Hal is able to reveal himself by stating how calculated his behaviour has been. Like the sun, he allows himself to be cloaked as if by clouds so that, when he reappears, the prince is all the more impressive:

> So when this loose behaviour I throw off
> And pay the debt I never promisèd,
> By how much better than my word I am,
> By so much shall I falsify men's hopes;
> And like bright metal on a sullen ground,
> My reformation, glitt'ring o'er my fault,
> Shall show more goodly and attract more eyes
> Than that which hath no foil to set it off.   (1. 2. 186–93, p. 1357)

Hal's tactic is to create false expectations which he can then defy, and gain legitimacy from doing so. As Greenblatt comments, the mark of true authority in the play 'is precisely the ability to betray one's friends without stain [on one's character]' (1988: 58). Rather than revealing something particular about Hal's personal trajectory from prince to king, Greenblatt sees the tactic as revealing a truth about the way power itself functions, 'creating' an opponent whose defeat confirms the legitimacy of the victor.

Greenblatt's reading differs from previous readings of the play by drawing particularly on a text with a religious dimension and a colonial context, Thomas Hariot's 1588 text *A Brief and True Report of the New Found Land of Virginia*. Hariot's text centres on the encounters between the Algonquian native Americans and the European colonists, noting the ways in which the Algonquians are encouraged to believe in the Christian God of the colonizers through demonstrations of the human inventions that they bring with them, including clocks, telescopes, guns and books. Thus, human powers of invention are used to 'prove' the power of divine creation. As Greenblatt notes, the text paradoxically deploys arguments used in Europe against the Church, that it is itself fundamentally a human invention. Those seeking to convert the Algonquians are thus using the structure of a subversive argument against religion to reinforce the power of religion. In this way, the structure that Hariot identifies maps on to the structure used by Hal in Shakespeare's plays. Like the colonists, Hal adopts behaviour which in other contexts would be considered subversive; however, he does this in order, ultimately, to strengthen his position: the reprobate is unexpectedly transformed into a paragon of political virtue. In the terms usually used to describe this argument, 'subversion' must precede the 'containment' of the threat posed by that subversion.

What then might the objections be to this reading? Firstly, there are some questions that have been raised around what has come to be known as the 'subversion and containment' model that is to be found in this essay, and which is often taken to represent the politics of new historicism more generally. However, there are potentially problems with the methodology of this essay, as well as in the results to which that methodology leads. Why, for example, is Hariot's text seen to be an 'appropriate' context for these plays? In talking about the context for plays set in the underworld of London, why doesn't Greenblatt say more about this world rather than colonial Virginia? There would certainly be lots of material available in the many pamphlets and prose texts that outline that criminal milieu. More significantly, perhaps, why is so little attention given to the most obvious context of all, that is, the other plays produced in the same theatres in which Shakespeare worked as both actor and writer? There is clear evidence that Shakespeare either read, played in or saw many of the plays written by his contemporaries, but Greenblatt – not only here but in his work as a whole – says little of that work. Greenblatt chooses the contexts which allow him to make his points.

'Race' and Ethnicity

One of the key elements of theoretical approaches to Shakespeare has been an increased awareness of the situations of those who have not traditionally occupied dominant positions within a society. In the largely historicist approaches that have employed a category of 'race' in order to think about Shakespeare, there has been an inevitable focus on plays that contain supposedly non-European characters such as Othello, Aaron the Moor in *Titus Andronicus*, the Indian boy in *A Midsummer Night's Dream*, or those such as Shylock in *The Merchant of Venice* who are taken to represent attitudes towards ethnic categories such as 'the Jew' (see Maley, this volume, Chapter 10).

I say 'supposedly non-European' because one of the most striking aspects of thought concerning identity – whether thinking here of personal identity, national identity or supra – and transnational entities such as Europe – has been the stress placed on the fact that identity formation is as much a negative as a positive process: people define themselves and find themselves defined as much by what they are not (or would like to believe they are not) as by their positive features and characteristics. From an historical perspective, Europeans traditionally – and still noticeably in debates being conducted as I write this on whether or not Turkey should be admitted as a member of the European Union – asserted their European identity in part by identifying themselves with Christianity, with ideas inherited from Ancient Greek and

Roman culture such as democracy, and with an ethnic whiteness. But the movement that accompanies this self-identification is one of identifying others, often in hostile ways: to be Christian is not to belong to another faith, especially not Judaism or Islam; the link to Greek and Roman thought often represses the extent to which that thought was preserved and mediated by Islamic scholars. The idea of a single European identity also tends to repress the differences between states and regions within Europe, not least linguistic ones. The identity that is created in this way is always relational, that is, it only emerges through simultaneous processes of identification and differentiation which continue to leave profound traces within the culture that thinks of itself as Europe.

In the context of this re-evaluation of identity, the play which has attracted most attention has been *The Tempest*. At the heart of the discussion has been the character of Caliban (for a survey of this material, see Vaughan and Vaughan 1991, and White 1999). Following a lead established by a series of writers from the Caribbean and other formerly colonized areas who have identified with Caliban in describing their own relation to the colonial history of Europe, critics have seen in Caliban, who precedes Prospero on the island, an embodiment of the colonial subject. Read in this way, the story hinges on issues of possession and dispossession. Caliban is turned into a slave and 'civilized' (he speaks Prospero's language in the play, not his own).

One speech in particular has come to stand for this colonial history. Called forth by Prospero, Caliban narrates the recent history of the island, staking a claim to its possession:

> This island's mine, by Sycorax my mother,
> Which thou tak'st from me. When thou cam'st first,
> Thou strok'st me and made much of me, wouldst give me
> Water with berries in't, and teach me how
> To name the bigger light, and how the less,
> That burn by day and night; and then I loved thee,
> And showed thee all the qualities o'th'isle,
> The fresh springs, brine-pits, barren place and fertile –
> Cursed be I that did so! All the charms
> Of Sycorax, toads, beetles, bats, light on you;
> For I am all the subjects that you have,
> Which first was mine own king, and here you sty me
> In this hard rock, whiles you do keep from me
> The rest o'th'island.   (1. 2. 334–47, p. 3065)

This sense of dispossession – even though it is denied by Prospero, who immediately counters that Caliban is a 'lying slave' in what is either an unfortunate or revealing choice of words – is clear, although Caliban's title to the island is not entirely convincing. It is his possession, he claims, through Sycorax, his mother. Ania Loomba suggests that the figure of Sycorax further genders the colonial situation – pitting a female figure against both Prospero and Miranda – and that Prospero also emphasizes her non-European origins as well as her witchcraft: 'Prospero's takeover is both *racial* plunder and a transfer to *patriarchy* [. . .] Prospero as colonialist consolidates power which is specifically white and male, and constructs Sycorax as a black, wayward and wicked witch in order to legitimise it' (Loomba in White 1999: 146, emphases in original).

Caliban's dispossession, in which he claims he has become a subject where formerly he was a king, is made explicit in this kind of reading at the point where Prospero lays claim to Caliban himself: 'This thing of darkness I / Acknowledge mine' (5. 1. 278–79). How we read this is a key to how we read the play. Is it a moment of reconciliation, in which Prospero offers some vision of forgiveness (Caliban has just been involved in a plot to kill him, of course)? Is it a further example of Prospero's power over Caliban, or of his desire to retain some power over him even as he prepares to leave the island? Is it a recognition of the extent to which Prospero's treatment of Caliban may have shaped him? All of these readings are possible, but their persuasiveness depends on how well they fit into a broader sense of the play as a whole.

As with the new historicist choice of contexts, choosing which is the most 'appropriate' reading presents problems, and this has led to some critical scepticism with respect to the colonial reading of *The Tempest*. Edward Pechter underlines that:

> New historicists often privilege their criticism by assuming that their version of history is the thing itself, as if they were doing *history*, but if we understand that they are merely *doing* history, then that privilege disappears. To say that the colonialist *Tempest* is superior because 'the Renaissance was an age characterized by the expansion of power' does not answer the question, it begs it. (Pechter 1995: 65–66)

If history is not an object that is somehow 'out there' waiting to be discovered, but is instead produced through and as a critical process, then an appeal to history is part of that process, not its end point. Similarly, critics such as Pechter would object that the relevance of the colonial reading comes from a sense that because this is a period witnessing significant activity that this fact *must* somehow be reflected in the text. But what is the purpose of reading the text, if it only reinforces something already independently known? There has to be a degree to which the 'already known' may be called into question by the reading of the text, if that reading is not to become a 'mere' repetition.

One of the further problems in attempting to deal with questions of ethnicity lies in the awkward critical status of the term 'race' itself. As Henry Louis Gates, Jr, puts it: ' "race" is a metaphor for something else and not an essence or a thing in itself, apart from its creation by an act of language'. So 'race' is not a descriptive term, it brings into being the object to which it supposedly refers. More disturbingly, he argues, ' "races", put simply, do not exist' (Gates 1986: 402–3). In this way, a play such as *The Tempest* urges us to revisit cultural habits of thinking and to interrogate their origins. Nonetheless, despite the problematic nature of 'race' as a concept, this is not a barrier to exploring how it has been deployed in a variety of contexts and discourses.

Gender and Sexuality

The opening pages of Kate Chedgzoy's *Shakespeare's Queer Children* circle around the statement 'This island's mine'. In this case, Chedgzoy is citing not *The Tempest*, but a 1988 play by Philip Osment for the Gay Sweatshop Theatre Company, entitled *This Island's Mine*. Starting from this statement, Chedgzoy asks two (or really four) questions: 'who may speak of/for Shakespeare? and for/to whom may Shakespeare be made to speak?' (Chedgzoy 1995: 1). As in the discussion of 'race', our answers to these questions depend to a great extent on our understanding of processes of identification. As we witnessed in our consideration of 'race', much is a matter of representation: how are women represented? Is a gay or lesbian audience member able to identify with the characters or situations that he or she sees onstage? Thinking about Shakespeare in terms of sexuality or gender amounts to much more than asking 'Is the Antonio in *The Merchant of Venice* or *Twelfth Night* gay?' or 'Was Shakespeare a misogynist?' As the quotation above from Ania Loomba regarding *The Tempest* demonstrates, issues of gender have been bound up in a range of studies that have not taken gender as their primary focus, as well as being at the heart of a critical industry (see Hopkins, this volume, Chapter 8). Questions of patriarchy, the representation of women (particularly in the context of a renaissance stage convention that had female parts played by boys, which has also inevitably attracted theorists of sexuality) (see Barker and Kamps 1995, and Ferguson and Vickers 1986), cross-dressing of characters such as Viola in *Twelfth Night* (Belsey 1988; Jardine 1983), the construction of female identity (Charnes 1993), the reading of Shakespeare by women (Thompson and Roberts 1997) or the use made of Shakespeare by women writers (Sanders 2001), have all attracted substantial bodies of work. This has been supplemented by works on masculinity, on sexuality and particularly by queer theory (Goldberg 1992; Smith 2000).

While much of the work that I have just indicated focuses on plays, some of the key work on sexuality, gender and Shakespeare centres on the sonnets.

Part of the attraction, of course, lies in the sense that the voice that speaks in the sonnets – because it is not obviously a dramatic character – might bring us closer to Shakespeare 'himself' (see Hiscock and Longstaffe, this volume). The largely post-Romantic association of a lyric voice with confession, self-expression, has led to much biographical speculation about a direct correlation between the situations and characters described in the sonnets and Shakespeare's life, fuelling much of the activity to identify the Dark Lady, the young man and the rival poet in the sequence. Though many have speculated about what some sonnets reveal about Shakespeare's sex life, one of the closest readers (and editors) of the sonnets, Stephen Booth, concludes that 'William Shakespeare was almost certainly homosexual, bisexual or heterosexual. The sonnets provide no evidence on the matter' (Booth 2000: 548). Instead, here I will explore how theories of gender and sexuality might help us to *read* the sonnets.

One of the key things to remember in reading Shakespeare's sequence of sonnets is that the 'I' who speaks is a persona, not a person (and certainly not Shakespeare 'himself'). The voice that we hear when reading the sonnets is a construction, as is any voice in a poem, but this is made particularly evident here. In Sonnet 144, we are told:

> Two loves I have, of comfort and despair,
> Which like two spirits do suggest me still.
> The better angel is a man right fair,
> The worser spirit a woman coloured ill. (p. 1972)

The simple supposition in these lines that the male must take precedence over the female does not exhaust what that can tell us about gender expectation. As Bruce Smith points out: 'The "I" who speaks through all the sonnets may seem to enjoy an independent existence, but he is constituted by this "him" and this "her". In poem after poem he defines himself with respect to them. He is quite unimaginable without them' (Smith 2000: 101). The speaking persona is thus always positioned in relation to the main subjects of the poems themselves, the Young Man who features in the opening part of the sequence and the Dark Lady of the latter part. Each sonnet uses relation to another – sometimes male, sometimes female – to define and redefine the speaker's masculine identity. As in readings that focus on the colonial or ethnic Other, this is often as much a negative process as a positive one. The sonnets thus establish two kinds of difference: that between the masculine and the feminine, and that between one male and another.

A staging of masculine and feminine difference takes place on (at least) two levels. Sonnet sequences tend to play on the idea of an unattainable female figure who is desired by the male persona (see Glossary). Shakespeare's sequence disrupts this by beginning with a male addressee – the Young Man – who is urged to reproduce in order to preserve his beauty from death and decay (on the relation between desire and death in the sonnets, see Dollimore 2001). The speaker seemingly urges the Young Man to have a relationship with someone else. This unusual starting point is compounded by the appearance of a female figure of desire who fits none of the standard expectations: she is all too attainable, and not just by the speaking persona, and the sonnets addressed to her are not chaste expressions of idealized love but frequently bawdy and punning in their sexuality. Indeed, the sequence ends with a poem that is usually taken to be about a sexually transmitted disease: 'Till my bad angel fire my good one out' (Sonnet 144, line 14). So while there is an expected distinction between the male speaker and the desired female, there is also a distinction between the male and female addressees, as well as between the figures that appear in Shakespeare's sequence and those that appear in more traditional sonnets (see Sonnet 130, for an example of this negative process of definition).

The division of one man from another comes across most clearly in Sonnets 133 and 134. Claiming that the lady has disdained his love and taken up with his friend, the speaker complicates matters by referring to the friend as 'my next self' (133, line 6) and 'that other mine' (134). But this entails the loss of the woman, the loss of the friend and the loss of himself: 'Of him, myself, and thee I am forsaken – / A torment thrice threefold thus to be crossed' (133, lines 7–8). Now we have a third difference that supplements and underpins the other two: we move from the difference between masculine and feminine, and that between one male and another, to that within one 'self'. Thinking of gender identity as an ongoing process, rather than a fixed entity, challenges us to identify our own relation to these processes, rather than standing at a safe distance from them. Subjectivity is constructed through exactly the linguistic and conceptual processes that can be seen at work in the sonnets. Identifying the nature of the relationships within the sonnets is thus also a matter of identifying our own relation to those processes.

Psychoanalysis and Deconstruction

The relation between Shakespeare and psychoanalysis is a complex one. While it is true that there have been many psychoanalytically informed readings of Shakespeare's plays, what is also important to recognize is the extent to which psychoanalysis is itself dependent on Shakespeare for some of its crucial insights. Its two main figures in terms of their influence on literary studies – Sigmund Freud, the founder of psychoanalysis, and the French analyst Jacques Lacan, whose own work represented a famous 'return to Freud' – both wrote about Shakespeare, and Freud in particular developed some of his most important ideas through thinking about drama and literature (we might think of the Oedipus Complex, for example, and its reliance on Freud's reading of both Sophocles and Shakespeare, or of the 'The "Uncanny" ' and its relation to Hoffmann's short story 'The Sand Man'; see Freud, 1997).

Many psychoanalytic readings seem incompatible with historicism, stressing universal rather than historically contextualized features of the human psyche. For Freud, it is possible to talk about an Oedipus Complex that is 'the same' for Ancient Greek culture (as in the Sophocles play from which he takes his model), early modern English culture (exemplified by a Shakespearean tragedy, *Hamlet*) and the late-nineteenth-century middle-class Viennese patients on whose analysis he based many of his findings. Such claims to universality are, of course, necessary for Freud's attempts to ground psychoanalysis as a science; it would be no good if the findings of psychoanalysis worked for only a single patient, just as a 'law' of gravity that was only valid in Chelmsford would be unlikely to meet with widespread acclaim.

Psychoanalytic criticism is most convincing in its handling of Shakespeare – as it is whenever it turns to literature – when it avoids the pitfalls of trying to psychoanalyse either the characters or the author (see Hopkins on Jones vs Rose, this volume, Chapter 8). No character in Shakespeare's plays has a 'life' in the usual sense, none has had a childhood, happy or unhappy, outside the text or the performance of that text. It is always possible to speculate, of course, about the sex life of the Macbeths, or about Lear's daughters as children, but this is not so much criticism as the creation of another text (see Hiscock and Longstaffe, this volume).

What, then, can psychoanalysis tell us about Shakespeare's texts? The cliché about psychoanalysis is that it is dominated by a concern with sexuality, and this might suggest that its appeal is limited to knowing what Macbeth is *really* thinking about when he wonders whether or not he sees a dagger before him, or explaining the symbolism of the fact that Juliet stabs herself with Romeo's 'happy dagger'. This version of Freudian reading underpins many approaches to *Hamlet*, and can be seen not only in critical readings but also in adaptations of the play such as Laurence Olivier's (1948) and Franco Zeffirelli's (1990) film versions. In Olivier's bedroom scene, Hamlet's reaction to his mother's remarriage so quickly after his father's death is clearly based upon an Oedipal structure in which the son fantasizes taking the place of his father in his mother's bed. Olivier's staging of the scene echoes Freud's own, reinforcing its plausibility as more than simply a theory. By contrast, Kenneth Branagh's 1996 film shows a sexual relation to Ophelia, sidestepping the Oedipal plot, and differentiating his version from earlier ones.

There are certainly characters in Shakespeare's texts who behave as if they were 'Freudian' readers (Othello or Leontes in *The Winter's Tale* might both be thought to suffer from extreme forms of jealousy that are fed by their ability to see sexual significance in apparently innocent everyday occurrences), but nevertheless to think that such concerns are the only contribution that psychoanalytic thinking might make to studies of Shakespeare is ultimately reductive. While Freud's early work tends to focus on questions of sexuality and childhood, it develops into a much more wide-ranging set of concerns. Perhaps most fruitfully, he allows us to think about time and knowledge in ways that provide a clear challenge to the interests of historicism.

Freud and Traumatic Knowledge

In a series of pieces written between the end of World War I and around 1920, Freud moved away from his concerns with sexuality towards a recognition that not all human actions were based on the pursuit of pleasure. Drawing in particular on the traumatic effects of wartime experience and the psychological (rather than physical) symptoms exhibited by those involved in accidents, Freud developed his much-discussed conception of the death drive. In the course of this work, he also described a particular relation between knowledge and time that he called *Nachträglichkeit*. While there is no direct English equivalent to this term, it encompasses senses of belatedness, and crucially, the idea that knowledge of an event does not necessarily coincide with the moment at which that event is 'experienced'. In the case of trauma – and Freud's key example is shell shock – there is a structure of unwilled repetition: those who suffer from trauma are compelled to go back over what has happened to them even though, each time they do so, they again feel pain and discomfort (what Freud calls 'unpleasure'). This repetition can be both psychological – nightmares, involuntary memories, and so on – and physical, including shaking or rocking back and forth. What Freud suggests, however, is that this repetition is necessary because at the time of the traumatic 'experience' it was impossible to know fully what was happening, and that since the extent of the event is so overwhelming, the mind effectively closes itself down as a form of self-protection. So the event is not experienced at the time of its occurrence, it must be gradually pieced together through repetitions in which slightly more can be seen each time. Our knowledge of such events is thus inevitably belated and has to be seen not as something which happens once and for all, but instead as a process. Reflect upon the ways in which these concerns with belatedness trauma and revelation (Nachträglichteit) may illuminate your readings of Shakespeare's texts such as *Twelfth Night*, *Hamlet*, and the sonnets, for example.

Let's return to *Hamlet*. One of the crucial dimensions of the play's longevity has centred on the fact that it raises more questions than it answers. The play begins with a question – 'Who's there?' being the opening line, but there are seven questions in the first twenty lines – and proceeds to tackle a series of problematic issues of knowledge, the most famous question in the play of course being 'To be or not to be?' To indicate only the most obvious difficulties, we might ask: Is the Ghost that of Hamlet's father? Was he murdered by Claudius? In other words, can we trust the Ghost's version of events? Does Gertrude know of the murder? Is Hamlet mad, or only pretending to be? Did he love Ophelia? Does Ophelia commit suicide? Is there a divinity that shapes our ends? Frequently we are asked as readers or audience members to judge a speech or character on the basis of evidence that is at best partial. (For two dazzling readings of the play that bring together Freud and questions of knowing in very different ways, see Cavell 1987 and Garber 1987). The play even stages this problem of perspective and perception, and, more particularly, the difficulties of comparison, in the exchange between Hamlet and Polonius about whether a cloud is the shape of a camel, a weasel or a whale. It may be that Polonius, in agreeing with all of these possibilities, is simply trying to say what Hamlet wants to hear. But then the question arises of how it is possible to know what someone else has in mind.

One of the techniques employed in the play to deepen this sense of partiality or perspective is the use of repetition. We may be led to feel or believe at certain points in the play, say, after the Ghost has told his story, that Hamlet is justified in taking revenge for the murder of his father. But what do we make of Laertes' position once Hamlet has killed Polonius? Is his desire for revenge equally well motivated? We may think that Claudius is an evil character because he plots to have Hamlet killed on his arrival in England. So how do we judge Hamlet's plan to have Rosencrantz and Guildenstern suffer in his place? Do we have to rethink our view of Hamlet? Hamlet's 'madness' must be compared with that of Ophelia. The play-within-the-play may be said to 'repeat' the murder of Hamlet's father twice (once with words and once without). There are many other examples of repetition in the play, from large questions of structure down to specific verbal echoes. The play thus stages a traumatic structure in the way that Freud describes it.

When read psychoanalytically, *Hamlet* has in turn influenced an extraordinary essay on Marxism by the French philosopher Jacques Derrida. Working through the legacies of Marxism in *Specters of Marx*, Derrida weaves a consideration of *Hamlet* into his discussion, finding in the play's stagings of identification, mourning and haunting a powerful textual embodiment of the problems of 'inheriting' Marxism:

Repetition *and* first time: this is perhaps the question of the event as the question of the ghost. *What is* a ghost? What is the *effectivity* or the *presence* of a specter, that is, of what seems to remain as ineffective, virtual, insubstantial as a simulacrum? Is there *there*, between the thing itself and its simulacrum, an opposition that holds up? Repetition *and* first time, but also repetition *and* last time, since the singularity of any *first time* makes of it also a *last time*. Each time it is the event itself, a first time is a last time. Altogether other. Staging for the end of history. Let us call it a *hauntology*. This logic of haunting would not be merely larger or more powerful than an ontology or a thinking of Being (of the 'to be', assuming that it is a matter of Being in the 'to be or not to be', but nothing is less certain). It would harbor within itself, but like circumscribed places or particular effects, eschatology and teleology themselves. It would *comprehend* them, but incomprehensively. How to *comprehend* in fact the discourse of the end or the discourse about the end? Can the extremity of the extreme ever be comprehended? And the opposition between 'to be' and 'not to be'? *Hamlet* already began with the expected return of the dead King. After the end of history, the spirit comes by *coming back* [revenant], it figures *both* a dead man who comes back and a ghost whose expected return repeats itself, again and again. (Derrida 1994: 10)

Don't worry if you find this passage difficult to understand. However, it is worth considering the way in which Derrida brings together moments from and features of the play – including references to the ghost, the dead King, the to be or not to be speech – with broader arguments about the death of Marxism, in both ideological and political terms. Derrida wrote in response to writers such as Francis Fukuyama, who had suggested that as the conflict between (Eastern) Marxism and (Western) Capitalism had been won by the latter, the driving force of recent history had disappeared. That particular history was therefore at an end – hence Derrida's comment on 'staging for the end of history', and his suggestion that, like Hamlet's father, Marxism might continue to haunt its successor. Derrida also asks fundamental questions about the nature of ghosts and the ways in which the line between life and death might be drawn. While psychoanalysis is not explicitly brought in here, the emphasis on repetition and identification is informed by Freudian notions of the compulsion to repeat. Derrida does not simply 'use' the play to reinforce his 'real' concern with Marxism. His reading of *Hamlet* allows him to see something that he could not have got to in other ways, and at the same time reading *Hamlet* in this context reveals something about the play and its political status that had not previously been seen (which explains the huge number of studies of ghosts in Shakespeare that appeared and continue to appear in the wake of the publication of *Specters of Marx*).

One of the consequences of the argument that Derrida mounts here is that any notion of the 'end of history' is untenable. Indeed, there is no position within history from which it might be possible to see history whole and completed. Part of the reason for this is the psychoanalytic insight that events may not be susceptible to being fully known at the moment at which they occur. The process of repetition involved in coming to know an event cannot be closed off, since it becomes impossible to know which will have been the 'last' repetition. This is further complicated by Derrida's suggestion, again following a Freudian pattern, that the last time is also a first time, and vice versa. This is perhaps most easily understood through the fact that each repetition reveals something that has not been seen before (as in the structure of trauma); conversely, the first time that something is experienced is also the last time that this experience will occur *for the first time*. In this context, the idea of reconstructing a historical moment (to the extent that such a thing is possible at all) cannot be seen as an end in itself, but only as part of a movement that might open a critical reading.

Shakespeare After Theory

You might be slightly disappointed to hear at this stage in the chapter that there is no longer any need to worry about theory. That, at least, is what many people will be happy to tell you. The dominance of historicism has led a number of literary critics to call themselves cultural historians – or some such equivalent – or else to declare that we now occupy a time (or perhaps more accurately an institutional space) that is 'post-theory' or 'after theory'. As Jonathan Goldberg – a critic who has at different points in his career been associated with some of most advanced theoretical work in early modern and Shakespeare studies, including new historicism, gender studies and queer theory and work on colonialism and race – puts it in *Shakespeare's Hand*:

> the demise of 'theory' – or, better, the demise of its promise, especially in early modern studies – has prompted moves 'after theory', which is also to say, before theory. New historicism, insofar as it is still practised, is virtually indistinguishable from old historicism; early modern cultural studies divide the world into prefabricated binarisms and think themselves liberatory in so doing. In Shakespeare studies, postmodernity has passed; conservatism has returned. (Goldberg 2003: x)

Goldberg performs a neat critical move here. To claim to be post-theory is not to advance but to return to a position that remains prey to all of the problems that led to an engagement with theory in the first place. There can be no wishing away of theory, only a denial of it that is basically an admission of defeat. The intellectual excitement generated by new historicism has led only to a retrenchment of old historicism (which now effectively equals new historicism minus theory). Even those who would claim to be following a theoretical path – and who would claim the credit of pursuing a critical mode linked to notions of freedom – have regressed into a conservative position. Goldberg proposed that there can be no pure un- or a-theoretical critical practice. To this extent at least, Shakespeare is always, in theory, in theory.

6 Shakespeare in Performance and Film

Stuart Hampton-Reeves

A Player's Hide

In 1592, aware that death was near, the playwright Robert Greene, until recently one of the luminaries of the Elizabethan theatre, wrote in his final book a poisonous invective against a new rival. This 'upstart crow', the only 'Shake-scene' in the country, was nothing more than a 'tiger's heart wrapped in a player's hide' (for further discussion see *Norton Shakespeare*, pp. 3321–22). Greene could think of nothing more scathing to call his new literary rival – undoubtedly Shakespeare – than *player*. A jumped-up player at that. Like many of his contemporary playwrights (Marlowe, for example), Greene had a university background and, as a good scholar, saw his own work as literature – *poetry*. It is as a player and a fraud that Shakespeare enters literary history – and the relationship between Shakespeare the player and Shakespeare the literary artist has haunted his reception ever since.

Shakespeare himself was not above playing with these contrasting identities as player and poet. Hamlet scorns players who perform *ex tempore* – off script – in words widely assumed to reflect Shakespeare's own theory of drama: 'let those that play your clowns speak no more than is set down for them' (3. 2. 34–35). But Shakespeare was not Hamlet, no matter how tempting an analogy that is. The players in *A Midsummer Night's Dream* worry about whether they should 'leave the killing out' of their tragedy to avoid offending their audience and agree finally to make it clear at the start of the performance that 'I, Pyramus, am not Pyramus, but Bottom the weaver' for this 'will put them out of fear' (3. 1 .13–20) – but Shakespeare is not Bottom either. In *The Tempest*, Shakespeare may be Prospero, who stages scenes on the bare stage of his barren island, but finally breaks his staff, abjures his magic and begs the audience to 'set me free' (Epilogue line 20) – but we know that he went on to write more plays in collaboration with John Fletcher such as *Henry VIII: or All is True* and *The Two Noble Kinsmen*.

In this case study, Shakespeare will again wear his player's hide. It is in players' hides that Shakespeare's plays live on the stages of amateur and professional theatre. And it is as a player, I will argue, that we should be able to *read* Shakespeare's plays. The study of Shakespeare in performance and on film breaks down into three related activities: reading the plays with an awareness of the staging conditions which shaped them when Shakespeare was a player; exploring the texts using theatrical techniques, whether this is done in our imaginations or (ideally) in workshop with others, in ways which give rise to an understanding of the complex interplay of text and performance; and, last but not least, studying the work of theatre practitioners and filmmakers as an art form in its own right.

Not everyone agrees that Shakespeare *can* be read theatrically. The assertion that Shakespeare 'wrote for the stage, not the page' has been frequently challenged and for many years critical practice deliberately scorned the theatre (see Hiscock and Longstaffe, this volume).

Charles Lamb on *King Lear*

Famously, Charles Lamb scoffed at the way eighteenth- and nineteenth-century theatre reduced the dark complexities of *King Lear* to melodrama. As he put it, '[t]o see Lear acted, as an old man tottering about the stage with a walking stick [. . .] has nothing in it but what is painful and disgusting'. He goes on to insist that 'the Lear of Shakespeare cannot be acted' for the 'greatness of Lear is not in corporeal dimension, but in intellectual' (Lamb 1818: II, 25).

Rediscovering Shakespeare in Performance

In the twentieth century, partly as theatre itself became more adventurous and experimental, criticism rediscovered the potential that studying Shakespeare in performance offers with its focus on possible interpretations rather than intended meanings (see Hiscock and Longstaffe, this volume). Research into the physical and cultural contexts of Shakespeare's stage also furthered understanding of what kind of theatre Shakespeare's plays were written for. J. L. Styan went so far as to announce a 'Shakespeare revolution' which, he argued, decisively moved away from Lamb's position to what he called 'staged-centred' criticism in which issues of stagecraft and performance would be at the forefront of any critical discussion.

To read Shakespeare theatrically involves a certain amount of experience of what theatre is, even if contemporary experiences of theatre are wildly different from anything that Shakespeare ever himself understood as theatre. While much can be gained by going to the theatre and watching critically, there is no substitute for the work needed to put a play into performance to realize the rich possibilities that Shakespeare's text provides for theatre or the deep understanding of performance – of what performance demands, of what can be demanded of performance. In the rehearsal room, the text is torn apart as actors, designers and directors work together to establish their version of the play, to activate the text's complexities, to turn the words from script into performance.

In the following sections, I will look at practical and theoretical ways of 'reading' plays theatrically, taking into account both the conditions of Shakespeare's theatre and the possibilities opened up by modern stagings, including film. To anchor this discussion, I will offer a case study on *Macbeth* and in particular on one scene in the play, when Macbeth hosts a banquet and is haunted by the ghost of Banquo, recently murdered on his orders. This scene will be approached in three ways: by reflecting on the staging conditions of the theatre that Shakespeare wrote for; by workshopping the scene and exploring some of its staging issues; and finally by looking at two performances which have dealt with these issues in different ways.

Shakespeare's Theatre

On 20 April 1611, three days before Shakespeare's forty-sixth birthday and nearly twenty years after Greene's death, Dr Simon Forman made a record of a performance of *Macbeth* that he had seen that afternoon at the Globe. His notes are among the most detailed records of the plays in performance at this time and it is likely that Shakespeare was one of the players crowded onto the stage for the banquet scene. The scene stood out for Forman, who recorded it in some detail:

> The next night, beinge at supper with his noble men whom he had bid to a feaste to the which also Banco should have com, he began to speake of Noble Banco, and to wish that he wer ther. And as he thus did, standing up to drincke a Carouse to him, the ghoste of Banco came and sate down in his cheier [chair] behind him. And he turninge About to sit down Again sawe the goste of Banco, which fronted him so, that he fell into a great passion of fear and fury, Utterynge many wordes about his murder, by which, when they hard that Banco was Murdred they Suspected Mackbet. (*Norton Shakespeare*, p. 3337)

Forman's summary of the scene gives us some valuable information about *how* Shakespeare and his company staged the scene. From this account we know that there *was* a ghost visible onstage (as we shall see, the scene can be played without the ghost physically appearing). We also know that Macbeth reacted with passion, fear and fury, and that the party at the feast 'suspected' Macbeth because of his ravings.

The theatre in which Forman saw this performance take place was very different from the modern theatre (see this volume, Chapter 3 – Globe theatre). Today, lighting effects are so key to creating performance that it is hard to imagine theatre without them: without the dimming of lights at the start of the play, without lights dividing the stage, setting atmosphere and tone, spotlighting key characters and rising at the end to signify that it is time to go home. For Shakespeare's Globe, the only light was the sun, so plays in the Globe were staged in mid-afternoon. This may have meant, in British wintertime, that the plays ran into dusk with interesting effects, especially for the tragedies.

Further Analysis: Darkness Visible in Shakespeare's Drama

Macbeth seems to get literally darker as the story progresses as if caught in a perpetual night. However, Forman saw the play in April in broad daylight and had no difficulty in recognizing the scene's imagined darkness, for he begins his account of this scene with the words, 'the next night'. Many critics have noticed the disjunction between the play's dark setting and its daylight performance at the Globe (see Kliman 2004: 1). In this context, you may like to reflect upon the ways in which the characters at the beginning of *Hamlet* repeatedly draw our attention *verbally* to 'this time of night', or those at

> the beginning of *The Tempest* make us experience the storm ('these roarers') in their desperate exchanges.

Viewing Shakespeare

Shakespeare's theatre was also less spectacular – although we have to be careful here about importing modern experience of spectacle into our judgement of what counts as 'spectacular'. Although Shakespeare would modestly draw attention to the limitations of theatrical representation, frequently tourists (we know from surviving accounts) were often impressed by what they saw. It was not the convention to construct realistic scenery, although props were used to create a sense of place and one surviving prop list includes an intriguing reference to the 'sittie of Rome' (Henslowe 2002: 319). Yet plays like *The Tempest* and *Macbeth* are clearly spectacular plays. *The Tempest* includes one theatrical trick which remains a challenge today. Prospero lays out a feast to tempt the shipwrecked sailors, and then makes the feast disappear. *Macbeth* is full of ghosts, apparitions and demons. As Gabriel Egan notes (see Chapter 9, this volume), most characters wore the same kind of clothes as the audience, even if the plays were set in other places or times. Some costumes, indeed, were sourced from courtiers. For many Elizabethans, these were as close as they could get to the high fashions of the court, even if they were last season's fashions. As well as costumes, the theatre also used live animals. Shakespeare employed a dog in *The Two Gentleman of Verona*, for example. However, sometimes realism could go too far, as in the 1613 production of *Henry VIII* (known then as *All is True*). The script calls for a cannon to be fired. The players used a real cannon for the scene, which must have been an impressive spectacle for an audience in a relatively confined space. Unfortunately, the discharge sparked a fire in the Globe's thatched roof, the audience was evacuated and the theatre burnt to the ground (two accounts of this are in *Norton Shakespeare*, pp. 3338–40). The scene that Forman saw was likely then to have been as realistic and spectacular as Shakespeare's company could manage. The nobles would have worn expensive costumes, the ghost would have looked terrifying, and Macbeth's hysterical reaction obviously had an impact on the other characters on the stage – and on Forman in the audience.

The performance that Forman saw in 1611 was probably quite different to the one staged in 1606 when *Macbeth* was premiered. Scholars have long been fascinated by the clear differences between what Forman saw and the performance that the text records. For example, Forman remembers Macbeth standing up from his seat, following which the ghost 'came and sat down' behind him, whereas in the text Macbeth is returning from his clandestine talk with Banquo's murderers when this happens. *Macbeth* was not a new play in

1611 (Shakespeare had written it, we believe, in 1606, around the time of the Gunpowder Plot); so, it is quite possible that the company made changes in performance that did not survive into the printed text. The first printing of the play, in 1623, is now generally thought to be Thomas Middleton's abridged and revised version of Shakespeare's play. Brown rightly argues that Shakespeare's texts are and have always been 'open' to alternative ways of delivery, but the choices made in delivery have critical consequences for both the part performed and the audience's understanding of the play as a whole (Brown 2002: 71). By understanding the context of *Macbeth*'s early performances, we are better able to appreciate the shaping architecture of the texts – but seventeenth-century performances are no more definitive than any other. In the next section, I will suggest some ways in which we can begin to open up the scene to our own contemporary exploration of the scene in practice.

Macbeth Workshop

The most productive way to begin to develop a critical imagination inflected, even infected, by performance is to just get up and do it. I have taught many students without acting ability in workshops which have opened up important insights into a text which would otherwise be static on the page. Shakespeare did not need a lighting rig or a public address system for his plays in 1611, nor are they are needed now. Instead, a suitable space, enough people to form a group, a little bit of courage, a lot of imagination and some patience are all that is required to start exploring Shakespeare in performance.

This workshop supposes an opportunity to work in groups on the scene – but the steps taken here can be imagined as well. In a written chapter, the shared experience of a workshop cannot be created – but with practice, and imagination, it is quite possible to start to read texts theatrically so long as the workshop in our minds identifies the kinds of problems and questions encountered in the theatre.

The Ground Rules
1 *The Space*. A workshop can take place anywhere. But of all the anywheres that they could take place, the traditional classroom is the least attractive: cluttered with desks and chairs, many hierarchically facing one way, designed for sages to lecture to disciples rather than for groups to embark on a shared exploration of a problem. So if this is where you find yourself, start by moving tables out of the way and doing what you can to make the room flexible in the ways it can be used. It will need to be flexible, because we do not know what we are going to do with it yet.

2 *The Time*. The time may be out of joint in *Hamlet* and it probably is in *Macbeth* as well, but most educational institutions will rigorously police

time, and you are probably not too sorry about that either. But time quickly disappears in workshops. Speeches which are skipped over in reading can take a couple of hours to unpack in the kind of detail that will serve our purposes. Assuming that you are bound within the two-hour traffic (maybe one!) of a seminar or school class, choose scenes carefully. One hundred lines is more than enough for an hour's work, so long as the context of those lines is taken into account.

3 *The Read-through.* The read-through is not strictly compulsory but it is useful. The words are difficult when spoken for the first time, the rhythms are strange, and it's not clear where the stresses should be, or why what is being said is being said. So, most of the read-throughs will be just that – a bland reading, perhaps excruciatingly so. Long speeches will take an age to get through, but at least you will be able to measure how far you have come later when reading starts to become performance. There are various strategies for read-throughs – some prefer to allocate parts from the outset, others to rotate parts around the room so that everyone is reading. Because I want to move forwards and backwards around the scene, we will read it in its entirety, though in workshop we will focus on a few lines.

4 *The Work.* A workshop is a place where things get made, where *work* gets done. Not everyone does the same work and it will be enormously helpful if there are more people in the workshop than there are parts to play. Someone will have to be brave and stand in the middle of the circle. Others will have to be tactful spectators, confident enough to direct the actors, bullish enough to push them when needed, diplomatic to recognize that it takes courage to stand up and enact a script.

5 *The Method.* Here is a simple method, useful for non-actors (including teachers). The 'directors', those who have not stood up to speak parts, take the responsibility to set the scene, to organize the space, to position actors and to decide on interpretation. Each line will have to be thought-through. Actors can join in the discussion, make suggestions, try different ideas, but it is the class as a whole that makes decisions. The scene must first of all be set. No elaborate props or costumes are needed, but the basic skeleton of the scene should be agreed: table and chairs for the banquet table and a clear sense of where the exits and entrances are. Once the scene is in play, the directors will have certain privileges. They can shout 'freeze' and the action must stop. This will allow space for new ideas to be aired, fresh doubts to be confessed and discussed. The action can be spooled back, played again, tried a different way. Anyone in the class can do this. Also, the director has the power to retire an actor if they think they can do better. If there is a teacher in the room they (or someone else) must take responsibility for making sure that these

privileges are used. The object of the workshop is not to get from the start of the scene to its end as quickly as possible. The object is to get to the end as *slowly* as possible, with understanding accruing. If the group is large, then the scene can be broken down into parts with different groups working on different aspects of the scene, playing at different speeds, experimenting with different character viewpoints and so on. (If the group is large then several tables can be set – see Tibbets 2004: 43).

6 *The Object*. Though there is no one *right* way to play a scene – there are no end of wrong ways. The object is to understand what the problems are, to formulate questions rather than arrive at definitive answers. The worst performance of Shakespeare is that executed without understanding, without grappling with the text, as if simply saying the words is enough. Peter Brook has a good name for this kind of theatre: Deadly Theatre (see Brook 1968). Nevertheless, a final performance will focus the work. This is what we are aiming for, a short performance to the class which makes sense of the scene and renders it in three dimensions.

7 *The Problems*. Shakespeare's scripts are full of endless problems for those performing them. Crucial information is missing, or at least appears to be. The group will need to make some early decisions. Where do characters enter from and where do they go to? Who do they speak to, who hears them and how do they react? These are not questions which the text directly answers, but the text is full of cues – and clues.

Practice

Actors are positioned, the scene is run, questions are asked and as the group pauses over a line, discusses an action, the text will gradually become a performance. The group should pay attention to the drama of the scene – what is being contested (because drama is *always* a conflict), who is contesting it and why? And they should attend to the personal and political dynamics evident in the stage pictures that they create as the text is built up, layer by layer, into a performance. Discussion can range back and forth across the play; it is even possible (with confidence) to suggest another part of the play to look at to help illuminate the scene. (For a detailed and theatrically focused analysis of this scene see Brown 2005: 51–56 and Worster 2002.)

The scene is deceptively simple. The occasion is a banquet in honour of the new king Macbeth, a man who has seized power unexpectedly, violently, secretly and without right. But Macbeth is balancing two different parties – the one in the open, with those he is now subjugating, who recognize that the politics of tyranny is to go along with the flow; and the one in the shadows, for not long into the scene, Macbeth skulks into the corner, anxious for news from the men he sent to murder his former ally Banquo. This is a striking scene. Macbeth is *meant* to be the triumphant host: as Chris Meads points out, the banquet is the culmination of Macbeth's display of new power (Meads 2001: 144). The occasion is awkward enough for those at the feast, all terrified by the way Macbeth has seized power. This is the moment for Macbeth to impose his command, to show he is a king – and instead, almost at the earliest opportunity, Macbeth absents himself from the main party. It is worth spending some time over this – the text only gives us the murderers' words, but the party is still there and, evident from their remarks when Macbeth returns, intensely curious about his absence.

Macbeth returns from his secret meeting with the murderers, troubled by the news of Fleance's escape, nervously rejoining the party. Macbeth says nothing, for it is Lady Macbeth who has the next lines and they are all directed at making him speak, making him perform the role of host, of King. 'My royal lord', she says, stressing that he is 'royal' as if he needed reminding, 'You do not give the cheer' – you are not toasting the feast, but also you are not creating a hospitable atmosphere. She goes on, for some lines, to chide him for this. The subsequent stage direction 'Enter the Ghost of Banquo, and sits in Macbeth's place' now governs the whole dramatic situation. While Macbeth ponders a 'Sweet remembrancer', Lennox nervously asks 'May't please your highness sit', gesturing to the *regal* seat from which Macbeth still stands back. At this point Banquo's ghost appears, but Macbeth does not see it. Rather, he ignores Lennox and continues with his toast. This is superficial cordiality, an over-the-top eagerness to be the host which ignores how uncomfortable his guests are that he will not simply take his place. But he cannot – it is not his place to take.

Ross has another go: 'Please't your highness', he says, 'To grace us with your royal company?' It is tempting to play Ross and Lennox in much the same way, but Brown points out interesting differences between the two characters. Lennox, young and ambitious, is simply trying to cover up an awkward moment; but Ross 'has sought help in coping with the "unnatural" aftermath of Duncan's death and so his words will be more carefully chosen' (Brown 2005: 52). Exploring the scene from a minor character's point of view can be an illuminating way of opening out its complexity. But Macbeth is not paying attention to them, for he is looking at the table, puzzled, for now he says, perhaps a little too casually, 'The table's full'. Macbeth sees that there are no places before he sees the ghost. Lennox tries again: 'Here is a place reserved, sir'. 'Where?' says Macbeth, dumbfounded. This time certainly gesturing, Lennox says, 'Here, my good lord'. This is the point at which Macbeth *sees* the ghost. We know that Macbeth must react – there are no stage directions, no lines, but Lennox's next line tells us – and the actor – all that is needed to establish what has happened: 'What is't that moves your highness?' What *is it* that moves Macbeth?

To answer this question, we need to step back a bit and consider the stage picture that Shakespeare has created for this action. At the start, Macbeth addresses his guests with the opening line of the scene, 'You know your own degrees'. Macbeth is simply saying, you know where to sit at the table, because you know your station. In other words, the guests seated at the table represent a social and political order of things, with the King (one presumes) in the centre of the table, the most powerful Lords either side of him, and the lesser Lords furthest away. There are probably many of them as well: the stage directions call for 'Lords and attendants', but Brown assumes that all 'the actors that the company can supply will crowd onto the stage, marking a major new event after a sequence of scenes that, for the most part, involved very few persons' (Brown 2005: 52). The play shifts gear, the stage is busier than ever before, but rather than rising to the occasion (this is, after all, what he has *killed* for), Macbeth becomes utterly isolated from the moment he steps aside to talk to the murderers. Given the layout of the Globe, a straight table with Macbeth's seat in the centre and everyone sat facing the audience would have made most sense – especially if Macbeth's seat were placed over a trap-door to allow for a ghost to appear magically. So Macbeth's reluctance to sit at the table, even before Banquo's ghost appears, signifies more than his unease; it also points towards his inability to assume that place in society which he has usurped. It is for this reason that the scene is not private but public for, as Richard McCoy argues, the unfulfilled banquet demonstrates the 'breakdown of social communion' in the world of the play (McCoy 2004: 29).

This line of thinking throws up an intriguing performance crux, one well worth exploring in a workshop.

Does Banquo Actually Appear, and How does Macbeth React?

The text, at least, is clear about this: 'Enter the Ghost of Banquo'. Yet the scene's drama lies in the different perceptions of those on stage. Macbeth sees the ghost. Lady Macbeth and the rest do not see it. If the ghost is onstage, Macbeth's terrified, deranged shouts make sense; without Banquo's ghost onstage, he rails at air, and the others' puzzled anxiety is plain. Suddenly, the stage direction seems less trustworthy. The scene can be played either way because there are two scenes, two plays: Macbeth's play, in which Banquo, gory locks and all, appears; and everybody else's play, for whom Macbeth's behaviour is not only strange but deeply worrying given the prevailing political instability, for which the feast was supposed to be resolving. For David Garrick, the leading actor of the eighteenth century, the scene was about Macbeth's reaction rather than the ghost's appearance. When he staged the scene, Macbeth held a glass of wine, which, on the ghost's second appearance, slipped gently from his hand without him realizing it: 'he should not discover the

---

least Consciousness of having such a Vehicle in his Hand, his Memory being quite lost in the present Guilt and Horror of his Imagination' (qtd in Vickers 1975: 132). Contemporary attempts to emulate such passion tend to be poorly received: for example, Peter Holland wittily rubbished Alan Howard, whose lines were 'screamed and chanted, twisted and fragmented, stretched and gabbled' (Holland 1997: 156).

In the rest of this case study, I will look at two ways in which actors and directors have grappled with this problem by using the resources of theatre *and* film.

Macbeth in Performance

To conclude this case study, I am going to discuss two contemporary stagings of the banquet scene which brought out very different perspectives on the play. My aim in both cases is to demonstrate how the theatrical and filmic interpretation of this scene decisively influences the whole production's approach to the play.

The BBC *Macbeth* (1982)

Directed by Jack Gold, this 1982 film was commissioned and broadcast by the BBC *Complete Works* series. The BBC *Macbeth* deliberately shied away from representing the supernatural as anything other than a figment of Macbeth's obsessive madness. The only ghosts here were in Macbeth's mind. The banquet scene had no part for Banquo's gory locks. Macbeth railed over the table, but only at an empty chair. There was no ghost outside his mind, no way for the audience to see into that mind, and so no ambiguity about whether Banquo is really there or not. The camera kept returning to the chair, as if straining to see the ghost, and then back to Macbeth, staring, his shaking arm pointing at absent space. Instead of situating the supremacy of fate, the scene was a tipping point in representing how unhinged Macbeth was. Some critics have been unconvinced by Nicol Williamson's hysterics which Bernice Kliman (for example) described as 'wearisome' (Kliman 2004: 101). This is always a risky strategy for an actor determined to explore Macbeth as a character full of sound and fury – or, as Forman put it, 'a great passion of fear and fury'. Williamson's Macbeth was teetering on the edge of madness even in his first appearance. Faced with the witches, he stood back, apparently proud, secretly afraid. Banquo taunted the witches, approached them, examined them, but Macbeth stood back, dumbfounded. Prophecies which amused Banquo unsettled Macbeth. His relationship with Lady Macbeth, superbly played by a snake-like Jane Lapotaire, was both sexual and violent. Reading his letter, Lady Macbeth rolled on a stone bed (recalling the witches' dolmen or stone table made from unhewn stones suggesting a prehistoric setting) speaking her soliloquy faster and faster until reaching orgasm, at which point Macbeth entered and she jumped on him, kissing him with intense passion. But this kind of passion was obviously unstable. Not much later Macbeth, suddenly enraged, started to strangle her. Their relationship could easily flip over into violent madness, its dynamics too easily perverted. As James Lusardi and June Schlueter point out, this Macbeth towers over Lady Macbeth, but after murdering Duncan he too easily falls into hysterics from which 'she must desperately seek to recover him' (Lusardi and Schlueter 2003: 82).

The banquet built on this relationship. Lady Macbeth played the perfect host, calming her husband, trying to contain his outbursts, trying to settle the table into some kind of convivial hospitality. It began with such a note, Macbeth welcoming his guests, sitting them at a small table of steel and stone. But after his brief dialogue aside with Banquo's murdered ghost he became more agitated. Before that, Lady Macbeth had already seemed ill at ease with the table. Everyone sat, there were three places vacant: Macbeth's at the head of the table, her seat opposite and a seat with the other nobles that they were entertaining. Offered her seat opposite the head of the table, she hesitated, declined to sit in it and instead joined the others – sitting, in fact, in Banquo's seat. Macbeth took his position and it was at this point that he raved at the seat opposite, which became Duncan's place, Lady Macbeth's place, his own place perhaps, all taken by Banquo's invisible ghost.

Such strategies created a sense of psychological claustrophobia which came to a head at the play's conclusion. With battles fighting outside, Macbeth stayed in his shadowy throne room. When Macduff appeared, silhouetted against a portcullis at the end of a corridor, Macbeth at first hid like a frightened child behind his throne, before coming out to face his nemesis. Williamson's Macbeth was always frightened and haunted, his wide-eyed speeches, his slow bitter ruminations, were all rooted in a fear of himself. Williamson's performance brilliantly captured this complexity. One of the highlights was his delivery of perhaps Macbeth's most famous lines. Told news of his wife's death, he was at first good humoured, even sanguine, saying 'there would have been time for such a word. /Tomorrow' but as soon as he said the word, a terrible thought struck him. Tomorrow . . . the weight of the word seemed to disorientate him. He said the word again differently and with each utterance of the word in the line, changed intonation and expression, as if being struck with new thoughts, new horrors, each time.

The 'Patrick Stewart' *Macbeth* (2007)

Rupert Goold's critically acclaimed 2007 production, in which Patrick Stewart played Macbeth, opened in Chichester and after a successful run transferred to the Gielgud Theatre on Shaftesbury Avenue in London. In this production, the banquet scene was the touchstone for the production's interpretation of the play: so important was it that, uniquely, the company played it twice, in two different ways, during the same performance. The production was full of innovations like this. Goold wanted to give *Macbeth* a contemporary feel without also losing a sense that the play takes place in another world, a recent past familiar and different, canny and uncanny. The permanent set suggested a wretched hospital basement, a morgue perhaps, a torture chamber maybe – one reviewer, John Lahr, guessed at a 'dingy field ward' (*New Yorker*, 3 March 2008), others noted its 'grimy, institutional sterility' (Ben Brantley, *The New York Times*, 15 February 2008). To the left of the stage, a tap and basin stood for characters to wash their hands in. In a play famously unclean, the basin was a stark object holding out the possibility of cleanliness, of redemption, but this possibility would, of course, turn out to be an empty one. In her last scene in the play, Lady Macbeth (played by Kate Fleetwood) would desperately try to scrub out invisible blood marks on her arm, trying to absolve herself of guilt. But more striking than this and the dirty white basement walls upon which, at times, Goold projected unintelligible postmodern images of electricity jerking wildly like a cardiometer hooked up to a man in his dying spasm, was a large central door. This was gated like an old-fashioned industrial lift and the characters who entered it did so as if to rise to the level above. Bright electric light flooded the stage from the lift when it appeared, emphasizing the claustrophobic world created by the set. In this way, Macbeth's world was mundane and functional, but could suddenly be transformed by such interventions into an unsettled, terrifying world paranoiacally obsessed by a fear of what lies beyond and above. Fear and the mundane intermingled, as Michael Billington noted in his review for *The Guardian*: 'Even when dressing for dinner with his wife, he [Macbeth] seems haunted by fear' (4 June 2007).

In a keynote opening, the set took on the role of a wartime emergency hospital, a role it never quite lost. Goold rearranged the text so that the play started with the Captain's message to Duncan which is a graphic rendering of war in a play that is otherwise preoccupied with politicized domestic violence. In this production, that message became instead a desperate death-bed story. Changing Shakespeare's text still has some capacity to provoke controversy and Goold took a risk by removing one of Shakespeare's most famous opening scenes from its context, but this allowed him to open with a scene full of energy and desperate panic. The stage cracked with an explosion and gunfire, soldiers, generals and nurses ran onto the stage pushing a wounded man on a makeshift hospital bed. (This mood of near-death terror was sustained through the whole, exhausting production.) Bleeding, his limbs quivering, his shirt bloody, clearly horribly mutilated, the soldier panted his story to Duncan, who listened concerned as the nurses bustled around the soldier, connecting him to ECG machines and morphine drips, preparing him for surgery. If Goold had started with the witches, he would have had a different performance challenge and a different play to deal with. Instead, this opening was deliberately violent both in what it staged and how it was staged. However, the witches were there. They were not obvious at first in the frantic bustle of the opening, but Duncan signalled that the Captain should be left alone now he had got crucial intelligence from him, and everyone left the stage except three nurses. As they quietly settled the Captain and finished connecting him to wires and tubes, so the audience, able to draw breadth, may have realized who these three nurses really were. One depressed the morphine drip to settle the soldier, but quickly it was clear that whatever was in the sac it was not morphine. The captain started to struggle in pain, the other nurses holding him down, his legs quivering violently before crashing into death, the ECG flatlining behind. Only now did one of the nurses start, 'when shall we three meet again', so signalling Goold's way into the play.

These were effective ways to disorientate an audience over-familiar with the play (and, for that matter, with Stewart's high-profile roles in Hollywood) and to set the tone for the production. Nonetheless, the banquet scene was literally the centre of the production, as the interval was placed at the moment that Macbeth sees Banquo's ghost; this was replayed from the beginning when the audience resumed their seats. This was a very effective technique, for the scene was played from two different points of view. In the first version, before the interval, Goold presented the scene from Macbeth's point of view. In the second, the audience saw the same scene, the same action, but from the point of view of the other guests at the banquet. To achieve this, Goold and his company had to choreograph the scene carefully in order to make it clear that the same actions were being repeated in both versions. There were gains and losses. The gap between Macbeth's reality and everyone else's was brilliantly theatricalized.

Yet some of Shakespeare's structure was lost in this revision. First of all, the clear political order which Macbeth invokes when he invites everyone to sit according to their degree was muddied, for the table was positioned so that the audience was seated behind the head of the table, the rest of which stretched back to the elevator door. This made it hard to see the political gap in Macbeth's world. The table was not grand, the occasion not stately. Rather, Goold chose to make the 'banquet' an intimate family dinner. The Macbeth family was two-faced. When alone, Macbeth and his wife hissed at each other, argued, fought. Lady Macbeth would hack at bread and meat with a carving knife and then wave the same knife at her husband, unaware of the ironic associations with their earlier butchery. Food, guests and murder textured the family scene. However, as soon as guests arrived, both assumed the manners of enthusiastic hosts. Lady Macbeth danced gaily, Macbeth teased his guests, charmed them, made sure that they were seated and fussed over them. Yet all this took place in the same dank kitchen cellar as the rest of the play, there was nothing kingly about Macbeth's celebration feast. Spying the crooks he had hired to murder Banquo skulking at the other side of the stage, Macbeth made his excuses and walked over to them, speaking to both in whispers. As he did so, the party continued silently in the background. Back at the table, Macbeth's cheerfulness seemed disproportionate, bordering on the manic. The table was waited upon by the nurses, whom Macbeth had hardly noticed at all as they put out plates and refilled glasses with wine. But as he started towards his seat, they suddenly stood together at the top of the table, blocking his way. Macbeth started, at last realizing who they were. The witches are not in Shakespeare's version of the scene; it is Banquo who, famously, stops Macbeth from sitting in the chair that he has murdered Duncan for.

In this staging, Macbeth does eventually take his place at the head of the table, so this aspect of Shakespeare's play was lost. However, it was a brief victory, for not long after he had sat down the stage turned into a horror show. Banquo suddenly appeared standing on the table as if he were part of the feast being eaten, his dead eyes staring, his shirt covered in blood. The other guests ignored the ghost, staring right through it, but Macbeth started back, stumbling from his chair in terror. At this point there was a blackout, and then the houselights were put on to signal the interval.

Goold's excessive theatricality robbed the scene of some of its thematic significance but gave to it a pivotal status for his production. It was the banquet where everything was meant to be made right, where Duncan's sacrifice could be finally buried. By making the scene into a domestic house party rather than a sovereign's formal banquet, Goold suggested that the banquet was Macbeth's way to make things normal, ordinary. This was their strategy all through the play, to offset the grotesque with the mundane. Washing their hands, getting ready for guests, preparing meals were all domestic routines which became progressively corrupted by the extraordinary actions that both Macbeths undertook to gain power.

But this was only the scene *as Macbeth saw it*. After the interval, the play picked up from the start of the banquet, as if time had been spooled backwards. Once again, Macbeth met his guests, once again he teased them, charmed them, once again he danced on the table. Only when the murderers arrived at the side of the stage did Goold's intent become clearer. Macbeth sidled over to them, but this time the audience heard nothing of his conversation. They saw him nod and worry and chide the murderers as he realized that Fleance had escaped, but words were only mimed, not spoken. As this dumbshow went on the party, which had been silent until this point, was this time staged with audible chatter. It was on odd moment, a risky departure from the text. This was the banquet as some one other than Macbeth would remember it: they might have seen Macbeth talking with strangers, but would not have heard him. Macbeth returned to the table and once again his way to his chair was at first blocked by the witches. He sat and suddenly started, falling off his chair as before, raving to the ghost – but the ghost did not appear. Instead, the domestic scene remained domestic, and the guests simply looked at Macbeth with alarm. The ghost was in Macbeth's mind all along. For John Lahr, this was 'a clever demonstration of Macbeth's splitting off of his guilt-ridden panic' (*New Yorker*, 3 March 2008). Nonetheless, not all reviewers appreciated the innovation: Benedict Nightingale worried that Goold's theatrical inventiveness was 'busy and sometimes distractingly fussy' (*The Times*, 27 September 2007).

Further Analysis: First Encounters with Shakespeare's Dramatic Worlds

By introducing the ghost, Shakespeare effectively endorses Macbeth's madness, for this is a play world in which ghosts do exist and witches do shape the universe in a place that is somehow beyond time. Modern productions often prefer to keep Macbeth in the material world and render this scene as a demonstration of his madness. By staging the scene twice, once with the ghost and once without, Goold kept open both possibilities and the performance never finally resolved whether Macbeth was mad, haunted or both. Consider the implications of reversing a play's opening scenes. In *Twelfth Night* and *1 Henry IV*, this would radically affect our introductions into the dramatic worlds and the nature of the bonds we forge with the characters.

Conclusion

Some critics are suspicious of performance criticism because it seems to be, on the face of it, another way of determining 'meaning' and blocking individual interpretation. But in truth, putting Shakespeare into performance – whether in our classroom, rehearsal room, in professional production or just in the mind's eye – is a powerful way to enable the text to breath the air of the present and capture the future in the instant. In this case study, I have tracked a scene through our own performance (real or imagined) and through two contrasting performances, one staged, another filmed for television. In each case, I hope I have demonstrated the centrality of that scene's interpretation to the overall production logic. In each case, different readings have important ramifications for the play as a whole. The choices made in performing the banquet scene shape what happens afterwards and help us to understand what went before. Unlike a text on the page, a script in performance is always for an audience, however small or large, and it is for an audience of moderns, not early moderns. In short, Greene got it wrong. Shakespeare was no superficial player prancing about fancying himself a poet. He had a player's heart, wrapped in a tiger's hide.

7 Key Critical Concepts and Topics

Adrian Streete

Chapter Overview

Setting the Scene

What do you need to know in order to get the most from studying Shakespeare at university level? There is no easy answer to this question. However, as a way of developing your confidence in coming to terms with Shakespearean studies, it will first be useful to consider the following three points:

- Like any academic discipline, Shakespeare Studies has its own critical vocabulary with its own key critical concepts and topics.
- Shakespearean critics use this vocabulary and these key concepts and topics in order to discuss Shakespeare's texts in a range of contexts, including Shakespeare's early modern context.
- This vocabulary and these concepts and topics may seem daunting and impenetrable at first. But like any vocabulary, with some effort on your part, its concepts and topics can be learnt and used successfully.

Elsewhere in this book, you will find chapters that deal with past and current critical approaches to Shakespeare. These show that the critical concepts and topics which Shakespearean critics use to discuss the plays and poems are constantly changing. Students sometimes assume that *any* book in the library – or worse, any document on the internet – on Shakespeare will help them when trying to prepare for a class or write an essay. For example, although still interesting and well worth reading, a book such as M. C. Bradbrook's *The Growth and Structure of Elizabethan Comedy*, which was first published in 1955, is a product of its time (see Hiscock and Longstaffe, this volume). Many of its critical concepts may still be valid: others will have been critiqued or long rejected. So, when you are trying to make sense of the terms that Shakespearean critics use, you also need to be aware that:

- The terminology of Shakespearean criticism has a history, has changed over time and is still changing.
- Shakespearean critics are aware of that history and work within it.

In what follows, I will outline and explain six key critical concepts and topics commonly used by Shakespearean critics writing today. These concepts and topics represent a snapshot of some important current concerns and interests within Shakespearean scholarship in 2008. As such, they offer neither an exhaustive list, nor should they be read uncritically. My aim is not to give you a series of 'readings' or provide you with failsafe 'methods' that you can 'apply' to any Shakespearean text. Rather, my aim is to encourage you to reflect critically on how these key concepts and topics might enable you to begin to explore other Shakespearean texts not covered elsewhere in this book. By developing a critical vocabulary of your own, I hope that you will feel more confident in adding to that vocabulary and expanding your understanding of it through independent research.

Key Concept One: Authority

The religious Reformation that swept sixteenth-century Europe has been understood in a variety of ways but one enduring critical approach to the Reformation is to say that it represented a crisis of authority. Up until the 1960s, the Reformation in England was often understood as a process of inevitable change: the authority of the medieval Catholic Church and the Papacy had diminished to such an extent that Reformation was unavoidable. Harnessing the new print technology, Protestant ideas swept across Northern Europe and changed forever people's attitude to kingship, church power, worship and identity. However, since the 1970s, this picture of the Reformation has been subject to question. Inspired by so-called revisionist historians, an alternative view has been proposed. Scholars have argued for a vigorous and well respected late medieval Catholic Church, widespread expressions of religious and lay piety, and no particular desire for change. It has been suggested that a series of Reformations were imposed on England for political reasons. These were closely connected to the political contexts of the various Tudor monarchs (see Engel, this volume, Chapter 2). Henry VIII's divorce, Edward VI's ardent Protestantism, Mary I's equally ardent Catholicism and Elizabeth I's adherence to a pragmatic form of Protestantism were, it is argued, the main determiners of what people believed.

This brief summary shows that there is no simple way of understanding the Reformation in early modern England. Some scholars maintain that the revisionists overstate their case, that the late medieval Catholic Church was not as vibrant as is claimed, that the Reformation cannot be reduced to what individual monarchs enacted, and that this approach underplays the theological impact of the Reformers' ideas on dominant modes of thought. Revisionists, on the other hand, will often point out that in England at least, the refusal of Catholicism to die out completely complicates this picture. Debate on this issue is ongoing, but it is clear that authority, or more precisely, the question of where authority resides, is central to both approaches (see Robson, this volume, Chapter 5).

In terms of Shakespearean study, a number of critics have debated the question of authority. In this section, I am going to introduce the work of one, Robert Weimann and mention briefly the work of another, Andrew Hadfield. I will offer a brief outline of their work as well as some of the central questions that they deal with, such as:

- Where does authority reside? With the Pope; with the monarch; with parliament; in books?
- What political power (if any) do the people have?
- What is the best way to govern a state?

I will also suggest some Shakespearean texts that you might examine in relation to these questions.

In his book *Authority and Representation in Early Modern Discourse*, Robert Weimann adopts an anti-revisionist position, arguing that the proliferation of print in the early modern period profoundly changed attitudes towards political authority. He argues that before the Reformation 'traditional locations of premodern authority persisted in [. . .] the ecclesiastical hold over religious writings' (1996: 5). But with the invention of the printing press and the ever increasing production of books, a new attitude to authority was born, 'one residing in the strength of personal beliefs and convictions, in the differentiating uses of knowledge, discussion, and a busier exchange of signs and meanings' (5). With such a shift, argues Weimann, and as different ways of *representing* authority became possible, 'there resulted an intense circulation, allowing for mutual interrogation among diverse locations, of authority' (18). Weimann focuses on Reformers like Luther and Calvin in his discussion, suggesting that Protestantism has a fundamentally antagonistic attitude to secular authority. This antagonism may not always be on show, but nonetheless, Weimann enables us to understand that the Reformation crisis in authority was as much a political issue as it was a religious one. As you can see, Weimann's writing can be dense and is not always easy to comprehend. But, like a number of Shakespearean critics, once you get past the sometimes complex language, there is much to be gleaned. How might we relate Weimann's ideas to Shakespeare's writings?

First, we might think of the way in which numerous Shakespearean figures read, interpret and challenge various forms of writing. These often take the form of letters and books, and they demonstrate how often the written word is open to interrogation in the plays.

Further Analysis: Shakespeare and Writing

For example, *Love's Labour's Lost* is a play saturated with books, letters, scholars good and bad, and is deeply concerned with questioning the authority of writing. Here are some sections that you might examine:

- In Act One, scene one, the King of Navarre and his court sign an 'edict' (1. 1. 11) committing them to three years solitary study. In what ways is the oath that the court takes compromised in the play?
- The edict forbids women to come within a mile of the court (1. 1. 119–20). In what way do the women in the play read, interpret, and negotiate this edict?
- You might examine the importance of letter writing, reading and interpreting letters, for example the letters that the braggart Armado writes as he tries to woo Jacquenetta. See 1. 1. 179–292 and 4. 1. 53–120. You might also like to consider the ways in which different forms of writing ask us to question the nature of erotic desire, judicial authority and intellectual ambition in plays such as *Henry IV, Twelfth Night, Hamlet* and *The Tempest*.

Another way of utilizing Weimann's work is with regard to monarchical authority. Shakespeare's history plays explore this question remorselessly. In historical terms, the Wars of the Roses start with the deposition of a rightful king, Richard II, and end with the assumption of the first Tudor monarch Henry VII. Traditionally, critics have read this narrative as implying the restoration of monarchical authority in the Tudors. However, since the 1970s scholars have found a much more complex set of attitudes towards monarchical authority at work in the histories. Here are some interesting sections to explore further:

- You might compare Act Three, scene three of *Richard II* when Richard submits to Bolingbroke, with the deposition scene in Act Four, scene one. Is monarchical authority given by 'divine right'? Or does authority derive from the application of political might?
- In *Richard III* we see a monarch who is a murderer and usurper. Yet the play presents us with at least six Kings or Queens, as well as any number of potential monarchs. What does this reveal to us about the idea of divine right? How does 'God's name' (5. 2. 22) operate in this play?
- How does Shakespeare's last history play (written in collaboration with John Fletcher), *All Is True* (*Henry VIII*) debate the relationship between Papal and monarchical power? Look at the trial of the Protestant Archbishop Cranmer in Act Five, scene two, and in particular the accusations made against him by the Catholic Gardiner (5. 2. 35–214). How does England's opposition to Rome inform this play's politics?

Finally, these questions about the location of authority might encourage us to think further about alternative political structures that may have been available in Shakespeare's time. The monarch was the most powerful single figure in early modern England. However, as Andrew Hadfield has shown in his book *Shakespeare and Republicanism* (2005), alternatives to this form of governance were also debated. By the sixteenth century England had developed a complex constitutional system of checks and balances combining the authorities of monarch and national representation – this structure is frequently discussed in terms of the power of 'King-in-Parliament'. Parliament (a grouping of peers in the Lords and mostly gentry in the Commons) participated in the monarch's law-making and taxation initiatives as well as voicing opinions on more divisive issues such as religious reform, foreign policy and royal marriage. If this form of 'mixed government' was celebrated by many political writers of the time, this was not universally the case. Republican thought, which drew upon classical sources as well as contemporary political writing, was a complex phenomenon. However, broadly speaking, it referred to 'the intellectual conviction that it was necessary to control the powers of the crown by establishing a means of ensuring that a coterie of virtuous advisors and servants would always have the constitutional right to counsel the monarch, and so influence and control his or her actions within the limits of the law' (Hadfield 2005: 17). This 'conviction' might take a variety of forms, ranging from the assertion that citizens should have rights and that parliament should be a more powerful force, to the promotion of doctrines of lawful resistance against a monarch. We might therefore ask:

* In what ways might Shakespeare's texts explore 'alternative' forms of government? There are a number of texts that draw directly upon republican history, such as *The Rape of Lucrece* and *Julius Caesar*, as well as many others that deal with deposition, rebellion and civil war – do these texts critique, reject or advance alternative forms of government? Is Shakespeare a 'republican'?

Key Concept Two: Carnivalesque

If the previous section on authority dealt with questions surrounding the maintenance of power, this section deals with those moments in early modern culture and literature when the power of the ruling classes is deliberately mocked, ridiculed and (temporarily at least) overturned. Many Shakespearean critics call these moments carnivalesque. In order to understand what this term means and how it might apply to Shakespeare's writings, we need first to consider where the term comes from and how it might operate within early modern culture.

The term carnivalesque draws upon the work of the Russian critic Mikhail Bakhtin. In his influential book *Rabelais and His World*, Bakhtin examines the importance of the feast days and festivals that structured the passage of the year across medieval and early modern Europe. In particular, he argued that these 'official' events were offset by the carnival. As he notes (1984: 10):

> The suspension of all hierarchical precedence during carnival time was of particular significance. Rank was especially evident during official feasts; everyone was expected to appear in the full regalia of his calling, rank, and merits and to take the place corresponding to his position. It was a consecration on inequality. On the contrary, all were considered equal during the carnival. [. . .] This led to the creation of special forms of marketplace speech and gesture, frank and free, permitting no distance between those who came into contact with each other and liberating from norms of etiquette and decency imposed at other times.

The carnival was a place where, for a while, the overturning of rigid social hierarchies could be celebrated. A different form of speech was permissible during the carnival. Rather than the monologic speech associated with official ruling ideology that was singular and dominant, the speech of the carnival was dialogic, that is to say, multiple, plural and 'liberating'. Though the carnival was invariably a temporary state, it could nonetheless give rise to all kinds of subversive behaviours. The carnivalesque celebrated what Bakhtin terms 'A second life [. . .] a "world inside out" ' (1984: 11). As such, it rejoices in parody, satire, inversion, travesty, profanity and a celebration of bodily excess, what Bakhtin terms the 'grotesque body' (1984: 317). Here, Bakhtin is not simply referring to extraordinary specimens of the human body which often attracted crowds to the carnival, but to a moment which signalled a collapse in human and self-government – a provisional time in which all kinds of appetite might be unleashed and undermine the day-to-day power structures which usually held that world in check.

In terms of Shakespearean criticism, Bakhtin's work on the carnival has proved fruitful for a number of critics. One such is Naomi Conn Liebler, whose book *Shakespeare's Festive Tragedy: The Ritual Foundations of Genre* (1995) uses Bahktin and others to examine the ways in which the genre of tragedy draws upon much older rituals such as carnival. Another critic who has utilized Bakhtin is Michael Bristol. In his discussion of *Othello*, Bristol argues that the carnivalesque environment which is generated during the course of the tragedy releases a 'latent social violence' (1996: 180) which had hitherto been repressed by the rigorous political order of the Venetian world. In this challenging essay, Bristol also attempts to recover, via Bakhtin, a reading of Othello not as tragic hero, but as a 'comically monstrous' figure, an 'abject clown' whose humiliation and death exposes the 'invidious racial sentiments' of the period that it was written in (1986: 181, 187, 186). This essay shows the way in which critics can use the inversion implied by the carnivalesque to read the plays and, in so doing, disrupt dominant critical readings of the Shakespearean text, which all too frequently have concentrated upon the psychological anguish of the protagonist, the catalytic role of the tempter Iago, and the pathos generated by the dramatization of victim experience.

What other Shakespearean texts might be read in relation to the carnivalesque? Here are some suggestions:

- Falstaff has a dramatic life outside the history plays and in the broad farce of Shakespeare's *The Merry Wives of Windsor* he could be seen as an embodiment of the carnivalesque. How might you read the attention paid to his 'grotesque body'? Look in particular at the exchanges between Falstaff and Ford in Act Two, scene two (especially Ford's 'jealousy speech' at 2. 2. 253–74) and Act Three, scene five (3. 5. 54–130). What do you make of Falstaff's disguise as an old woman in Act Four, scene two? Does Falstaff's wooing represent a 'world inside out'? Is the carnivalesque used against Falstaff as a punishment in Act Five, scene five?

- Look at the use of holidays and feast days in *Julius Caesar*, starting with Act One, scene one – how does this scene introduce the relationship between carnival and political upheaval? You might then contrast Brutus and Cassius's discussion of when to kill Caesar in Act Two, scene one with Caesar's concerns about the calendar in Act Two, scene two – how are ritual and carnival connected? Lastly, what of the role of the plebeians in the play – do they embody the carnival or its worst excesses?

Key Concept Three: Colonialism and Race

Attitudes towards race in the early modern period were complex and were invariably religiously inflected. One important post-Reformation strand of thought, which was sometimes articulated but in other places simply assumed, held that to be English was also to be Protestant and thus superior to all other races and religions. However, while these attitudes could often be jingoistic and/or stereotypical, they did not preclude serious and (in early modern terms) respectful study of and exchange between foreign nations.

The examination of race – and indeed, the questioning of these very terms – is an extremely vibrant one within Shakespearean studies. Scholars such as Stephen Greenblatt, Ania Loomba, Kim Hall, Daniel Vitkus and Jyotsna Singh have advanced our understanding of this area in important ways. For example, and developing a point I made earlier, Ania Loomba has pointed out that the ways in religion and race are intertwined in the early modern period. Writing of English attitudes towards Islam, she notes:

> Literary texts are crucial indices of cultural complexities, rather than fictions superimposed upon them [. . .] our analysis of racial ideologies and stereotyping has to go beyond identifying 'positive' or 'negative' images and taking these at face value. English writers acknowledge Turkish military superiority, civic organisation, and patriarchal control. They envy and even want to emulate these attributes, but at the same time, they see these as evidence of an alien and threatening culture. Evidence of Muslim power only feeds into the construction of Muslim alterity in the period. (2002: 73)

Loomba here points out that literary texts themselves are a way into the complexities of culture. She urges critics to move beyond looking for simple 'positive/negative' portrayals, and recognize the complexities of, for example, English images of Turkish people. 'Alterity' here means 'other-ness' (as in *alter ego*). Loomba helps us to see that representations of other races in Shakespearean texts need to be examined for the various cultural assumptions that they might make. Alternatively, we might ask ourselves to what extent Shakespearean texts accept those assumptions: to what degree are figures of different races also figures of 'alterity' in Shakespeare's work? Here are some ideas for further study:

- Look at the construction of race in *Othello*. Look at the racialized language of Iago and Roderigo in Act One, and also of Desdemona's father Brabantio – what does this reveal to us about racial stereotypes? To what extent is Othello aware of these stereotypes, e.g. at 3. 3. 262–81? Is Othello seen as a Christian, a Muslim, a convert or an amalgam of each?
- How might we read Aaron in *Titus Andronicus*? Is he a simple 'villain'? Is he complex? Look in particular at Act Five, scene one.
- What about the construction of the Jew, Shylock, in *The Merchant of Venice*? Is this an anti-Semitic play? Does it interrogate anti-Semitism? Look at Shylock's various speeches in Act One, scene three, Act Three, scene one, as well as at the 'trial scene' in Act Four, scene one. Do we understand Shylock's 'conversion'?

Key Concept Four: Desire

When approaching the issue of desire in the work of Shakespearean text, it might be tempting to think that human impulses do not change much over time, and that sexual desire is much the same now as it was in the sixteenth and seventeenth centuries. Indeed, some psychoanalytic approaches to Shakespeare begin from that very assumption. While the biological apparatus through which humans enact sexual desire might have remained the same, the cultural meanings have changed radically since Shakespeare's day. Therefore, coming to terms with how desire operates in Shakespeare's texts will first involve some consideration of what kind of cultural meanings sexual desire had in early modern culture.

In order to do this, we first need to consider early modern understandings of the human body. Attitudes drew heavily upon religious doctrine. According to the biblical book of Genesis, 'God created man in his *own* image' (1:27). The emphasis on 'man' points to the fact that woman is not created independently in Genesis as Adam is, but rather from one of Adam's ribs. Woman is an adjunct of man and, as such, subordinate to him. When Eve is beguiled by Satan and persuades Adam to eat of the tree of knowledge, the consequences are quite specific: Adam and Eve become aware of their nakedness as a mark of their transgression; Eve is condemned to bring forth children 'in sorrow' and have Adam 'rule over' her (3:16); Adam will have to work for their food; both will suffer death; and both are cast out of Eden. This biblical narrative underpinned early modern attitudes to the body as a marker of original sin. Moreover, as Adam and Eve were the 'first family', their narrative also underwrote the patriarchal attitudes that dominate early modern sexual and familial relationships, subordinating women to men.

Early modern attitudes to the body were also deeply informed by the writings of the ancient Greek physician Galen, whose theories were widely accepted across Europe. The Galenic system was based on the idea that the body contained four principal humours. These humours were Phlegm, Blood, Choler and Black Bile. If an individual's body maintained each humour in balance with the others, all would be well. But if one humour predominated, the imbalance would cause an ill humour. For example, too much Black Bile would lead to melancholy (see Bradley on Hamlet's melancholy in Hiscock and Longstaffe, this volume). Central to this system was the idea of heat. Men, it was believed, should be active, energetic and vigorous, and all these states required the exertion and production of heat. Masculinity, in other words, was associated with warmth. Females, on the other hand, should be passive, inactive and reserved. Femininity, therefore, was defined in relation to coldness.

Both religious and medical theory in the early modern period served to maintain the patriarchal order that placed women in a subordinate position to men. Where, then, does this leave us with respect to desire? Is it the case that the expression of human desire might problematize these discourses? The answer is yes. For one, to desire another human being is to potentially put oneself into an active position, and as we have seen, activity is traditionally associated with masculinity. During the early modern period, it was believed that one human's desire for another was conveyed through the eyes. A man would look at a woman, and via his 'eye beams' his gaze would convey his desire for that woman, via her eyes, into her soul. As the historian Stuart Clark writes: 'The dominant role of the eye in love imagery was also matched by the themes of "possession with the eye" and voyeurism that flourished more darkly in contemporary misogyny' (2007: 23).

Further Analysis: Which role for the audience?

In *The Rape of Lucrece*, the narrator describes the sleeping Lucrece before her rape by Tarquin. Are the 'lewd unhallowed eyes' (392) someone else's or ours? To what extent are we as readers implicated in this scene? Is the description of the sleeping Lucrece intended to mirror Tarquin's desire or, more problematically, to invoke desire in us as readers?

However, there are also numerous instances where Shakespeare overturns the 'contemporary misogyny' of such discourses, invoking instead desire as enabling female self-assertion. In a number of the comedies, for example, the role of men's poetry in constructing women as objects to be looked at is subjected to scrutiny. For example:

- In Act Three, scene two of *As You Like It*, you might examine how Rosalind questions the patriarchal assumptions inherent in Orlando's love poetry. You might also look at Act Three, scene three where the Clown Touchstone and Audrey's discussion of the value of Ovid's *Metamorphoses*. This was one of the most important 'classical' texts for literary writers in Shakespeare's time, so think about the responses of Jaques who overhears this discussion – what do they reveal about different social attitudes towards poetry and desire?
- Think too about the Epilogue to *As You Like It*. How does it question the role of looking in constructing gender roles? What might it reveal to us about the role of desire in theatrical performance and looking?
- Another play worth examining is *A Midsummer Night's Dream*. How does Oberon's 'juice' (2. 1. 170) facilitate the play's exploration of contemporary attitudes to the gaze and sexual desire? Titania the fairy queen, the upper class lovers and the lower class 'mechanicals' are all entangled by the application of the juice to their eyes – what might this reveal to us about desire and class?

To finish this section, I want to draw briefly upon the work of one critic, Catherine Belsey. Much of Belsey's work on desire is heavily indebted to the work of the French psychoanalyst Jacques Lacan. Desire, for Lacan, far from being a positive experience, is inevitably about lack – as the connotations of the English word 'want' show. As the sense of lack is produced by the split between conscious and unconscious that takes place during every child's development, it can never be satisfied for long.

These Lacanian principles underpin an essay by Belsey entitled 'Cleopatra's Seduction', published in *Alternative Shakespeares, Vol. 2*. In this essay, Belsey sets out to examine 'the dramatic representation of seduction' by Cleopatra in Shakespeare's *Antony and Cleopatra* (1996: 41). She looks at how, throughout the play, Cleopatra repeatedly refuses to be located where others expect her to be. Writing of Enobarbus's famous description of the Queen aboard her barge in Act Two, scene two, Belsey observes that this is a recollected account of an event that has already taken place. In this way, the play describes but at the same time refuses to show us how the very air 'had gone to gaze on Cleopatra too' (2. 2. 223). As Belsey puts it: 'Cleopatra's erotic power is seen as mysteriously elsewhere, deferred, indefinable, irreducible to language, identified only as a transcendent and thus inevitably absent present' (1996: 44) – a principle that you might usefully explore in relation to other Shakespearean plays.

- Look at Act Five of *The Winter's Tale*. In what ways does the seemingly dead Hermione still communicate erotic and political meanings for Leontes and others? How do works of art represent erotic desire? How does the final scene test the relationship between desire and looking?
- Consider the function of the 'name' in Act Two, scene one of *Romeo and Juliet*. Can language ever embody erotic desire, or is it always doomed to fail in this task?

Key Concept Five: Religion

In terms of the literary culture of early modern England, many scholars have suggested that Protestantism gave writers new ways of thinking about a whole range of topics, such as monarchical authority, the relationship between subject and ruler, attitudes towards the family, or attitudes towards money and trade. But perhaps the most pervasive feature of Protestantism for many critics is the way it shaped early modern thinking about subjectivity. Sinfield argues that Protestant theology was a harsh and unyielding system that asked individuals to scrutinize themselves inwardly for signs of their spiritual status. He calls this 'a self-conscious deployment and cultivation of self-awareness; it is part of a project for actualizing interiority. [. . .] Envisaging one's fate at the hands of the Reformation god of incomprehensible love and arbitrary damnation must have been a great provoker of self-consciousness' (1992: 159–60). Sinfield's term 'interiority' refers to Hamlet's 'that within which passeth show' (1. 2. 85), his private inner being; for Sinfield, Protestantism is about producing a certain kind of (inner) self. While this is not to say that individuals did not experience inwardness in the medieval period or earlier, it is to say that Protestant theology has a particular kind of investment in the practice of inwardness and its consequences for the individual. It is also important to remember that both Sinfield and Dollimore are operating within a British version of Marxism known as Cultural Materialism and that they argue that such religious practices also had a broader political purpose, namely in Dollimore's words to 'provide the bases for a materialist understanding of the interrelations between the social, the political and the subjective' (2nd ed. 1989: 174). Both Dollimore and Sinfield thus hold that Protestantism was a crucial political tool during the early modern period, for the individual, and his or her relationship to state power.

In terms of Shakespeare's texts, you might begin by thinking of the relationship between the soliloquy and Protestantism. It is a theatrical convention that characters tell the truth in soliloquy. When characters speak directly to themselves and/or to the audience, do they scrutinize the inner self they display? How aware are they of what their words reveal? You might look at the following:

- Macbeth's 'dagger' soliloquy at 2. 1. 33–64 in *Macbeth*.
- Compare Richard's opening soliloquy at 1. 1. 1–40 with his 'dream' soliloquy before the battle of Bosworth at 5. 5. 131–60 in *Richard III*.
- Adriana's speech (not a soliloquy, but nonetheless concerned with inward scrutiny and the self in relation to an Other) at 2. 2. 110–46 in *The Comedy of Errors*. Are inner selves different in a comedy as opposed to a tragedy? Can we distinguish between different kinds of inwardness and interiority?

Key Concept Six: Textuality

When you study a Shakespearean text at university, in all likelihood that text will be a scholarly edition that your tutor has recommended. But what exactly do we mean by a 'scholarly edition'? And why might it be important for you to be interested in how the text you came to be holding got there in the first place? Such questions relate to what scholars call the textuality of the early modern book. We might think about the production of early modern books, examining how, by whom and where they were printed, marketed and sold. We could think about the dissemination of literary texts like plays and poems. What cultural status did such books have relative to other books? How much did they cost? Who might have bought them? We could also think about the relationship between the staged play and the written play. How did a play text come to be printed? Who owned the text: the playwright, the playing company, the printer or the bookseller? And, given all of this, how might we edit a Shakespearean play? These issues centring around the early modern book – and your Shakespeare edition – come under the catch-all term 'textuality'.

A generation or so ago, such questions were not widely asked, except perhaps by editors and historians of the book. However, such questions are now part of the mainstream within Shakespearean studies. It is no longer good enough to simply assume that what you are presented with in a scholarly edition simply reflects 'what an author wrote'. In the first place, many Shakespearean texts come down to us in a variety of versions. Take the example of *Hamlet*. The earliest versions of this play are the first quarto of 1603, the second quarto of 1604–5 and the first folio edition of 1623 (see Glossary).

Editing the Shakespearean Text

For an editor of this play, the interesting if problematic fact is that each of these versions differs from the other. In the case of the first quarto, these differences are extremely wide. For example, Polonius is called Corambis, Ophelia is Ofelia and Gertrude is Gertred. As an editor, how might you deal with these differences? Do you ignore them, incorporate them or find a mean between the two? Up until fairly recently, the answer to this question was thought to be a relatively simple one. An editor's job was to recover, as nearly as possible, an authentic text that was a close as possible to the author's original. Some editors were explicit about this aim: others simply assumed that this was their job.

However, since the 1980s, editors and scholars have begun to question radically this assumption. The majority of early modern play texts were not written by a single author, but instead in collaboration (see Egan, this volume, Chapter 9). But what the *Norton Shakespeare* (1997: 65) terms 'The Dream of the Master Text' – that is, the text faithfully recording the recoverable intentions of a single author – is no longer viable, then how are editors to proceed? In terms of *Hamlet*, the most recent answer has also been one of the most radical. One of the premier scholarly editions of Shakespeare is the *Arden Shakespeare*. When the scholars Ann Thompson and Neil Taylor came to edit this *Hamlet* for this series, they noted that:

> For as long as editors are seeking to establish a single text of *Hamlet*, they are driven to regard each of the three early texts, Q1, Q2 and F, as imperfect to some degree and, with extremely few exceptions, have produced a fourth, improved, eclectic text. (Shakespeare 2006: 91)

Instead of doing the same as previous editors, Thompson and Taylor's solution was the logical conclusion of the shift in editorial practice that I have been outlining. As they explain:

> We are not assuming that William Shakespeare was necessarily the sole author of every word in those early seventeenth-century texts, nor that we know the degree to which any of them represent the author's or authors' intentions, nor how it was that they came to be in print. We do know, however, that they have a claim to be regarded as separate plays as well as separate versions of the same play. Our approach to editing them

ultimately lacks intellectual purity, since the 'dream of the original text' invariably informs every editor's mind and, therefore, practice. But we nevertheless offer three *Hamlets* rather than one. (Shakespeare 2006: 93)

So while the *Arden Shakespeare* offers a single volume of the play based on the second quarto, it also offers a companion volume that reprints the first quarto and first folio editions of the play.

Further Analysis: Shakespeare's Competing Texts

- How might our reading of *Hamlet* as a series of 'versions' alter our thinking about the play?
- You might usefully compare Hamlet's soliloquies in Q1 and Q2, for example the 'To be or not to be' speech at 3. 1. 55–87 and 7. 115–36 (in the *Arden*). These are very different 'versions' of this speech – what are these differences and do they alter your reading of the play?
- Lukas Erne has argued in his book *Shakespeare as Literary Dramatist* that the difference between Q1 and Q2 is down to the fact that the former was a text that was performed and the latter an expanded text designed not for performance but for reading (2003: 192–219). Do you agree? What difference does this argument make to our understanding of the play? Have a look at the early publishing history of the Shakespearean text you are studying. Are there very different versions of the play circulating in the early modern period? Would you have adopted the same decisions that your edition has taken? To explore this process in detail, look at the way in which *The Norton Shakespeare* reproduces quarto, folio and conflated texts of *King Lear* (2307–2553).

Conclusion

Throughout this chapter, I have introduced you to some of the key critical concepts and topics animating Shakespearean studies today. This is by no means an exhaustive list, and there are many other areas that you may wish to investigate with the aid of other chapters in this book. However, I hope you have seen some of the possible applications of these terms as well as how you might develop your own research in relation to them. I hope you have also seen the ways in which the use of key critical concepts and topics is not divorced from a broader consideration of early modern cultural and social context. To my mind, the most successful students in Shakespearean studies are the ones who manage to integrate close critical analysis of the texts, judicious and self-reflective use of appropriate critical terminology, and an understanding of these broader contexts that I have been referring to throughout. This chapter therefore offers you a start in developing your own critical vocabulary: the rest is up to you.

Part III
Shakespeare Studies Now

Recent Critical Responses and Approaches

Lisa Hopkins

Chapter Overview

Since the mid-1980s, Shakespeare studies has seen an explosion in both the number and the impact of 'theorized' approaches, with a bewildering array of theoretical approaches brought to bear on Shakespeare's plays and poems. This section will briefly survey a number of these: psychoanalysis, feminist criticism and queer theory, New Historicism, cultural materialism, and Bakhtinian approaches, postcolonialism and British Studies, and presentism, ecocriticism, performance criticism, and 'post-theoretical' approaches.

Psychoanalysis

Psychoanalysis has been a force in Shakespearean criticism since at least the 1920s, when Ernest Jones offered a controversial Freudian analysis of Hamlet's behaviour, but it is fair to say that the new prominence given to 'theorized' analysis of Shakespeare has given fresh impulse to psychoanalytic criticism. It is not surprising that *Hamlet*, with its famously complex hero, should have attracted the lion's share of the attention (see Hiscock/Longstaffe, this volume). A good example is Jacqueline Rose's essay 'Sexuality in the Reading of Shakespeare: *Hamlet and Measure for Measure*'. In the essay, Rose poses as her central question

> What fantasy of the woman has figured in readings – psychoanalytic and other – of *Hamlet* and *Measure for Measure*, plays which have repeatedly been defined as a 'problem', as requiring an interpretation which goes beyond their explicit, or manifest, content? (1985: 95)

Rose here unusually couples two plays of different genres on the grounds that even if only one of them is usually classed as a 'problem play', both have in fact been perceived as problems, and the reason for this, she implies, is to be sought in the way they represent women, the covert suggestion being that it is women and their representations that our culture is most likely to find problematic. In order to answer her own question, Rose suggests that 'psychoanalytic and literary criticism share with the literature they address a terrain of language, fantasy and sexuality – a terrain in which the woman occupies a crucial, but difficult, place': Rose is, in effect, here performing some psychoanalysis of her own not only on the plays but also on the critics who have apparently struggled with them, and as always in classic Freudian analysis, the mother is at the heart of the problem. Therefore,

> the fact that *Hamlet* constantly unleashes an anxiety which returns to the question of femininity tells us above all something about the relationship of aesthetic form and sexual difference, about the fantasies they share – fantasies of coherence and identity in which the woman appears repeatedly as both wager and threat. (1985: 115)

It is instructive to measure the difference between Rose's approach here and that of Ernest Jones, who offered the first serious and sustained psychoanalytic reading of *Hamlet* (see Robson, this volume, Chapter 5). For Jones, psychoanalysis was solely and simply a way to understand the character of Hamlet himself, and he writes about Shakespeare's fictional Prince of Denmark in exactly the same terms as he might write about a real person, saying for instance that 'This conclusion, that Hamlet at heart does not want to carry out the task, seems so obvious that it is hard to see how any open-minded reader of the play could avoid making it' (1949: 45). For Rose, much more critically sophisticated, the characters in a drama are not in any sense the equivalents of real people, but rather individual components in an artistic design; thus her use of psychoanalysis, unlike Jones's, tells her not so much about the 'character of Hamlet' but rather about the nature of dramatic narrative and sexual difference.

Hamlet also occupies about half of Philip Armstrong's book *Shakespeare in Psychoanalysis* in the important New Accents series, and he too is attentive to gender. For Armstrong, the big names of psychoanalytic history are explicitly treated not as gurus but as objects of enquiry in their own right. His argument is that

> Shakespeare preceded psychoanalysis epistemologically [that is, in terms of knowledge], just as he does historically: that is, the modes of narrative, rhetoric, imagery and characterisation that Freud, Rank and Jones encounter in Shakespearean drama help to shape the development of psychoanalytic notions about dreamwork, the operations of the unconscious, and the nature of the self. (2001: 40–41)

Armstrong focuses on 'what happens if the avowed psychoanalytical fascination with the peripheral, the scarcely mentioned or the silenced is turned back on [the] three psychocritical forefathers [Freud, Rank, Jones] themselves. One notion that emerges as a result is that of an underlying femininity in Hamlet or – more disturbingly – in Shakespeare' (2001: 49), and he suggests that this is because those three early psychoanalytic theorists' shared emphasis on the Oedipal makes them all uncomfortable with any suggestion either of homosexuality or of effeminacy, which they equate with homosexuality (2001: 50). (A charge recurringly brought against psychoanalytic approaches is that they are powerless to account for any patterns of desire which do not accord with Freud's heterosexually-oriented Oedipal theory, and are forced to treat them as aberrational or deviant.) Armstrong himself does not pursue this line of enquiry very far; for him, what psychoanalysis calls attention to in *Hamlet* is above all its interest in memory (2001: 148), and this certainly is a crucial faculty in Freudian theory and something given much prominence in the play, as is evidenced by the fact that there are more entries in the index of Peter Holland's recent edited collection on *Shakespeare, Memory and Performance* for *Hamlet* (2006) than for any other Shakespeare play. [see Robson, this volume, Chapter 5]

Further Analysis: Hamlet and Femininity

Do you agree that the feminine is in some sense at the root of the problem in *Hamlet*? If so, is the feminine something which proves

> problematic for Hamlet the character or for *Hamlet* the play, or in fact for both? And is this a 'problem' really more prominent in *Hamlet* than in other plays, or is the attention paid to it a function of the high status that *Hamlet* has been accorded in the critical tradition?

Feminist Criticism

A surprisingly similar conclusion to Jacqueline Rose's on *Hamlet* and *Measure for Measure* emerges in another essay reprinted in the same volume as Rose's, Catherine Belsey's 'Disrupting sexual difference: meaning and gender in the comedies', but Belsey turns her attention to very different texts, and uses a methodology which she explicitly identifies as feminist, declaring that 'I want to suggest that Shakespearean comedy can be read as disrupting sexual difference, calling in question that set of relations between terms which proposes as inevitable an antithesis between masculine and feminine, men and women' (1985: 167) (see Streete, this volume, Chapter 7). For Belsey, Shakespeare's conception of gender roles is fluid rather than fixed, particularly in *Twelfth Night*. She observes that

> Of all Shakespeare's comedies it is perhaps *Twelfth Night* which takes the most remarkable risks with the identity of its central figure . . . it is only in *Twelfth Night* that the protagonist specifically says, 'I am not what I am' (3. 1. 143) where 'seem' would have scanned just as well and preserved the unity of the subject. (1985: 185)

The implication, it seems, is that Viola's adoption of male clothing is more than merely a matter of outward disguise. Indeed, one view which was culturally available in the Renaissance, even if we cannot know how widely it was subscribed to, suggested that the boundaries of gender were in fact potentially so permeable that cross-dressing, or even perhaps a member of one sex behaving in a way considered appropriate only for members of the other sex, might actually be enough to tip you from one gender to the other. This idea, known as the 'one-sex model', originated with the Greek physician Galen and proposed that male and female were in fact only separate outward manifestations of the same underlying structure. It lies behind a remarkable story recounted by Stephen Greenblatt:

> In September 1580, as he passed through a small French town on his way to Switzerland and Italy, Montaigne was told an unusual story that he duly recorded in his travel journal. It seems that seven or eight girls from a place

called Chaumont-en-Bassigni plotted together 'to dress up as males and thus continue their life in the world'. One of them set up as a weaver, 'a well-disposed young man who made friends with everybody', and moved to a village called Montier-en-Der. There the weaver fell in love with a woman, courted her, and married. The couple lived together for four or five months, to the wife's satisfaction, 'so they say'. But then, Montaigne reports, the transvestite was recognized by someone from Chaumont; 'the matter was brought to justice, and she was condemned to be hanged, which she said she would rather undergo than return to a girl's status; and she was hanged for using illicit devices to supply her defect in sex'. The execution, Montaigne was told, had taken place only a few days before.

I begin with this story because in *Twelfth Night* Shakespeare almost, but not quite, retells it. (1988: 66)

Greenblatt follows this up with an even more surprising anecdote, telling of how the sixteenth-century French physician Ambroise Paré

recounts the story of 'a fifteen-year-old peasant girl who one day was "rather robustly" chasing her swine, which were going into a wheat field. As Marie in midpursuit leaped over a ditch, "at the very moment the genitalia and male rod came to be developed." After consulting with physicians and the bishop, Marie changed her name to Germain. (1988: 81)

For Greenblatt, awareness of this model helped to make sense of the paradoxical journey of Shakespeare's cross-dressed heroines, who have to 'become' men to become women.

My second example, Dympna Callaghan, also focuses on *Twelfth Night*, but to rather different effect. Announcing her intention as being 'to focus on the absent-presence of female genitals in *Twelfth Night*' (2000: 30), which she sees as being evoked by a lewd pun implicit in Malvolio's fantasy of himself as a count, Callaghan argues that

the monstrous female genitalia in the play's representational register are not merely a localized 'theme' but rather depend on and produce the exclusion and denigration of women and the ridicule and punishment of men who attempt to change their status in the social hierarchy. This is nothing less than the maintenance and reproduction of patriarchy. (2000: 35)

It may seem surprising to associate the punishment of *men* with an overt focus on *female* genitalia, but for Callaghan, the two issues are linked by the fact that Shakespeare created roles such as Viola and Olivia for performance by boy actors:

> in the carnivalesque world of *Twelfth Night* the female body's capacity for resistance and disruption is severely curtailed by the fact that the transvestite actor is 'as likely to be portraying women with contempt as with respect' and the fact that the male body, 'the very instrument of the art of the theatre' (Gibbons 1980: 64), repeatedly and ritually enacts the displacement, exclusion, and discipline of its female counterpart. (2000: 32)

She therefore argues that 'In accordance with its carnival theme, *Twelfth Night* places female genitals at the heart of Malvolio's gulling, the play's most famous scene' (36), in that she expounds the reference to 'cut' as a play on a standard term for the female genitalia and to argue that count and cunt were probably pronounced in the same manner in Elizabethan English, so that Malvolio's desire to be a count further equates him with the displaced feminine element of the play. Callaghan sees this as also operating on another level: she argues that the strictness of Renaissance 'sumptuary laws' means that 'Malvolio's cross-gartering, his "transvestism", is [. . .] structurally and symbolically related to gender inversion' (33) (see Longstaffe, this volume, Chapter 3). This is an argument developed by Mihoko Suzuki: postulating that 'the comic form works to repress anxieties about unruly women to displace them onto male scapegoats' (2000: 130), she argues that in *Twelfth Night* 'the comedy manages residual anxieties about unruly women by displacing them onto the "effeminate" social climber Malvolio, who is excluded from the concluding marriages as a convenient scapegoat – marked as such by the telling prefix "Mal" – for the other offenders' (2000: 140) and that

> The play displaces its disapproval of all the transgressors onto Malvolio, who is punished not only as the obnoxious social climber in the place of more innocuous Sebastian, but also in the place of Olivia, who succeeds in evading patriarchy's control, and of Viola, who transgresses gender divisions through her cross-dressing. (2000: 139)

Interestingly, Callaghan notes that 'the only record we have of a Renaissance performance of the play does not so much as mention Viola's transvestism' (33), and suggests that this is because 'class transvestism is more threatening than that of gender, which can be resolved rather more readily' (34).

In the course of her argument, Callaghan cites a number of anecdotes and legal cases about men displaying women's genitals in the sixteenth century (2000: 40–41). Here, as so often elsewhere, feminism is linked to historicism: it is interested not so much – or only secondarily – in the conditions of women *now* and primarily in the conditions of women *then*. More broadly, the historicist emphasis in feminist studies bears witness to the massive influence that New Historicism had on Renaissance studies in the last decades of the twentieth century.

New Historicism

New Historicism is interested above all in power; indeed it is sometimes accused of fetishizing power, and of fostering political quietism by suggesting that the established order will always fend off any challenges and will in fact use them to bolster its authority, so that it is not worth the trouble of rebelling against it (see Robson's Chapter 5 and Streete's Chapter 7, this volume). Thus David Scott Kastan strikes a note typical of New Historicism when he argues that 'If 1 *Henry IV* can be said to be "about" anything, it is about the production of power, an issue as acute in the early years of the reign of Henry IV as in the final years of the aging Elizabeth when the play was written' (1991: 241), and by implication still of interest to us in our own historical moment. Kastan does find a crack in the hegemonic surface:

> The play [. . .] insists that history is not identical with state politics, indeed that the history of state politics inevitably and purposefully erases other histories – histories of women or the poor, for example – histories whose very existence contests the story that the hegemonic state would tell of itself. (1991: 245)

In contrast, Stephen Greenblatt's extremely influential reading of the play sees the dramatic narrative in terms of

> the odd balance in this play of spaciousness – the constant multiplication of separate, vividly realised realms – and claustrophobia – the absorption of all of these realms by a power at once vital and impoverished. The balance is almost eerily perfect, as if Shakespeare had somehow reached through in 1 *Henry IV* to the very centre of the system of opposed and interlocking forces that held Tudor society together. ([1985] 1992: 98)

For Greenblatt, 1 *Henry IV* is not an exploration of character or even of a specific moment in English history, but an investigation of a phenomenon which – ironically in view of his self-labelling as a 'historicist' – he essentially conceives of as essentially the same throughout history, even though the specifics of its modes of operation may vary at different times and in different places (see Robson, this volume, Chapter 5).

New Historicist analyses also often involve reading against the grain; thus Leonard Tennenhouse declares that 'One might be tempted to declare a generic difference between *Hamlet*, a tragedy, and the history plays [. . .] but I will argue against the wisdom of doing so for those who want to understand Shakespeare's genres as political strategies' (1986: 93), while Francis Barker asks of the giving to Laertes leave to go to Paris: 'does this episode not serve to reformulate the scene, and to manage a transition from the public space to the personal and domestic argument with Hamlet that is to follow? To think so would be to commit a signal historical mistake' ([1984] 1992: 158). Having deliberately used the construction 'does this [. . .] not' to trick us into thinking that the answer will be yes, Barker then uncompromisingly switches tack to inform us that this apparently plausible supposition is in fact completely erroneous. Rather he argues that 'The public and the private as strong, mutually defining, mutually exclusive categories, each describing separate terrains with distinct contents, practices and discourses, are not yet extant' ([1984] 1992: 161) and that

> At the centre of Hamlet, in the interior of his mystery, there is, in short, nothing. The promised essence remains beyond the scope of the text's signification: or rather, signals the limit of the signification of this world by marking out the site of an absence it cannot fill. It gestures towards a place for subjectivity, but both are anachronistic and belong to a historical order whose outline has so far only been sketched out. ([1984] 1992: 163–64)

Here, a number of factors which previous critics would generally have considered important – genre, the apparently multi-faceted character of Hamlet – are summarily dismissed as at best illusions and at worst distractions from more appropriate modes of reading. This is typical of New Historicism, which is characterized by its ingenuity and above all by its claims for its own innovativeness as much as by its interest in specific historical circumstances.

Bakhtin

The Russian philosopher and language theorist Mikhail Bakhtin (1895–1975) has been influential in two interrelated respects. One of Bakhtin's two key concepts is that of heteroglossia, a word derived from ancient Greek and meaning literally 'many-voicedness'. Of course, the basic structuring principle of drama is the interaction of different voices, but nevertheless New Historicism, as we have just seen, has been able to see Renaissance drama as a whole as articulating a seamless discourse of power. A Bakhtinian approach, however, is likely to find something very different; thus Ronald R. Macdonald (2001), reading *1 Henry IV* in terms of heteroglossia, finds that it 'reveals a world that seems to have many more meanings than any single, monoglot language can readily dispose of' (81). Although not explicitly using Bakhtinian terminology at this point, David Scott Kastan draws on its fundamental assumptions when he writes of *1 Henry IV* that

> Criticism has delighted in demonstrating the play's aesthetic unity
> by showing how the comic plot 'serves' the historical plot, functions
> as a *sub*plot clarifying the 'main' plot. But the play seems to me less
> coherent – not therefore less interesting or good, but less willing to
> organize its disparate voices into hierarchies – than such demonstrations
> of its putative unity would allow. The formal coherence that critics have
> demanded from the play can be achieved only by subordinating subplot
> to main plot, commoners to aristocrats, comedy to history – by imposing,
> that is, the same hierarchies of privilege and power that exist in the
> state upon the play. But the play does not so readily subordinate its
> comedy. (1991: 244)

Kastan's reference to the 'disparate voices' of the play leaves us in no doubt that what he is talking about is essentially heteroglossia, though in a sophisticated further development of the idea he posits a chorus of different voices from not only the individual characters but from the different plot strands of the play: indeed he suggests that 'the very existence of a comic plot serves to counter the totalizing fantasies of power, to expose and disrupt the hierarchies upon which they depend' (245). Kastan is certainly not the first critic to note that the subplot of *1 Henry IV* does strongly compete with the main plot for attention: indeed as he observes, 'throughout the seventeenth century, the play was as likely to be called *Falstaff* as *Henry IV*' (244), and even when Falstaff is not busy attracting the lion's share of the audience's interest, they are almost certainly going to find the nominal hero of the play, Henry IV, less interesting than his son Prince Hal (see Hiscock and Longstaffe, this volume).

'sub' plot

This raises the larger question of the relationship between subplot and main plot in Shakespeare's plays. The most famous example of a play with a prominent subplot is arguably *King Lear*, where the way in which the subplot repeats the events of the main plot has often been seen as inviting us to read a sense of inevitability into the play. But sometimes subplots may actually seem to pull in the opposite direction to the main

> plot rather than echo or chime with it: think, for instance, of the way Caliban's conspiracy interrupts Prospero's masque, or the indifference of the gravediggers in *Hamlet* to the concerns of the characters in the main plot.

Allied to Bakhtin's theory of heteroglossia is his interest in the phenomenon of carnival (see Streete, this volume, Chapter 7). In Bakhtin's hands, the idea of carnival takes on a resonance far greater than the mere idea of a period of feasting and merrymaking preceding the forty days of Lent. It acquires connotations of the popular as opposed to the aristocratic, holiday as opposed to work time, and licence as opposed to control (although New Historicism would have it that the 'licence' is, precisely, 'licensed', that is deliberately allowed to happen because doing so ultimately serves the interests of authority), since it offers a safe and contained defusion of energies which might otherwise build up a much more dangerous head of steam. Thus François Laroque declares in his important book *Shakespeare's Festive World*, which draws explicitly on Bakhtinian ideas and terminology, that 'The clown is one of the foremost representatives and spokesmen of popular culture' (1988: 42), and proceeds to pay attention to the 'low' rather than the 'high' characters of the plays, while Terence Hawkes reads *Twelfth Night* in terms of carnival and sees it as exemplifying Northrop Frye's three-stage structure of prohibition/confusion/emergence of a new society. For Hawkes, too, this leads to an attention to the low rather than the high: 'The most obvious effect of this structure is to focus attention upon Malvolio and to make him a central figure at every stage. As a result, his predominant anticarnival, antiplaying stance serves to foreground the playing / carnival dimensions of the play' (1991: 172).

In the hands of New Historicists, this idea takes a further twist. In their characteristic way of invariably finding containment rather than subversion in Shakespeare's plays, they propose that the apparent licence afforded by carnival ultimately serves only to reinforce the stranglehold of authority. Thus Leonard Tennenhouse argues that in the logic of the *Henriad*, 'history is nothing else but the history of forms of disorder, over which Henry temporarily triumphs', and that

> Such a rhetorical strategy guarantees the figures of carnival will play a particularly instrumental role in the idealizing process that proves so crucial in legitimizing political power. It cannot be accidental that the *Henriad*, which produces Shakespeare's most accomplished Elizabethan monarch, should also produce his most memorable figure of misrule. (1986: 82–83)

The underlying logic of such a coupling inevitably dictates that however much they appear to embody oppositional values, in fact 'The figures of carnival ultimately authorize the state'.

Cultural Materialism

Cultural materialism is in some ways so like New Historicism that it is sometimes confused or amalgamated with it, but in other ways the two are significantly different. Whereas New Historicism typically finds plays working to produce an apparent subversion which is ultimately co-opted to serve the ends of power and thus contained, cultural materialism typically finds an authentic form of subversion. Kiernan Ryan argues that the *Henry IV* plays 'are designed to withdraw through formal implication what they avow through overt statement and action'; consequently, he argues that the 'low' scenes comment on the 'high' scenes in ways which have not really been observed, in that 'The spectators are encouraged to recognize majesty as a rehearsed production and reminded of the gulf between the performed events before their eyes and the remote past realities they presuppose' (1995: 121, 106–7 and 110). As can be seen from the links between this point and David Kastan's quoted on 155, Bakhtinian thought has been a notable influence on much cultural materialist work, as when Graham Holderness argues of *1 Henry IV* that 'The king is supremely contemptuous of people, things and values which inevitably constitute an element of his state: he expresses an aristocratic scorn for "vulgar company", "the common streets", "popularity", "community", "participation" ' (1992: 100) and that by contrast 'Falstaff is at the centre of a popular comic history, located within the deterministic framework of the chronicle-history play, which challenges and subverts the imperatives of necessitarian historiography' (1992: 130). For Holderness, 'Falstaff *is* Bahktin's "material bodily principle" writ large: his enormous size and uncontrolled appetite characterize him as a collective rather than an individual being' (1992: 139). One might in fact object to this assertion on the grounds of Falstaff's ruthless selfishness, a trait commented upon by many early-twentieth-century critics (see Hiscock and Longstaffe, this volume), but Holderness has an ingenious counter-argument to that:

> Falstaff is often associated with the individualism of soliloquy, since some of his most memorable utterances belong to the mode. It is worth pointing out that in *Henry IV Part One* he hardly uses it at all. In this particular scene, for the first sixty lines he does not even use the pronoun 'I': but speaks of 'we' and 'us', invoking his identity as member of a collective. The Prince consistently employs the first person singular, and with the departure of Falstaff and Poins he is able to turn aside from the action and address the

audience directly, displaying his capacity for detachment and egoistic self-assertion. (1992: 150)

Cultural materialism is on the whole more likely to pay attention to historical specifics and also to questions of form than New Historicism; thus Holderness reads *Henry IV Part One* very much in terms of its echoes of *Richard II*, declaring that 'Insofar as *Henry IV* is a chronicle-history play, it extends the historical vision of *Richard II* into a new regime' (101), and also notes that

> The Lollard rebellion is an absence in *Henry IV*; an omission which, despite the importance attached to it by the chronicles, would not be strikingly surprising or significant (matters of religion were not lightly dealt with on Shakespeare's stage [. . .]) if it were not for the presence of Falstaff. (1992: 159)

Only a historicizing approach of one stripe or another could read to find what is *not* there that historically might have been.

Silencing and the Text

The difference between the two dominant modes, New Historicism and cultural materialism, is that New Historicism would be more likely to read such an omission as a tactful suppression whereas cultural materialism, as here, is more likely to conclude that it is a silence to which audience attention is deliberately drawn.

However, what cultural materialism does strongly share with New Historicism is a tendency to find the early modern period highly repressive, at least in its purposes. For instance, in one striking passage, Holderness declares that 'the revelry and satire of Falstaff constitute kinds of social practice which were afforded a legitimate space in medieval culture' (130), which effectively displaces a Tillyardian 'merrie England' a couple of centuries back in time in order to make a sharp contrast with Shakespeare's historical moment. Yet for cultural materialists the oppressive early modern regime is not monolithic in its power and structures, but could be – and was – challenged, not least by early modern dramatists.

Queer Theory

The basic aim of queer theory is to make same-sex love and attraction visible within literary works, on the grounds that its presence has too often been ignored. Although in some ways it may seem to resemble feminism in explicitly focusing its interest on one particular group of characters in the text, and also like feminism often drawing an equation between the identity and experiences of characters and critic, queer theory is significantly different in that it emerged later in the theoretical moment, and so tends to be in dialogue with a wider range of other theoretical paradigms than feminism, or at least than feminism in its early days (see Robson, this volume, Chapter 5). It is no surprise that *Twelfth Night* has proved a particularly happy hunting ground: Pequigney, for instance, observes that 'the given name Sebastian recalls the martyr traditionally pictured as a handsome youth – a kind of Christian Adonis – with a nearly nude body pierced by arrows' (1995: 181) and argues that there is no evidence that Sebastian is proposing to separate himself from Antonio at the end of the play (182), while Valerie Traub argues that Olivia's desire for Viola is serious. Less obviously, Traub also finds in *1 Henry IV* a 'contained homoerotic desire' (1992: 93). Arguing that Falstaff has some qualities Shakespeare's culture typically gendered 'female' and also that 'Such a focus on the bulging and the protuberant, the openings, permeabilities and effusions of Falstaff's body situate him as "grotesque body" ' (1992: 56), she declares that 'it is apparent that homoerotic desire infuses the relationship of Falstaff and Hal, signaled both by Falstaff's "feminine" qualities and Hal's predominant lack of interest in women' (59). It is this dangerous desire, she suggests, that makes Falstaff's ultimate banishment inevitable: 'When homoerotic exchanges threaten to replace heterosexual bonds, when eroticism is collapsed into anxiety about reproduction, then homoeroticism is exorcized at the same time as the female gender is resecured into the patriarchal order' (1992: 139).

Building on Traub's analysis, Jonathan Goldberg, declaring that 'The *Henry IV* plays are, no doubt, history plays, yet their relationship to at least one kind of history – the history of sexuality – has gone largely unexamined' (1995: 37), argues that 'The opening scenes of *1 Henry IV* locate Hal's career – his desire for the throne – in the context of others' desires for his arrival there' (1995: 43). Since those others are the exclusively male groupings around Hal and at his father's court, Goldberg therefore cautions against simply seeing Falstaff through his 'femininity', as Traub largely does, and indeed argues for a much more complicated view of gender identity altogether. For Goldberg, Hal and Falstaff are in every meaningful sense lovers – 'what keeps the play from making more overt the love relation between Hal and his fat companion is the proximity of their relation to sodomy: the terms *stain*, *riot* and *rebellion* suggest as much' (1995: 49) – even if the relationship is not technically consummated, which we can in any case never know: 'Are Hal and Falstaff bed companions? It is perfectly clear why the plays can never answer that question directly. For while the king could sleep with men, he could not be a sodomite' (1995: 56).

Nevertheless, even if the question cannot be answered, it is still important for Goldberg that it should be asked, for a queer theorist will regard it as essential to encourage readers and audiences of Shakespeare's plays not always to read from an unthinking heterosexual perspective, just as in the early days of feminism there was much insistence on simply reminding people not simply to assume that all those who mattered were male.

Presentism

In the inaugural issue of *Shakespeare*, the journal of the British Shakespeare Association, Hugh Grady contributed a piece entitled 'Shakespeare Studies, 2005: A Situated Overview'. Hugh Grady declares the piece's foundational premise to be that

> With numerous signs that the era dominated by the new historicism is coming to an end, Shakespeare Studies in 2005 appears to be at a crossroads [. . .] In addition, it seems clear that the new historicism has split into two different streams. One, epitomized by the new materialism has foregone an orientation toward our contemporary world, preferring to recreate Shakespeare's historical context empirically. The second has arisen as a reaction to this tendency and self-consciously interprets Shakespeare in the context of our own culture, even when it is involved in situating Shakespeare historically. (2005: 102)

The father of New Historicism, Stephen Greenblatt, famously declared that the aim of his criticism was to speak with the dead. In his book *Shakespeare in the Present*, Terence Hawkes challenges Greenblatt to offer what might well stand as a presentist manifesto:

> If an intrusive, shaping awareness of ourselves, alive and active in our own world, defines us, then it deserves our closest attention. Paying the present that degree of attention might more profitably be judged, not as a 'mistake', egregious and insouciant, blandly imposing a tritely modern perspective on whatever texts confront it, but rather as the basis of a critical stance whose engagement with the text is of a particular character. A Shakespeare criticism that takes that on board will not yearn to speak with the dead. It will aim, in the end, to talk to the living. (2002: 3–4)

Not only is this a more direct and energizing aim than New Historicism's notorious self-abasement in the face of power, but many presentist critics have also argued that we can in fact only ever read from a presentist perspective, whether we choose to do so or not, because we are simply not equipped to read from the point of view of a past so utterly alien to our own experiences: as Grady has it,

> Presentist criticism [. . .] assumes that all our knowledge of the past, including that of Shakespeare's historical context, is shaped by the ideologies and discourses of our cultural present and that far from being an impediment to our knowledge, this understanding is its enabling foundation. (2005: 114)

Certainly, we do need to recognize that there were many points of difference between Shakespeare's historical moment and our own: Stephen Greenblatt notes, for instance, that atheism, 'the stance that seems to come naturally to the greenest college freshman in late twentieth-century America [,] seems to have been almost unthinkable to the most daring philosophical minds of late sixteenth-century England ([1985] 1992: 84)' (see Maley, this volume, Chapter 10). On the other hand, Peter Womack finds in *Henry IV* a construction that is recognizably 'Brechtian', despite the three centuries separating Brecht and Shakespeare. Womack here implicitly calls for us to recognize that it is just as legitimate to call Shakespeare 'Brechtian' as it is to call Brecht 'Shakespearean' (1995: 138). Ewan Fernie, whose abstract announces that 'the current climate of terror casts a strange light on extreme action in Shakespeare', similarly does not hesitate to propose a comparison which Shakespeare could never have intended when he compares the self-destructive urges of Angelo, Othello and Macbeth to the practice of 'barebacking', that is having unprotected gay sex for the sake of the thrill of flirting with infection with the HIV virus (2006: 95 and 110).

In *Shakespeare in the Present*, Hawkes begins his analysis of *Hamlet* by noting that in Berlin in 1945, the Office of Military Government in the American sector appointed Theatre Officers and circulated a list of what was and was not suitable for performance. *Coriolanus* and *Julius Caesar* were not; *Macbeth* and *Hamlet* were, because they were felt to illustrate the workings of justice and the downfall of criminals (66). This leads Hawkes to observe the characters in *Hamlet* that 'It is almost a commonplace that most of them engage in some sort of policing or supervising activity' (70) and to focus his analysis accordingly, concluding that 'To exaggerate only slightly, the proposal that *Hamlet* was at this juncture preferable to *Coriolanus* heralds nothing less than a new world order. In it, the United States, not Britain, effectively speaks for a triumphant and belligerent Anglo-Saxon order' (76). Here, Hawkes's far-reaching argument is that attention to the history of Shakespeare production can help us better understand the world. There might indeed be times when presentist readings effectively force themselves upon us. In 1992, for instance, Graham Holderness could write without further comment that

'Henry IV Part One begins with the image of the crusade, a characteristic Lancastrian symbol of social unity and harmony in the pursuit of piety and violence' (89); now, it would be difficult to forget that the image of the Crusades has been appropriated by Al-Qaeda as a prompt and justification for what they see as their own holy war against the West, and one would consequently not simply be able to pass over this passage but would have to linger and consider it. At present, representations of Islam in Shakespeare are the focus of a great deal of critical activity, so that as I write a special issue of *Shakespeare*, the journal of the British Shakespeare Association, is proposing to concentrate entirely on 'Shakespeare and Islam', an emphasis that simply would not have occurred to the Anglo-American subject community twenty or so years ago.

Postcolonialism

A different kind of reading explicitly from within the present is offered by postcolonialism. Postcolonialism, like British Studies slightly later in the theoretical moment, is acutely aware of Britain's place in the wider world, but it is also aware of temporal as well as of the geographical positioning which has been the principal interest of British Studies (see Streete, this volume, Chapter 7). Thus, Francis Barker and Peter Hulme declare that

> texts can never simply be *encountered* but are, on the contrary, repeatedly constructed under definite conditions: *The Tempest* read by Sir Walter Raleigh in 1914 as the work of England's national poet is very different from *The Tempest* constructed with full textual apparatus by an editor / critic such as Frank Kermode, and from the 'same' text inscribed institutionally in that major formation of 'English Literature' which is the school and university syllabus and its supporting practices of teaching and examination. (1985: 192–93)

For Barker and Hulme, 'The ensemble of fictional and lived practices, which for convenience we will simply refer to here as "English colonialism", provides *The Tempest*'s dominant discursive con-texts' (198). UK-based critics who write about this rather dark moment in their own nation's past often betray a slight queasiness about Shakespeare's role in it. For Barker and Hulme, *The Tempest* is a play that supports the English colonial enterprise, and yet they suggest that 'The lengths to which the play has to go to achieve a legitimate ending may [. . .] be read as the quelling of a fundamental disquiet concerning its own functions within the projects of colonialist discourse' (203–4). More starkly, Ann Thompson writes that

Reading the play as a woman and as a feminist, it is possible to feel good about delineating and rejecting its idealization of patriarchy, and one can go beyond the play to consider the conscious and unconscious sexism of the critical and stage history. Reading as a white British person, my conscience is less clear: women as well as men benefited (and still benefit) from the kind of colonialism idealized in *The Tempest*. (1995: 176–77)

One could well argue, though, that this *angst* is misplaced, because it is by no means clear that *The Tempest* actually *does* idealize colonialism (see Robson, this volume, Chapter 5). Certainly this is by no means guaranteed to be the case in performances of the play, which are much less likely to be driven by a single dominating idea which everything must be found to fit. The other criticism which is often levelled at postcolonialist approaches is that they may be too quick to assume a one-size-fits-all model in which all previously and presently colonized countries are understood as having had essentially the same experiences. In the case of *The Tempest*, the Shakespeare play to which such approaches are most often applied, this tendency is exacerbated and complicated by the play's own notorious geographical indeterminacy, which has led different critics to relate it to Ireland, the Mediterranean and North America with equal ease, despite the fact that these three areas had such very different colonial histories. Indeed Dympna Callaghan argues that this very indeterminacy is central to the meaning of the play, in that 'What is at stake in relating Ireland to *The Tempest* is not [. . .] a matter of direct and specific correspondence between Ireland and the isle, but precisely the play's resolute nonspecificity, its haziness and imprecision on matters of both geography and, especially [. . .] of history; its deliberately bad memory' (2000: 100), though for Callaghan there is no doubt that 'Ireland provides the richest historical analogue for the play's colonial theme' (2000: 137). For Callaghan, the play's 'resolute' lack of reference to the most obvious contemporary parallel is in itself telling.

British Studies

More geographically specific is the emerging discipline of 'British Studies'. In recent years, many critics have followed the lead of historians in paying increasing attention to the fact that during the second half of Shakespeare's career England was being forced to reassess quite radically its position in the world (and this process was in fact already in train in some respects, and being anticipated in others, throughout his writing life) (see Engel, this volume, Chapter 2). At home, the ongoing wars in Ireland and the accession in 1603 of a Scottish king who introduced for the first time the idea of 'Great Britain' meant a radical reappraisal of England's traditional borders; abroad, the push to acquire overseas colonies was making the new 'Great Britain' acutely aware of its position on the world map, and particularly of its location within what is now often called 'the Atlantic archipelago'. Willy Maley's survey of Shakespearean criticism is influenced by these ideas: ' "A Thing Most Brutish": Depicting Shakespeare's Multi-Nation State'. It appeared as a review piece in *Shakespeare*, and begins with an extremely punchy abstract which gives an excellent sense of the types of topic such criticism has tended to cover:

> In recent years, anglocentric and royalist readings of Shakespeare have yielded to colonial and republican perspectives. The placing of the plays within a problematic early modern British context has been a distinctive feature of this criticism. This essay surveys recent work on the British and Irish dimensions, addressing the broad issues entailed in situating Stuart Shakespeare: succession, union, plantation, the reinvention of Britain, and the expansion of England. This criticism, concerned with questions of colonialism and nationalism in the context of British state formation, focuses on the Nine Years War in Ireland (1594–1603), the succession crisis that led to the Union of Crowns (1603), the Flight of the Earls (1607), and the Ulster Plantation (1609). (2007: 2)

Many of Shakespeare's plays have proved amenable to being understood within this new paradigm, but it is no surprise that some have attracted more analysis than others: as Maley observes in the second half of his abstract,

> Although this work has touched on all of Shakespeare's corpus, it has tended to centre on a group of plays, namely the 'British tetralogy' – *Hamlet, King Lear, Macbeth* and *Cymbeline* – book-ended by *Henry V* and *The Tempest*. This work, part of the 'new contextualism', a revised and enlarged version of new historicism and cultural materialism, mixes the empirical methods of the old historicism with the theoretical insights of the new, and adds the urgency, the 'very now' of Presentism. Four related features emerge: the rethinking of genre, in the extending of the category of history play to include tragedies such as *Macbeth* and *King Lear*, and romances like *Cymbeline* and *The Tempest*; the rethinking of history, in a concomitant extension of the terms 'Jacobean' and 'Stuart' to all of Shakespeare's late and post-Elizabethan work; the rethinking of the relation between new historicism and cultural materialism in the twinning of topicality and presentism as critical approaches; and the reorientation of the field in the recollection of, and reconnecting to, an earlier tradition of (old) historicist criticism preoccupied by geography and place. By going beyond the histories and reorienting the tragedies and romances, this new criticism is challenging genre boundaries as well as national borders. (2007: 20)

British Studies, then, does considerably more than it says on the tin: it addresses a wide range of issues and invites some far-reaching reassessments and recategorizations of some of Shakespeare's most important plays.

Particular attention has been paid by British Studies to *The Tempest*, with its obvious nod in the direction of the English colonial enterprise (see Maley, this volume, Chapter 10). Indeed, Maley classifies *The Tempest* as the Irish play (he also calls *Hamlet* as 'the Scottish Play', on the basis principally of work by Stuart Kurland and Andrew Hadfield). Callaghan found in a variety of parallels falling short of direct reference: that 'Ireland was quite literally full of noises, a culture of sound', that 'scamel' and 'gabble' can both be understood as specifically as Irish words, and that 'English attacks on Irish dress also correspond with the representation of Caliban as misshapen and inhuman' (2000: 107, 108, 116–17, 130). To these Maley adds 'Ariel as an Old English figure, that is, as a representative of the descendants of the Catholic colonists of the twelfth century' (2000: 95). Even more important have been the histories, which explicitly address the question of the processes by which Shakespeare's England and its neighbouring countries have been formed. Again British Studies invites recategorization here: Maley takes issue with critical perspectives which subsume Scottish, Welsh and Irish characters into the English.

> According to Ania Loomba: 'Shakespeare's "others" are remarkably few in number – Othello, Caliban, Shylock, Jessica, Cleopatra and her train, Aaron, Tamora if we wish, and Morocco' (180). This list leaves out as others the likes of Fluellen, Glendower, Jamy, Macbeth and Macmorris, in other words those non-English others who are both foreign and familiar.
> (2000: 82)

For Maley, then, British Studies makes us see that the increasingly important category of 'Otherness' is applicable not only to the usual suspects of postcolonial criticism but to the histories too. Thus David Scott Kastan observes of *1 Henry IV* that 'Henry rules over a nation whose boundaries are insecure and whose integrity is under attack from within. He is at war with the Scots in the North, the Welsh in the West, and the very nobles that helped him to power now oppose his rule'. (1991: 242)

In the case of many analyses, there prove to be two principal consequences of reading Shakespeare's representations of English history within the set of contexts to which we are alerted by British Studies. One of these, unsurprisingly, is a refusal to automatically read from an 'English' point of view, and a willingness to take the non-English characters of the play more seriously than has often been done in the past. Thus Joan Fitzpatrick argues that 'The magical powers that Glyndwr boasts of appear to be genuine at least once in the play' (2004: 125), and argues that 'Far from undermining Glyndwr in particular, the overall effect of the scene set in Wales is to undermine the rebels in general' (2004: 127), while Terence Hawkes similarly remarks that 'It may well be that an acquaintance with Welsh people in London accounts for Shakespeare's portrayal of Glendower as more sympathetic than his sources would encourage' (2002: 33). Secondly, reading Shakespeare's 'English' history plays within a 'British' context often tends to sensitize critics to issues that were prominent not only in the mediaeval Britain *of* which Shakespeare wrote but also – and in some cases more so – in the early modern Britain *in* which he wrote: thus David Scott Kastan writes that 'The unitary state, "All of one nature, of one substance bred" (1. 1. 11), would be produced in opposition to an alien and barbaric "other," almost precisely the way an idea of an orderly and coherent English nation was fashioned in Elizabethan England largely by reference to the alterity and inferiority of the Irish' (1991: 242). Nor need the political issues on which British Studies touches be solely confined to the sixteenth and seventeenth centuries. Willy Maley suggests that

> It is worth remembering that in the Commons vote on the Iraq war on Tuesday 18th March 2003, a majority of Scottish and Welsh MPs voted against the war, but thanks to the votes of English MPs, and a helping hand from Ulster Loyalists, the imperialist venture was endorsed. A thing most brutish indeed. (2007: 96)

In this respect, British Studies can indeed look like a powerful fusion of an unusually particularized form of historicism with an unusually energized and motivated form of presentism.

Ecocriticism

It is a powerful testimony to the relatively sudden emergence of this new critical position that the influential journal *English Literary Renaissance* should devote its 2007 survey of recent developments in a particular field to an article by Karen Raber on 'Recent Ecocritical Studies of English Renaissance Literature'. Ecocriticism certainly makes no bones about reading Shakespeare from within our own historical moment rather than his. In the first major ecocritical approach to Shakespeare, *Green Shakespeare* – surely also the first work of Shakespearean criticism to contain a diagram of James Watt's steam governor – Gabriel Egan argues that 'Our understanding of Shakespeare and our understanding of Green politics have overlapping concerns and can be mutually sustaining' (2006: 1). To apply Green thinking to Shakespeare, for instance, can, Egan argues, alert us to the fact that 'Although he would not, of course, have used these terms, Shakespeare's plays show an abiding interest in what we now identify as positive- and negative-feedback loops, cellular structures, the uses and abuses of analogies between natural and social order, and in the available models for community' (2006: 50). Egan also suggests that 'Virtually all Shakespeare criticism has been written according to the Enlightenment's scientific principles, and these are currently being revised. It is worth taking notice of the revision' (2006: 33), since 'a number of seemingly naive old ideas about our relations with the natural world – for example, that the Earth itself is alive and that what we do can change the weather – have turned out to be true' (2006: 4). Egan therefore suggests that we might want to reassess current critical orthodoxy in certain respects. Specifically, he suggests that writers such as Tillyard, with their focus on a holistic and ordered 'world picture', should not be uncritically discarded. Indeed, we need to 'discard certain prejudices that recent Shakespeare criticism has fostered. One such prejudice is that analogies between the natural world and human society, and between different levels of human society, are reductive and politically con-servative' (2006: 4): in fact

> Shakespeare's analogies between human society and the wider cosmic order should not embarrass us, as they seem to have embarrassed late twentieth-century criticism that chose to avert its gaze. The latest ideas from science offer us ways to understand these analogies as politically progressive. (2006: 16)

When it comes to specific texts, Egan suggests that

> we can read *The Tempest* in a couple of historical contexts that have recently become available, and within which it seems even more grimly pessimistic than recent (especially postcolonial) criticism has allowed. The new contexts are concerned with the knowledge of science, and with the costuming of the play. (2006: 149)

The point which Egan makes about costuming is a slightly separate one, but his point about the history of science takes us right to the heart of the ecocriti-cal project, since Egan suggests that to read the play in this light could show us that the play's 'recurrent arboreal [tree] imagery has a very real point in the play, for Prospero's main activity since his arrival on the island has been its deforestation' (2006: 155) and that 'Shakespeare's play links colonization, deforestation, and extreme weather in ways that can now be seen as prescient' (2006: 171). Like presentism and British Studies, then, ecocriticism is inter-ested not only in Shakespeare but in the ways in which the critical discourse it fosters can intervene in contemporary political debate, but its agenda is specifically a Green one.

Further Analysis: Green Readings

Perhaps the most obvious application of a Green agenda is in those plays which feature what C. L. Barber called the 'green world' – *A Midsummer Night's Dream*, *Two Gentlemen of Verona*, *The Merchant of Venice* and *As You Like It* being the most obvious examples, especially since *A Midsummer Night's Dream* contains a speech specifically remarking on recent severe disruptions to weather patterns. In the recent BBC series *Shakespeare Retold*, which jettisons the original language and updates the plays to a contemporary setting, Oberon actually uses the phrase 'global warming' when describing the effects of his conflict with Titania on the natural world – do you think that it is a legitimate interpretation?

Performance Studies

Related to presentism is the increasingly prominent study of Shakespeare's plays in performance and related issues (see Hampton-Reeves' Chapter 6 and Egan's Chapter 9, this volume). Performance may seem by its very nature to be fleeting, impermanent and ephemeral: even a long theatre run will finish, and however copiously it has been documented, it is difficult if not impossible to record or reconstruct it in every detail or to give any real sense of what it was like to be present at a performance. However, critics often make reference to performance in their explorations of plays and performance is also often now the focus of interest on its own account, as in the important Manchester University Press *Shakespeare in Performance* series. Introducing his volume on *Hamlet* in the *Shakespeare in Performance* series, Anthony B. Dawson declares,

> I am writing as part of a series called *Shakespeare in Performance*, published by a well-established university press. This context automatically confers an air of authority on the book that may be misleading because it suggests that 'Shakespeare', '*Hamlet*' and 'performance' are all stable entities; plus it assumes that when I describe a production I am somehow able to convey what really took place. But there is something crucial left out of such an assumption, something that is foregrounded in the text of *Hamlet* itself. And that is that all such certainties are to some degree illusory [. . .] all meanings, as the play reminds us, are provisional and temporary, a result of negotiation and cultural struggle as well as individual effort and creativity. (1995: 3)

For Dawson, 'making meanings is a cultural practice inseparable from performance in whatever arena' (1995: 4), and awareness of this allows us not only to appreciate the range of meanings that may be liberated in performance, but also to grasp something fundamental about drama in general and *Hamlet* in particular:

> Only recently have scholars begun to emphasize the performance aspects of [Shakespeare's] work. This in turn is related to cultural changes in which the idea of performance in all its senses (encompassing politics, teaching, communications and information exchange as well as theatre) has become dominant. In our post-modern world, selfhood itself has come to be seen as primarily a matter of performance, rather than as something 'real'. (1995: 4)

In this way, *Hamlet* becomes a play which speaks on a basic level to our present understanding of our own condition (see Hiscock/Longstaffe, this volume, Chapter 1). That *Hamlet* in turn is both a key text in English-speaking culture, and a key element in the self-definition of 'great Shakespeareans' such as Garrick, Irving or Olivier, indicates the importance of 'performance' in many senses and indeed Dawson suggests that an important factor

> in accounting for the play's cultural centrality may be the prominence the text and its performances confer on the individual self. Born at a time when the emerging forces of Protestant theology, capitalist enterprise and humanist individualism were combining to form what has come to be called the 'modern subject', Hamlet seems to embody the struggles and aspirations of the individual soul set afloat in a sea of troubles and uncertainties. (1995: 7)

To some extent, moreover, this is a self-perpetuating condition, since Dawson further argues that

> In this regard, too, the prominent cultural position of certain actors, such as David Garrick in the eighteenth century, Henry Irving in the nineteenth, or Laurence Olivier in the twentieth, makes itself felt. (1995: 8)

To think about *Hamlet* in this way is far more than to think about a few ephemeral and long-gone performances; it is to engage with how society has both shaped and been shaped by a central cultural icon of our civilization.

Michael Cordner applies a rather differently slanted kind of performance analysis when he examines Macbeth's injunction to Lady Macbeth to 'hold thee still':

Seventeenth-century usage authorises an intriguing line-up of possible meanings for [these words]. If we interpret 'still' as an adverb carrying its common early modern sense of 'constantly, always, continuously', one plausible paraphrase is: 'always, and in all circumstances, keep yourself under tight control'; while an equally credible option, deploying the same adverbial meaning for 'still', would be: 'stay loyal to the same mode of conduct – and the same firm resolve – as you have done throughout our attempt on the crown'. If, however, we invoke the adjectival meanings for 'still' available to Shakespeare, further possibilities open up. For instance, 'still' could mean, then as now, 'motionless', which could here generate 'stand still', but also, by extension, 'don't let your physical control lapse'. 'Still' could also signify 'silent, taciturn', and from that might be educed: 'stay tight-lipped, be careful to say nothing to betray us'. Another current sense was 'soft, subdued, not loud', which might suggest: 'keep your behaviour normal, unemphatic'. And finally, it could mean 'secret', which might lead to: 'take care you remain unreadable', thus generating a provocative – and (depending on the actor's choice of intonation) possibly barbed – echo of Lady Macbeth's earlier criticism that his face 'is as a Booke, where men / May reade strange matters'.

Cordner declares that

> When Shakespeare penned these lines, he presumably had in mind a clear idea of how he intended them to be inflected. Despite the pressured rehearsal circumstances under which Jacobean actors worked, he may have carved out time to instruct Richard Burbage in those intentions and secured the latter's agreement so to perform them. But no evidence of these preferences survives in the bare words printed upon the relevant page of the First Folio, which is all we have to work from. Consequently, modern readers and actors, while remaining strictly faithful to early modern usage, can construct a rich array of interpretative possibilities from this brief phrase. (2006: 91–92)

For Cordner, using a historical understanding of how meanings could be made in performance is crucial to understanding the possible range of meanings for the play (see Hampton-Reeves, this volume, Chapter 6).

However, not everyone is entirely convinced by the rise of performance criticism. Lukas Erne in his influential book *Shakespeare as Literary Dramatist* claims that

> The greater part of performance criticism has been salutary and beneficial, and this book has no quarrel with it. What does need to be questioned,

however, are some of the more dogmatic claims that have been made about the importance of performance for our understanding of Shakespeare's plays. When performance critics claim, for instance, that 'the stage expanding before an audience is the source of all valid discovery' and that 'Shakespeare speaks, if anywhere, through his medium,' they are simply ignoring one of the two media in which Shakespeare's plays exist and existed. (2003: 22)

Performance criticism, then, polarizes opinions. For some, it is an essential tool for reading and understanding the plays, but for a critic like Erne, it actually threatens the integrity of that process rather than assisting it.

Beyond Theory?

It is perhaps not surprising that one response to the plethora of competing theories has been the emergence of what can be loosely described as a 'post-theoretical moment'. In 1992, Graham Holderness remarked scathingly that 'The editor of the Arden Shakespeare texts of *1 Henry IV* is able to quote approvingly from both Dover Wilson and Barber, and to support the idea of the plays as a "unified vision" with the names of New Critics Cleanth Brooks and Robert B. Heilman' (144), but such ideological pluralism is increasingly less likely to be avoided or to attract attention if it is practised. Thus, for instance, Laurie Maguire argues in her book *Studying Shakespeare: A Guide to the Plays* (2004: 190) that *Hamlet* 'provides an extended examination of death and grief, with transhistorical emotions about death embedded in a localized Reformation crisis about rituals of mourning'. Aware of history, Maguire nevertheless feels able to regard the play as dealing with what we might call 'eternal verities': 'Hamlet divides his world into good versus bad, genuine versus false, but the tension is actually dead versus alive' (2004: 194), while of *Henry IV* she declares that 'The difference between Henry IV's and Hal's strategies is that the latter's involves using and disposing of people' (2004: 97). There is also a new willingness among many modern critics to engage with the figure of the author. Many early theoretical approaches rigorously eschewed discussion of the author himself on the grounds of the 'intentionalist fallacy' – that since we cannot actually know what the author was thinking, there is no point speculating about it – so that Stephen Greenblatt, for instance, declares that 'it may be that Hariot was demonically conscious of what he was doing [. . .] But we do not need such a biographical romance to account for the phenomenon: the subversiveness [. . .] was produced by colonial power in its own interest' ([1985] 1992: 89). However in recent years the idea of the author has been making something of a comeback, as the title of a book like the Kozuka and Mulryne edited collection *Shakespeare, Marlowe,*

Jonson: New Directions in Biography (2006) attests. Thus in *Studying Shakespeare* Maguire also observes that 'Shakespeare's father died in 1601; the death of fathers is prominent in Shakespeare's writing in 1600–1' (2004: 195), and the growing body of work by critics interested in Shakespeare's possible Catholicism almost invariably draws on biographical evidence. This can be problematic, however, because in many areas of Shakespeare's life biographical evidence is sadly lacking. Though this is no more than is to be expected for a figure of the period – in the case of a slightly later contemporary of Shakespeare's, the dramatist John Ford, we do not even know when he died – Shakespeare's fame has inevitably led too many critics to substitute speculation for evidence when faced with these tantalizing gaps, and work in this area may consequently need to be treated with caution. In the bewildering variety of theoretical approaches presently available to us it is perhaps inevitable that any one individual theory should find it difficult to maintain its claim to primacy and truth-value, but it is equally inevitable that it is no longer acceptable to read these plays in a way which claims to be wholly innocent of theory.

9 New Contexts for Shakespeare

Gabriel Egan

Chapter Overview

This chapter is concerned with recently-emerged new contexts for the work of Shakespeare and how these have affected, and may continue to affect, the criticism of his works. In particular, it will focus on his biography and working habits, his surviving texts, and the archaeological work on the buildings in which his plays were first performed.

Shakespeare and Biography

Several new biographies appeared in the first years of the twenty-first century, despite the fact that initially no new knowledge about his life had emerged in the preceding decades. Thus, it might seem that all biographers can do is fit the existing pieces of an incomplete jigsaw into new configurations, shaped not so much by the facts as by the kind of Shakespeare they want to construct (see Hopkins, this volume, Chapter 8). Thus Katherine Duncan-Jones's *Ungentle Shakespeare* (2001) is driven largely by the desire to dispel the longstanding myths of his unworldly goodness and to show that, like any ambitious and increasingly wealthy man of his time, Shakespeare was class-conscious and capable of sharp-dealing when his personal fortunes were at stake. That so many of his contemporaries called him 'gentle' Shakespeare should not cloud our judgement of the empirical evidence about his behaviour – such things as his purchase of a title, his enclosure of common land – which need to be understood within the contexts of the business activities which structured his life.

One of the reasons that the realities of Shakespeare's life have been glossed over is that, because he wrote dramatic poetry, he was for many years treated as a poet – and poets are supposed to be other-worldly. However, since about the mid-twentieth century the drive to have Shakespeare understood as essentially a man of the theatre has tended to strip away this assumed poetic unworldliness. The theatre of early modern London was a cut-throat business operating outside the protection and control of the guild structure of the city. Thinking about the existing facts of Shakespeare's life in these terms, a biographer may combine the pieces of the jigsaw with a respect for the necessary domestic and professional arrangements that a successful playing company sharer such as Shakespeare must have made.

To take a straightforward example, it is commonly asserted that Shakespeare retired to Stratford-upon-Avon some time around 1613, when his career in the theatre was over. The central biographical facts that underpin this assertion are that Shakespeare died in Stratford in 1616 and that none of the surviving plays in which he had a hand can be dated later than 1613. But in order to retire *to* Stratford Shakespeare would have to have been living elsewhere, and as Stanley Wells (2002: 28–38) points out we simply do not know where Shakespeare lived most of the time. It is a reasonable assumption that his work in the theatre industry kept him in London, and there are records of his being resident at certain times, but a life of constant travel between Stratford and London was quite possible. As Wells notes, the essential requirements for his work were a well-stocked library and relative peace in which to read and write, and it is at least as easy to imagine him finding these in Stratford, where he owned a grand house, as in London. Underlying an image of Shakespeare retiring to Stratford may well be an assumption of his long-term abandonment of his wife and family for the duration of an exciting career in the metropolis, and most potently of him giving up this life when he completed his last sole-authored play *The Tempest* in 1611. Prospero's farewell to the audience in the epilogue to the play is pleasingly read as Shakespeare's farewell to the stage but, of course, it can be no such thing, for he went on to co-write three more plays with John Fletcher: *All is True, Cardenio* and *The Two Noble Kinsmen*. We will shortly come back to this matter of collaboration, and how it bears upon interpretation of the works.

Further Analysis: Shakespearean Romance

Plays that Shakespeare wrote in the last years of his career are sometimes called the Romances. Find secondary material that gives you the current scholarly opinion on the dates of composition of each of his plays – a good Complete Works edition should have this – and make a list of the plays from *Pericles* (1607) to the end of Shakespeare's career. Beside each play title give a brief account of the play's genre, taking into account when it is set, the nature of the plot, and especially such things as whether any bad characters die, whether any good characters die, and whether the outcome is a happy one for the protagonists. Do these late plays fall into clear generic categories?

Catholic Shakespeare

The biggest biographical news has been the claim recently advanced by several scholars that Shakespeare was secretly a Catholic, and hence he lived his life in permanent tacit opposition to the state-enforced Protestant orthodoxy. This idea first achieved widespread currency when E. A. J. Honigmann (1985) attempted to explain the so-called 'lost years' between 1585, when the baptism of Shakespeare's twins is recorded in Stratford-upon-Avon, and 1592, when allusions to his London theatre life begin. For this missing period, Honigmann placed Shakespeare in the family home of a wealthy Catholic landowner Alexander Hoghton in Lancashire, whose will referred to a William Shakeshafte lodging with him. At the end of the twentieth century, Richard Wilson (1997; 2004a; 2004b) discovered further connections between Shakespeare and recusant activity. The validity of these connections remains a matter of dispute, and Richard Bearman's research has undermined the evidential value of there being a 'Shakeshafte' in Hoghton's will by showing that it was a common name in Lancashire (Bearman 2002).

However, what would it matter if Shakespeare were secretly Catholic? How would this affect the interpretation of his plays? For one thing, it would put an end to the long-cherished idea that Shakespeare saw both sides of every argument, and indeed was capable of articulating both sides, without ever finally coming down in favour of either. This alleged neutrality of Shakespeare is sometimes known as his 'negative capability', a phrase coined by the poet John Keats, who saw Shakespeare as having an unusual capacity to suspend judgement, 'of being in uncertainties, Mysteries, doubts, without any irritable reaching after fact and reason' (White 1987: 34). But the idea of a Shakespeare who secretly favoured one side in the greatest intellectual argument of his day not only forces us to reconsider his representations of religious controversies – say, in *1 Henry VI* where Cardinal Beaufort dare not appear at court in his robes until Henry V is long buried (Wentersdorf 2006) and in *King John* where the king overtly denies the power of Rome and comes to regret it – but also to reconsider all those moments where he seems to refuse final conclusions to any debate. Could it be that we are just too insensitive to the subtle hints that tell us which side he was on? In any event, the very fact that he had assiduously buried his own feelings (else he would not have so long passed as the poet of 'negative capability') would require a re-examination of every longstanding critical assumption of neutrality.

Let us take a concrete example. The ghost in *Hamlet* claims to come from Purgatory:

> GHOST   I am thy father's spirit,
>   Doomed for a certain term to walk the night,
>   And for the day confined to fast in fires
>   Till the foul crimes done in my days of nature
>   Are burnt and purged away.
>
>   (1. 5. 9–13, p. 1684)

Only Catholics believed in Purgatory and rejecting the idea of a fixed-duration for certain sins – a 'time' to be paid for each 'crime' – was a key tenet of the new Protestant faith and philosophy initiated by Martin Luther (see Engel, this volume, Chapter 2). Three scenes before this one, the audience was made aware that Hamlet himself was educated at the epicentre of Luther's influence ('going back to school in Wittenberg', 1. 2. 113), so the play offers something to adherents of both the old and the new religions. If we imagine a Shakespeare who was secretly attached to the old faith, Hamlet's own education is a new departure from the truth and the father, not the son, represents correct theology.

Further Analysis: Shakespeare and Religious Division

Find other moments in Shakespeare's plays where the difference between Protestant and Catholic doctrine seems important. (If you are stuck finding examples, search an electronic text of the plays for the word 'puritan'; this will not find every relevant moment but it should turn up at least four scenes in which extreme Protestantism is mentioned.) Reading these moments in the light of the characters' preceding

---

> dialogue and behaviour, can you tell if the audience is encouraged to see either side of this Christian schism as being in the right?

Hamlet is generally understood to be both forward and backward looking, with old Hamlet personifying medieval principles made to clank noisily onto the stage in full armour and presumably carrying a broadsword. At the same time, the younger generation looks forward to the Renaissance present, in which martial skill is transmuted into ceremonial combat with finely wrought weapons: 'French rapiers and poniards [. . .] girdle, hanger [. . .] most delicate carriages' (5. 2. 109–12). The 1990 film of the play makes explicit this contrast of old and new ways when Hamlet (Mel Gibson) chooses as his weapon for the final contest not a delicate rapier but a medieval broadsword, and self-mockingly collapses under its weight (Zeffirelli 1990). The old and the new, in theology as well as philosophy and wider cultural practice, are thus put into dramatic conflict, so the play might be thought quintessentially the work of a dramatist sceptical of past and present ideas. But if Shakespeare was a secret follower of the old religion we have to suppose that he was deeply opposed to the Elizabethan present, with its enforced attendance at Protestant mass.

According to Richard Wilson, this long-engrained necessity to conceal his beliefs is itself the reason that Shakespeare's personal views seem so markedly absent from the works. Extinguishing one's personality in order to mouth views that one did not believe was a habit that secret Catholics learnt in order to survive. When Shakespeare came to write plays this habit manifested itself as a highly developed capacity to inhabit the points of view of others and articulate them as though from within. The ventriloquism of drama was especially suited to Shakespeare's religious outlook, if (and the matter is far from settled) he was indeed a Catholic.

Shakespeare as Collaborator

The traditional view of Shakespeare's dramatic career has been that, unlike many of his contemporaries, he generally worked on his own. According to G. E. Bentley (1971: 197–234), most drama was composed by pairs or teams of writers collaborating, but we tend to think of Shakespeare as a loner. Work on evidence for his occasional collaboration was considerably suppressed for most of the twentieth century by a thunderous British Academy lecture by E. K. Chambers (1924–25) that denounced the early, relatively crude statistically-based investigations of F. G. Fleay and J. M. Robertson. Despite this, the evidence gradually accumulated and Brian Vickers's 2002 book on the subject counted amongst Shakespeare's collaborative works *1 Henry VI,*

Titus Andronicus, Timon of Athens, Pericles, All is True (Henry VIII) and *The Two Noble Kinsmen.*

Vickers does not dwell upon the dating of these plays, which in the chronology of the 1986 Oxford Complete Works is 1592 for *1 Henry VI* and *Titus Andronicus*, 1605 for *Timon of Athens*, 1607 for *Pericles*, 1613 for *All is True*, and 1613–14 for *The Two Noble Kinsmen* (Wells et al. 1987: 113–34). Between 1592 and 1605, Shakespeare seems not to have collaborated and yet he wrote twenty-one plays, over half the canon. Shakespeare slowed down towards what we now know – even if he did not – was to be the end of his career. The first ten plays in the Oxford chronology, from *Two Gentlemen of Verona* to *Richard II*, were written between 1590 and 1595, about two a year. The last ten plays, *King Lear* to *The Two Noble Kinsmen*, were written between 1605 and 1614, about one a year. (In those counts I exclude the lost plays *Love's Labour's Won* and *Cardenio* and ignore the poetic output.) So, Shakespeare began and ended his career as a collaborator, working quickly at the beginning and slowly at the end.

An obvious explanation for this behaviour offers itself. At the start of his career, the novice was keen but needed to work with others, like an apprentice, acquiring skills and perhaps being somewhat exploited. Although Thomas Nashe was three years younger than Shakespeare, he had established himself as a published writer in the late 1580s and was already part of a well-defined circle of Oxford and Cambridge graduates in London (including Christopher Marlowe and Robert Greene) when he worked with Shakespeare on *1 Henry VI* in 1592 (Smith, Stephen & Lee 1937–38: 101–9). Likewise, George Peele was connected with this circle of graduates when he worked with Shakespeare on *Titus Andronicus* the same year and he was somewhere between five and eight years Shakespeare's senior (Bowers 1987a: 242–53). When Shakespeare collaborated again it was in 1604–6 on *Timon of Athens* with Thomas Middleton (Shakespeare & Middleton 2004: 5–6), who was fifteen or sixteen years his junior (Bowers 1987b: 196–222), and in 1607 on *Pericles* with George Wilkins. Wilkins's age is unknown and his certain dramatic output to that date was a share in *The Travails of the Three English Brothers* and sole authorship of *The Miseries of Inforced Mariage*. His body of work was much less than Shakespeare's thirty-one plays written over the preceding fifteen years or so. We may suppose that in this second phase of collaboration Shakespeare no longer had to prove himself, could afford to slow down (as he undoubtedly did towards the end), and worked with others as a master imparting his skills and benefiting from the junior partner's keenness.

Shakespeare ended his working life somewhat as he began it, but as the master rather than the apprentice. According to Gary Taylor (2004b) the first few years of the 1600s were hard on Shakespeare, and, mid-career and (early) middle-aged, he returned to collaboration to revive his flagging output by breaking a run of mediocrity that began after *Hamlet*. Whether he achieved this with *Timon of Athens* we cannot directly tell because nothing is known of its stage history before the Restoration (Shakespeare & Middleton 2004: 89), although we might take this fact itself as indirect evidence that it was not a hit. But indisputably his next known collaboration, *Pericles*, written probably in the winter of 1607–8, was an immediate, huge, and enduring success (Shakespeare 2004: 2–4, 54–62).

What difference does it make to our interpretation of a play if we decide that Shakespeare collaborated on it? A reader who finds herself disappointed that at the end of *1 Henry VI* Joan of Arc turns out to be precisely the witch and harlot that the English said she was may be comforted by the knowledge that Shakespeare did not write this part of the play (Taylor 1995). The Shakespearean parts of the play seem to be those especially concerned to show that men hurl accusations of impropriety at women who threaten their masculine military dominance, and in particular that being accused of witch-craft was a risk taken by women who refused to conform to prevailing rules of female submissiveness. Someone with a less subtle touch seems to have finished off the play, and by confirming all the English accusations this writer drains from the character of Joan some of the radical power she has in the middle scenes of it.

In another of the early plays, the problem occurs right at the beginning. It has long been a matter of concern to critics that Titus's killing of his son Mutius in a row over Lavinia is out of character and seems too easily forgot-ten about in a play intensely concerned with family cohesion. One could argue that this is artistically intentional, since Titus embodies the strictest Roman values and places honour above all else. Recent work on the author-ship of the play, however, explains the killing of Mutius as an incident added to the play by its co-author George Peele without Shakespeare's knowledge or agreement (Boyd 2004). What should we do about such a case? There is an argument for undoing such interventions in a text if we think that the main author would not have approved of them, but what if (as seems to be the case here) Peele was entrusted with writing certain scenes and simply failed to keep to the agreed plot?

Further Analysis: Piecing Together a Shakespearean Text?

Read the first two scenes of *Measure for Measure*, making a list of the problems with the dramatic material, in particular repetitions and con-fusions in the events. (Editors often try to fix these things, so you may want to read the text as it appeared in the first, virtually unedited, edition: the Folio of 1623. You will find images and electronic texts of this online in a number of places, including the Internet Shakespeare Editions.) Then read the account of Thomas Middleton's interference in the play after Shakespeare's death (Taylor 1993); does this account explain all the problems you listed? How would your reading of the play differ if, as has recently been claimed, the original setting were not Vienna in Austria but Ferrara in Italy (Taylor 2004a)?

Shakespeare as Author?

For some scholars, authorial collaboration is just one expression of the generally collaborative nature of drama in which individuals necessarily submerge their personalities within the group. Others believe that in the act of collaborative writing the individual writers' voices might not be entirely blended. After all, if the voices were utterly merged we would be unable to detect that the ending of *1 Henry VI* or the beginning of *Titus Andronicus* were the work of writers other than Shakespeare. To take an example from near the end of Shakespeare's career, the subject matter of *All is True* (a collaboration between Shakespeare and John Fletcher) is the reforming Protestant king Henry VIII who himself had persecuted Protestant heretics before his conversion to the new faith. As we have seen, if Shakespeare was a secret Catholic then this would be a topic about which he had decided but covert opinions. John Fletcher, on the other hand, was the grandson of a man who assisted John Foxe on the 1583 edition of the standard account of Protestant martyrs called *Actes and Monuments* (Merriam 2005: 39).

Foxe's *Actes and Monuments* is itself a source for *All is True* – also known as *Henry VIII* – as can be seen in these extracts, in which the shared words and phrases are highlighted:

> Oh *Lord, what manner a man be you?* What simplicity is in you? I had thought that *you would rather have* sued to us to have *taken the pains to have heard you and your accusers* together for your trial, *without* any such *indurance*. (Foxe 1597: 8B1ᵛ)

> [KING HENRY]
> *What manner of man are you?* My *lord*, I looked
> *You would have* given me your petition that
> I should have *ta'en some pains* to bring together
> Yourself *and your accusers*, and *to have heard you*
> *Without indurance* further.
> (5. 1. 118–22, p. 3180–1)

This one page of *Actes and Monuments* is used for a whole sequence of borrowings in the play, some in scenes attributed to Shakespeare and some in scenes attributed to Fletcher. As Thomas Merriam (2005: 35–40) pointed out, this has been given as an example of the dramatists working so closely together, drawing on the same materials so extensively, that any thought of untangling their labours is futile. But what if we do not assume a division of labour by scenes and instead try to work to a finer reticulation, investigating collaboration within scenes?

Merriam used Chadwyck-Healey's Literature Online (LION) database to test the rarity of certain combinations of words in the Thomas Cranmer episodes in 5. 1 that use Foxe as a source. The phrases 'There are that' and 'For so I know' appear in the parts of this play normally attributed to Shakespeare, but nowhere else in Shakespeare, but they appear often in the works of Fletcher. By a series of such tests, Merriam redrew the boundaries between the Shakespeare and Fletcher parts of the play, and showed that '[. . .] the Cranmer episodes in Act 5 of *Henry VIII* were written by Fletcher and not by Shakespeare' and that Shakespeare did not use Foxe's book (2005: 39). This removes the difficulty of imagining a Catholic Shakespeare using as his source a vitriolic anti-Catholic, anti-Papal work. We may have been seeing ambivalence or neutrality in Shakespeare's work only because we mistook as his writing parts of the plays that were by other people, and that in truth he was more partial, more opinionated, than we have hitherto imagined.

Textual Transmission

For a long time a hierarchy existed amongst Shakespeare's texts, with the longer versions found in the posthumous First Folio usually considered to be superior to the shorter quarto versions published in his lifetime (see glossary). A set of particularly short quarto versions were for most of the twentieth century labelled 'bad' quartos because they seemed textually corrupt and inexpertly cut down versions of the familiar texts. The most notorious of these is the 'bad' quarto of *Hamlet* that includes a speech beginning, familiarly enough, with 'To be, or not to be' but continuing 'Ay, there's the point, / To die, to sleep – Is that all? Ay all' (Shakespeare 1603: D4ᵛ). There are 'bad' quartos of *The Merry Wives of Windsor*, *2* and *3 Henry VI*, *Romeo and Juliet* and *Henry V*, and at times the early printings of *King Lear*, *Richard II* and *Richard III* have fallen under suspicion too. Although the means by which these texts were compiled was never fully discovered, the general assumption was that minor actors who had performed in them had got together and produced surreptitious texts by recalling their lines and the lines of the other actors, selling the resultant text to a publisher for an easy and illicit profit.

Although occasionally critics expressed concern that the 'bad' quartos were not so bad after all (McMillin 1972), from the 1980s more and more critics argued that we simply cannot tell where these short versions of the plays come from, and that they might simply be alternative versions with dramatic merits of their own (Urkowitz 1988; Werstine 1990; Werstine 1999; Irace 1994; Maguire 1996). Most recently, Lukas Erne (2002; 2003) has presented an entirely new thesis that might account for the 'bad' quartos. Contrary to the orthodoxy that began to emerge in the 1950s and achieved dominant expression in the 1986 Oxford Complete Works of Shakespeare, perhaps the plays were not, after all, essentially scripts for the theatre. What if Shakespeare consciously wrote for readers of his plays rather than (or perhaps as well as) for performers?

Further Analysis: Which *Hamlet*?

Find the 'to be or not to be' soliloquy in *Hamlet* in your edition and compare it with versions you can find from the quartos and/or Folio. (You will find facsimiles of 'bad' quartos at the back of recent Arden Shakespeare editions, and also at various places online including the Internet Shakespeare Editions.) Does the 'bad' quarto strike you as merely a garbling of the good text, or can you see merits as well as corruptions in its differences from the text we usually read?

Man of the Theatre?

The idea of Shakespeare as essentially a man of the theatre writing scripts for actors – the idea that Erne would overturn – is worth considering for a moment before we lose sight of it. English studies as a university subject is largely a twentieth-century invention, although universities have been around for hundreds of years. The newly emerging discipline greatly valued practical criticism and close reading, attending to 'the words on the page', and seeing Shakespeare primarily as a literary writer (see Hiscock and Longstaffe, this volume). From about the 1950s, this view of Shakespeare was increasingly undermined, especially in the new university departments in Bristol and Birmingham that studied drama as a subject in its own right, and this approach rapidly spread to other centres. Under the influence of Allardyce Nicoll and John Russell Brown especially, the University of Birmingham's Shakespeare Institute in Stratford-upon-Avon treated what happened on the theatre stage as every bit as important as what appears in the text. Research in theatre history bolstered the idea that as a working actor,

Shakespeare would have considered the mounting of a successful performance as the whole point of his writing (and indeed the way to make money)
and that sales of books would be at best a sideline and at worst a distraction
from, even an injury to, his main business. After all, three thousand people
could pay to see one's play on any given afternoon in a theatre, while total
sales of a book were limited by statute to the fifteen hundred copies that no
print-run could exceed. In utter reversal of today's economics, theatre was the
mass medium and book-reading the minority activity.

This new man-of-the-theatre role for Shakespeare influenced attitudes and
practices in various ways. Within education, an active and participatory ('on
your feet') mode of instruction could now replace sitting at desks and reciting
lines of dense poetry (see Hampton-Reeves, this volume, Chapter 6). In the
theatrical profession, lack of an English degree need no longer be felt a handi-
cap, for was not Shakespeare himself a working actor with no more than a
grammar school education supplemented by adult auto-didacticism? Within
academic Shakespeare studies, the re-centring of attention upon the theatre
meant the stripping away of textual elements that belonged to the study
not the stage. An often-quoted example of just how far from the stage editors
had taken their texts is the opening words of John Dover Wilson's New
Shakespeare *Titus Andronicus*:

> [1.1] *An open place in Rome, before the Capitol, beside the entrance to which there
> stands the monument of the Andronici. Through a window opening on to the
> balcony of an upper chamber in the Capitol may be seen the Senate in session.*
> (Shakespeare 1948)

Not a word of this appears in the two early printings of the play, the 1594
quarto and the 1623 Folio editions that are our only authorities for the text; the
above is all the editor's invention. As Stanley Wells (1984: 84) commented '...
it reads more like a direction for a film than for a play on the Elizabethan
stage' (see King, this volume, Chapter 11).

Editing Shakespeare

Wells, fresh from graduate study at the Shakespeare Institute, worked on the
New Penguin Shakespeare with T. J. B. Spencer in the 1960s and developed
new ideas about stage-centred editing that received their fullest expression in
the 1986 Oxford Complete Works. Whereas their predecessors seemed to
want to help the reader imagine the fictional location in which the action took
place, the new stage-centred editors wanted their readers to imagine the
action occurring on the kind of stage that Shakespeare would have assumed
he had at his disposal. Knowing that for most of Shakespeare's career

performances were uninterrupted by intervals, these editors marked act-breaks as unobtrusively as possible, rejecting the 'start a new page' layout that had long governed editions of Shakespeare. When it began to be apparent in the 1970s that Shakespeare tended to return to the plays he had written and revise them, the new stage-centred editors had to decide just what it was they were trying to represent: the play as originally conceived, or the play as Shakespeare later preferred it, perhaps with changes made in the light of rehearsals and early performances.

Ever since editorial practices began to be properly theorized in the late-nineteenth century, it had been assumed that the ideal to which one was editing – the document, now lost, that one would like to recreate – would be the text as it stood in the first complete authorial version. But with Shakespeare now conceived as a working and practical man of the theatre, this ideal needed to be adjusted. Radically, the Oxford Complete Works attempted to represent the play as it was first *performed*. If there were two early printings, say a quarto that seemed to be based on authorial papers and a folio text that seemed to be based on a document used in the theatre, the latter might well be preferred even if it omitted passages in the quarto. Thus, Hamlet's soliloquy beginning 'How all occasions do inform against me' (usually appearing at the end of IV. 4), from the second quarto but absent in the folio, is demoted to an appendix in the Oxford Complete Works, on the grounds that (good as it is) it seems not to have made it into the first performances.

These are the practical editorial implications of insisting on a stage-centred study of Shakespeare (see Hampton-Reeves' Chapter 6 and King's Chapter 11, this volume). However, Lukas Erne's theory that Shakespeare, at least from about 1600 when he wrote *Hamlet*, had readers as much as playgoers in mind, challenges the idea that texts should attempt to record early or first performances. In the five years since Erne announced his theory there has been no serious attempt to refute it and we are currently in a period of uncomfortable vacancy: flaws in the theatre-centred orthodoxy have been revealed, but no new overarching paradigm has been proposed. What seems likely to occur next is at least a partial rehabilitation of literary-critical sensibilities within Shakespeare studies. Edward Pechter (2003) has argued that misguided ideas about radicalism and theatrical anti-elitism undervalue the literary in relation to theatre. In essence this, like Erne's, is an argument for a revaluation of Shakespeare's literariness. The argument that the short quartos are theatricalized (cut for a fast pace, losing the wordy stuff not needed in the theatre) is, Pechter claims, based on an impoverished sense of what the theatre can do. Fourth acts are often reflective, giving space to female characters, and cutting there (as many shortened versions do) does not just increase the pace, it changes the gender balance. Thus, we should not be afraid to laud the plays' literary qualities. Politics also gets in the way: we are supposed to reject the literary as conservative and elitist and the theatrical as radical and demotic, but in many cases to champion a short (formerly, 'bad') quarto text because you think it more radical than the folio is to give up the folio's more interesting political material such as the complexities of Henry V's heroism and Desdemona and Emilia's discussion of the gender double standard.

The Globe

While the stage-centred thinking held unchallenged sway, the thing most obviously missing from Shakespeare studies was a clear idea of just what that stage looked like. The American actor Sam Wanamaker's project to build a replica Globe theatre near to the site of the original in London had one watchword: authenticity. The aim was not to build the kind of theatre we would like to think that Shakespeare used, but rather, by using the best theatre-historical scholarship available, to build the closest possible representation of the theatre he actually used, and then to put on performances that adhere as closely as possible to the original practices. The project was comprehensively mocked by mainstream British Shakespeareans in the 1980s, many of whom were Marxists with deep suspicions that the whole thing was an exercise in worshipping the Bard (what George Bernard Shaw, writing much earlier in the twentieth century, wittily dubbed 'bardolatry'). The project came to fruition in the late 1990s with the opening of the replica Globe in south London and it has become the most successful theatre in the country, judged by how often the 'house' is 'full'.[1]

For the first ten years, the new Globe operated a policy of experimenting with academically intensive, deeply researched 'original practices' of performance. This meant such things as using teenage boys to play the female roles and wearing clothing that accurately reproduced what the sixteenth and seventeenth-century actors wore, which was essentially what everybody wore in those days. That is to say, there is overwhelming evidence that performances in Shakespeare's time were in 'modern dress' in the sense that the actors wore much what the audience wore, rather than trying to reproduce the clothing of the times in which their plays were set. We have to imagine the ancient Romans of *Julius Caesar* wearing hats, capes, doublets, and hose, not togas and sandals, if we want to picture the first performances. Likewise, we have to picture Juliet or Cleopatra played by a boy, and if 'her' gown is designed to show off a bust the boy actor must be put into a corset that pulls the male torso so as to produce one. Or rather, at the Globe we no longer have to imagine these things since the skills of making functional early modern clothing have been recovered and refined so that actors may experience for themselves just how their characters' movements and postures were constrained by the clothing worn in the first performances. An aristocratically dignified upright posture maintained even during the act of sitting down was, it turns out, not so much a matter of training in deportment as the constraining of the body wedged into the figure-hugging shapes popular for both men and women of high status. This kind of realism has struck many as historical fetishism, but it has an intellectual rigour, and a socio-historical practical usefulness, that we can contrast with the imprecision of early modern 'costumes', held together by velcro and zippers, used by other troupes such as the Royal Shakespeare Company.

The design team led by Jenny Tiramani that brought this discipline and expertise to the Globe left the project in 2006, and productions there now have much less claim to academic rigour than those mounted in the first ten years. The theatre building itself, however, remains an academically rigorous replica of the original, and if we think that theatre buildings have an important effect on the performances that take place within them then the project has much more to uncover about early modern theatre practice. A difficulty arises, however, because it is hard to show that a theatre building has an important effect on the performances, other than in the most general terms. Certainly, the dramatic aesthetics of open-air performance by daylight in the midafternoon are different from those of indoor evening performance by artificial light. When one factors in the spatial relationships between the actors and the audience – at the Globe the stage is surrounded on three sides by standing spectators whom the actors cannot ignore, and who cannot ignore one another as they do in dark indoor theatres – it is clear that modes of address (such as soliloquy and aside) and their associated psychological states (self-communion, appeal to the world outside the fiction) are quite different at an open-air amphitheatre when compared to a conventional indoor proscenium-arch theatre.

However, beyond these main differences, it is hard to justify the Globe's attention to detail, since it is difficult to argue that the authentic practices of its builder Peter McCurdy have a lasting impact on the actors' use of the theatre now. This is the case with the interior decoration which, in fact, should be (from what we know of Elizabethan public buildings) as bright and gaudy around the full span of the auditorium as it currently is on the stage. It is difficult to justify extending the decoration to the auditorium on the grounds of anything other than rigour, since it does not seem from performances to date that theatre decoration has a noticeable effect upon the play, beyond the occasional reference such as Othello's 'yon marble heaven' (3. 3. 463) and Hamlet's 'this majestical roof fretted with golden fire' (2. 2. 291–2) – both referring to the painted underside of the cover over the stage.

Arguably, this point was effectively conceded several years ago when a crucial compromise was made. During an academic seminar on the subject in the early 1980s, John Ronayne presented evidence that the interior decoration of the Globe must have been something between 'the English tradition of the ornamented facade, low relief decorating flat surfaces, and the innovation of classical sculptural principles' (1983: 22). Ronayne pointed out that in exterior views the 1599 Globe appears white with stone walls, although it must have been timber-framed. The contract for the Fortune theatre, modelled on the Globe, explains why. It specifies that the building was to be 'sufficiently enclosed without [that is, outside] with lath, lime and hair' (Henslowe 1961: 308). This exterior treatment led to the conclusion that at the new replica Globe 'a magpie black and white half-timbering is not acceptable' (1983: 23), it would have to be likewise covered up with plaster. By 1997 Ronayne's position had shifted:

> Our re-creation of the 1599 Globe is a timber-framed building, and we have elected to leave the 'green' oak exposed to weather and fade to grey over the years. The majority of buildings in pre-fire London had their timbers exposed (Claes de Jongh's painting of London Bridge, of about 1612, now at Kenwood House, shows this vividly). As our reconstruction is the first major timber-framed building in the capital since the Fire, our decision, on balance, was to expose the structure of what is a rare sight in London, rather than cover it up as the Elizabethans may have done, taking for granted the frameworked appearance. For them, outer rendering was grander. For us, half timbering is more generally evocative. (997: 122)

This shift represents a radical change in the theoretical underpinning of the project, since the stated aim was always recovery of 'what had been' in the Elizabethan period and not 'what is now evocative' of the period.

We can reach further back into the project and find that, despite McCurdy's authentic construction practices, compromises were built into the initial conception of the replica theatre. After all, if it were to operate as a professional theatre it would have to meet twentieth-century safety standards, just as McCurdy's building workers had to use hard-hats, harnesses and light-weight sturdy scaffolding unavailable to the builders in 1599. As the first couple of bays of the replica theatre were being put together by McCurdy's team, Terence Hawkes mocked the project, linking it to the futility of textual work that has similar ambitions to recover the past:

> The less than edifying spectacle of scholars in pursuit of authenticity is familiar enough in the field of Shakespearean textual scholarship, where the quest for what the Bard 'originally' wrote in pristine and unsullied manuscript form has its own comic and ideologically

illuminating history. [. . .] The good news is that, to conform to modern fire regulations, the [project's two] theatres will have illuminated Exit signs. Light one for me. (1992: 142–43)

That is to say, for all the meticulous scholarship about the archaeology of the Globe, the need to put in modern safety lighting reveals the intellectual bank-ruptcy of the entire project. We cannot go back to the past, Hawkes insists, at least not without bringing our modern selves along too (see Robson, this volume, Chapter 5). For all the architectural work, 'What can never be reconstructed', he wrote, 'is the major ingredient of all Shakespeare's plays [. . .] their original audience' (1992: 143). This means that our historical knowledge is always mediated through the concerns of the present, not least the concern to get out alive in the event of a fire. Hawkes went on to develop this insight into what has become the latest trend in Shakespeare studies – or at least the latest to have a single catchy name – which he dubbed Presentism (Hawkes 2002; Fernie 2005; Grady & Hawkes 2007) (see Hopkins, this volume, Chapter 8).

This might seem the last word on the subject, but in fact there were objec-tions along these lines well before the project began to assemble the replica's giant timbers. One school of thought had always been that a 'good enough' replica – outdoors, playing in daylight, with boy actors – would be a more useful tool for learning about Shakespeare's dramaturgy than an intensely authentic reconstruction. Indeed, a 'good enough' Globe might be made from flexible units so that if new knowledge emerged the replica could be adapted to take account of it, or indeed if a particular experimenter wanted to try something unusual – say, to lower the stage balcony so that Romeo could leave Juliet's bedroom in a single manly bound – it could be accommodated. At the Wanamaker replica an early argument between architectural experts and theatre practitioners about the proposed location of the stage-posts resulted in a redesigning of the stage cover, which cannot now be moved again. For all its usefulness as an experimental theatre, the existing replica Globe is hamstrung by its very authenticity, since no-one wants to alter it greatly for the sake of further research.

Virtual Shakespeare

There may be an emerging technical solution to this dilemma. In the 1990s the techniques of Virtual Reality (VR) modelling enabled theatre historians to build replica theatres inside computers. Once built, these theatres could be used to test theories about theatre design, answering such questions as 'what view of the stage could be had from the top gallery?' and 'how is audibility in the stalls affected if we cover the walls with this paper?' In the case of the replica Globe, such a model enabled a fresh testing of the interpretation of the archaeological evidence from the site of the original Globe, which revealed that the Wanamaker Globe is not quite so securely the best 'reading' of the evidence as was once thought (Egan 2004). In the past couple of years, Virtual Reality modelling has developed from an academic discipline into a widespread and inexpensive medium for recreation, with millions of users spending time inside virtual worlds such as Second Life.

The THEATRON project that built Virtual Reality replicas of ancient Greek and Roman theatres, as well as a replica Globe based on the Wanamaker project, is now moving its buildings into Second Life. Once there, these buildings may be used not only for academic experimentation but also for 'live' virtual performance by 'actors' (avatars) controlled by computer users who might never meet in real life. The technology is in its infancy, and the human-computer interfaces are notoriously clumsy: most users are limited to a mouse and a keyboard. However, Virtual Reality headsets are available that immerse the wearer in the virtual experience by controlling everything that is seen and heard, and combined with wirelessly-connected gloves and socks these enable an actor-avatar inside the simulation to adopt approximately the stance and gestures of the wearer. It seems likely that performances inside Virtual Reality worlds will become increasingly of interest to playgoers and academics. Even those with sympathy for the Presentist insistence on the thoroughly mediated nature of historical knowledge may wish to engage with such experimentation, and the present author (who has such sympathy) is currently advising on the removal of the illuminated Exit signs from the THEATRON Globe so that the Second Life version may approach even more closely than the full-size replica to the conditions prevailing at the 1599 original, and yet remain adaptable (as the full-size building cannot) to accommodate new discoveries.

10 Recent Issues in Shakespeare Studies: From Margins to Centre

Willy Maley

What's at Issue?

In his 'Afterword' to Jonathan Dollimore and Alan Sinfield's *Political Shake-speare* (1985), Raymond Williams addressed the issue of politicizing an author whose work attracts a body of criticism unparalleled in world literature:

> Recording a certain wariness, an unease, about the main title of this volume of essays, I found myself back in the North Wing of Cambridge University Library, in the autumn of 1939. I was there to pick up a couple of books on Shakespeare for an essay. My first impression of those hundreds of volumes, tightly stacked in what looked like an industrial warehouse, can be best understood if I add that this was the first time I had been in any library larger than a living room. Wandering in and out, trying to decipher [. . .] the complicated system of classification, I came across a section which induced a kind of vertigo. I don't, fortunately, remember all the actual titles, but a quick scan showed me Shakespeare as royalist, democrat, catholic, puritan, feudalist, progressive, humanist, racist, Englishman,

homosexual, Marlowe, Bacon and so on round the bay. I flicked the pages
of some of the more improbable ascriptions. The compounded smell of
disuse and of evidence rose to my nostrils. I got out and went for a walk.
(Dollimore & Sinfield 1994: 231)

Shakespeare studies in the past was caught between excessively specialized
studies of the sort derided by Williams, and all-encompassing theories like
E. M. W. Tillyard's *Elizabethan World Picture* (1943), an attempt to construct an
inclusive historical context for Shakespeare's age. In the age of cable, satellite
and the web, new approaches and interests are collapsing these specialist and
generalist distinctions. In her contribution to *Political Shakespeare*, 'How Brecht
Read Shakespeare', Margot Heinemann cited Nigel Lawson, then Chancellor
of the Exchequer in Margaret Thatcher's Conservative government, who confidently declared that, like him, 'Shakespeare was a Tory' (203). Shakespeare
was certainly taught as a Tory for a long time, as a great symbol of Empire and
Englishness. He has also been read and taught as a royalist.

Further Analysis: Shakespeare and Political Debate

The first extract is from *1 Henry IV* and the second from *The Tempest*.
Consider the ways in which Shakespeare's writing might be seen to
stimulate debate in the audience's mind about monarchy as a political
system.

1 Henry IV, 4. 3. 54–107

> HOTSPUR: The king is kind; and well we know the King
>   Knows at what time to promise, when to pay.
>   My father and my uncle and myself
>   Did give him that same royalty he wears;
>   And when he was not six-and-twenty strong,
>   Sick in the world's regard, wretched and low,
>   A poor unminded outlaw sneaking home,
>   My father gave him welcome to the shore;
>   And when he heard him swear and vow to God
>   He came but to be Duke of Lancaster,
>   To sue his livery, and beg his peace
>   With tears of innocency and terms of zeal,
>   My father, in kind heart and pity moved,
>   Swore him assistance, and performed it too.
>   Now when the lords and barons of the realm
>   Perceived Northumberland did lean to him,
>   The more and less came in with cap and knee,

> Met him in boroughs, cities, villages,
> Attended him on bridges, stood in lanes,
> Laid gifts before him, proffered him their oaths,
> Gave him their heirs as pages, followed him,
> Even at the heels, in golden multitudes.
> He presently, as greatness knows itself,
> Steps me a little higher than his vow
> Made to my father while his blood was poor
> Upon the naked shore at Ravenspurgh,
> And now forsooth takes on him to reform
> Some certain edicts and some strait decrees
> That lie too heavy on the commonwealth,
> Cries out upon abuses, seems to weep
> Over his country's wrongs; and by this face,
> This seeming brow of justice, did he win
> The hearts of all that he did angle for;
> Proceeded further, cut me off the heads
> Of all the favourites that the absent king
> In deputation left behind him here,
> When he was personal in the Irish war.
> SIR WALTER BLUNT: Tut, I came not to hear this.
> HOTSPUR: Then to the point.
> In short time after, he deposed the King,
> Soon after that deprived him of his life,
> And in the neck of that tasked the whole state;
> To make that worse, suffered his kinsman March –
> Who is, if every owner were well placed,
> Indeed his king – to be engaged in Wales,
> There without ransom to lie forfeited;
> Disgraced me in my happy victories,
> Sought to entrap me by intelligence,
> Rated mine uncle from the Council-board;
> In rage dismissed my father from the court,
> Broke oath on oath, committed wrong on wrong,
> And in conclusion drove us to seek out
> This head of safety, and withal to pry
> Into his title, the which we find
> Too indirect for long continuance. (pp. 1209–10)

The Tempest, 2. 1. 147–58

> GONZALO: (*to* Antonio) I'th' commonwealth I would by
> contraries

> Execute all things. For no kind of traffic
> Would I admit, no name of magistrate;
> Letters should not be known; riches, poverty,
> And use of service, none; contract, succession,
> Bourn, bound of land, tilth, vineyard, none;
> No use of metal, corn, or wine, or oil;
> No occupation; all men idle, all;
> And women too – but innocent and pure;
> No sovereignty –
> SEBASTIAN: Yet he would be king on't.
> ANTONIO: The latter end of his commonwealth forgets the
> beginning. (p. 3073)

Before we rush to replace Shakespeare the conservative royalist imperialist with Shakespeare the queer catholic republican we should pause a moment. Hamlet's hesitation has its virtues. Shakespeare is, for some recent critics, a writer preoccupied, even obsessed, with issues of race, class and gender in ways that have been glossed over by conventional criticism. Jacques Derrida, who has written on *Romeo and Juliet*, and whose *Specters of Marx* (1993) can be read as an extended meditation on ideas of time and justice in *Hamlet*, spoke before his death of his dream of becoming a 'Shakespeare expert', saying that he would like to live for two hundred years in order to achieve that status. We who are young shall never see so much nor live so long. For Derrida, 'everything is in Shakespeare' (Derrida 1992: 67). Derrida's own reading practice can be summed up in one line from *Hamlet*, 'The time is out of joint', because it consists precisely in 'deconstructing, dislocating, displacing, disarticulating, disjoining, putting "out of joint" the authority of the "is" ' (Derrida 1995: 25). Thus, for Derrida, anything which is viewed as being present ('is') requires close scrutiny and interrogation.

In this chapter, I intend to take the reader on a walk, a guided tour of key issues in Shakespeare studies in the period since Dollimore and Sinfield's *Political Shakespeare*. His anecdote is interesting for a range of reasons, not least its date, for 'the autumn of 1939' marked the outbreak of the Second World War in Europe, and the beginnings of a decline of the British Empire that brought with it the kind of questioning of nation and monarchy we see in recent Shakespeare criticism. Those old chestnuts of 'Shakespeare as royalist, democrat, catholic, puritan, feudalist, progressive, humanist, racist, Englishman, homosexual, Marlowe, Bacon' and so on have been reheated, and other irons thrust into the fire. So, let us wander round the bay and the bend to see how far the improbable and the disused have become new orthodoxies.

Much of the new material on Shakespeare shares a concern with the culture and society that produced him as much as the plays that he produced, and so it can appear less sympathetic, less appreciative, than the work of earlier generations. One critic who manages to be both new and to do a lot of very close reading of Shakespeare's plays is Patricia Parker. The title of her best book – *Shakespeare from the Margins* (1996) – encapsulates much recent issue-based Shakespeare criticism, which focuses on what appear marginal or minor aspects of the canon, or at least aspects considered marginal by traditional criticism: minor characters; lesser known works; or themes and issues that might have been, if not unthinkable for earlier generations of critics, then buried in footnotes or glosses or editorial asides or presented as notes and queries. These hitherto marginal enquiries are now becoming central to the study of Shakespeare. However, many of the fresh findings in Shakespearean criticism have earlier analogues and sources, and so it is as much a question of renovation as innovation. There is also a tendency in recent criticism to see Shakespeare as a writer closer to Joyce than Jonson, so that richness of texture supplants clarity of vision or any insistence on universal accessibility. Wordplay in *Twelfth Night* might repay as much attention as the pun fest that is *Finnegans Wake*.

Some of the most interesting work on Shakespeare in the last generation has come from what is generally referred to as 'Theory': theory with a capital 'T'. If that term implies abstraction then it should be pointed out straight away that the main plank of much of this theoretical criticism has been 'historical', but not in terms of the old approach that saw history as making up merely a 'background' or 'context' (see Robson's Chapter 5, Engel's Chapter 2, Hiscock and Longstaffe, and Hopkins' Chapter 8, this volume). Rather, this new material opens up the plays to a variety of 'contexts' in the plural, as well as blurring the distinction between a text and its historical context, which is always made up of other texts. Francis Barker and Peter Hulme in their 'Nymphs And Reapers Heavily Vanish: The Discursive Con-Texts of *The Tempest*' (1985) hyphenate the word context, to give 'con-text', in order to make the reader aware of the degree to which every context is also another text (236, n. 7). Likewise, the new historicist 'co-text', a text read alongside a canonical literary text in order to bring out something important but obscured in the culture at large, is another complication of the text/context divide. For Stephen Greenblatt, 'history cannot simply be set against literary texts as either stable antithesis or stable background, and the protective isolation of those texts gives way to a sense of their interaction with other texts and hence to the permeability of their boundaries' (1985b: 165). However, this does not mean that anything goes. Historical readings are fine and fashionable, but topicality – placing, locating and contextualizing specific parts of particular plays – is still a risky business.

Issue: Family, Lineage, Succession

There is no end to the 'issues' to be found, or pursued, in Shakespeare's texts. In mapping out apparently oblique and eccentric areas, Shakespeare sets the agenda as much as the critics. For example, one of the issues in *1 Henry IV* is 'issue' itself – the production of children as heirs and how they succeed their parents – a topic particularly pressing under the unmarried queen Elizabeth I. Under James Stuart, after the Union of Crowns (1604), the focus of the monarchy switched from 'England' to the 'Britain' which succeeded it (see Hopkins, this volume, Chapter 8). So, although the first allusion to 'issue' is to the issue of military success – Westmoreland's 'Uncertain of the issue any way' (1. 1. 61) – that issue is bound up with others in a way that makes it difficult to untangle the play's concerns. Although another messenger, Sir Walter Blunt, brings more emphatic word of an English victory, the news of Hotspur's 'conquest for a prince to boast of' (1. 1. 76) irks the king insofar as his own issue – Hal – is not 'the theme of honour's tongue' (1. 1. 80). Northumberland's issue is certain, Henry's less so. Northumberland's son, Harry Hotspur, issues forth into battle while that other Harry, Hal, Prince of Wales – and ales – is profligate with his time. When we see Hal jesting, and Ned Poins asks of him, 'Come, what's the issue?' (2. 5. 84–85), we see his father's problem. It's a fine time to be jesting when the kingdom's at war with itself and neighbouring 'others', the Scots and Welsh. Hal's subsequent speech shows that he knows what kind of issue Hotspur represents, and his decision to 'play Percy' (2. 5. 100), that other Harry, as bloodthirsty boaster rather than conquering prince shows that he has the measure of his mirror-image. Significantly, Hal is Prince of Wales at a time when the Welsh leader, Owen Glendower, is in the field, overpowering the English Mortimer:

> A thousand of his people butcherèd,
> Upon whose dead corpse' there was such misuse,
> Such beastly shameless transformation,
> By those Welshwomen done as may not be
> Without much shame retold or spoken of.   (1. 1. 42–46, p. 1158)

Here the question of issue and otherness is plainly presented. Genital mutilation of English soldiers by Welshwomen brings the issue into sharp relief. The King's plans to start a war 'in strands afar remote' (1. 1. 4) is short-circuited:

> It seems then that the tidings of this broil
> Brake off our business for the Holy Land. (1. 1. 47–48, p. 1158)

The issue of the monarch's uncertain issue and shaky claim to the crown, the issue of civil war, the issue of conflict between the nations of the Atlantic Archipelago – a term many now prefer to the 'British Isles' – and the issue of a deferred effort to displace these struggles onto a crusade are gathered together in this opening scene.

'Issue' in the reproductive sense also features prominently in the sonnets. In Sonnet 9 the speaker exclaims 'Ah, if thou issueless shalt hap to die', and offers a kind of immortality in Sonnet 13, 'When your sweet issue your sweet form should bear' (8), as protection against the 'barren rage of death's eternal cold' (12). Later in the sequence, the speaker complains that hopes for 'this abundant issue' of the beloved's presence turn out to be 'But hope of orphans and unfathered fruit' (Sonnet 97, 9–10). Feminist and queer readings of the sonnets are interested in the issue of issue. Valerie Traub, in 'Sex Without Issue: Sodomy, Reproduction, and Signification in Shakespeare's Sonnets', analyses sodomy in the sonnets as 'simultaneously a construction of and reaction to gender and erotic difference' (1999: 432). Traub's conclusion underlines the complexity of the topic: 'Historically, Shakespeare's attempt to reserve sodomy as a signifier of heteroeroticism loses out; since the seventeenth century, sodomy has signified acts performed, legislated, and prosecuted primarily between men' (447). Traub insists that the failure or forgetting of Shakespeare's original project does not detract from its legacy. 'Sex without issue' remains on the agenda (see Hopkins, this volume, Chapter 8).

Sodomy

Taking their cue from Michel Foucault's allusion to 'sodomy – that utterly confused category' (Foucault 1978: 101), critics have analysed the messy, multiple meanings of sodomy in Shakespeare's day (Goldberg 1992; Halpern 2002). Jonathan Goldberg recovers the early modern synonym, 'sodometrie', in order to suggest that sodomy is 'a measure whose geometry we do not know', while for Richard Halpern it 'constitutes a kind of empty hole in discourse, about which nothing directly *can* be said' (Goldberg 1992: xv; Halpern 2002: 9). This complicating and opening up of confused category of marginalized transgression has extended our understanding of the cultural and discursive nature of a sodomy, and sexuality more generally, in the period, but this broadening of perspective still does not go far enough for some scholars, including feminists. According to Valerie Traub, ' "female homosexuality" was not only *not* criminalized, it did not exist as a legal category in early modern England. That women were prosecuted under sodomy statutes on the Continent (but only then in cases of passing as a man and using a

---

dildo) suggests that we must account for national differences in the recognition of what *counts* as sexual transgression' (Traub 1997: 540–41). In other words, sodomy cannot be separated from questions of gender and nation.

Speaking of Claudius, Horatio tells Hamlet:

It must be shortly known to him from England
What is the issue of the business there.   (5. 2. 72–73, p. 1748)

Imagining Horatio's lines spoken or written in 1600 just before Elizabeth's death, with James VI of Scotland waiting offstage to enter as James VI of Britain, gives 'issue' a particular topicality. In *The Tempest*, the question of issue is raised, then racialized:

Thy mother was a piece of virtue, and
She said thou wast my daughter; and thy father
Was Duke of Milan, and his only heir
And princess no worse issued.   (1. 2. 56–59, p. 3058)

Later, Ferdinand hopes 'For quiet days, fair issue, and long life' (4. 1. 24), to which Prospero responds 'Fairly spoke' (4. 1. 31). Juno's blessing is that Ferdinand and Miranda be 'honoured in their issue' (4. 1. 105). This 'issue' does not just unite two families, and two states. It also contributes to the construction of national identity in the colonial margins (Brown 1985). Gonzalo's words late in the play make explicit its concern with the reproduction of a humanist self against the alternative barbarous Other:

Was Milan thrust from Milan, that his issue
Should become kings of Naples? O rejoice
Beyond a common joy! And set it down
With gold on lasting pillars: in one voyage
Did Claribel her husband find at Tunis,
And Ferdinand her brother found a wife
Where he himself was lost; Prospero his dukedom
In a poor isle; and all of us ourselves,
When no man was his own.   (5. 1. 208–16, p. 3103)

The progress of Prospero's issue has been interrupted by usurpation and exile; many of those temporarily 'othered' by their experience on the island are transformed into selves. Other Shakespearean texts hitherto read for their exploration of 'selfhood' – *Hamlet*, the sonnets, *The Tempest* – are increasingly read in terms of the relations between self and other.

Nationalism, Colonialism and Race

If the notion of nation, always accepted as a key feature of the histories, has been expanded and expounded upon, race remains a more complex issue in Shakespeare studies (see Robson, this volume, Chapter 5). Critics have long argued over whether the term can be applied to Shakespeare's time. Some see notions of ethnicity as modern developments, inapplicable to early modern Britain, while others regard race as at issue in English state formation. Moreover, such questions do not only come into play when considering the inhabitants of distant lands as they are dramatized in Shakespearean drama. Ireland is now almost an issue in its own right in Shakespeare studies, with *The Tempest* fast becoming the Irish play (see Hopkins, this volume, Chapter 8). According to Lynda Boose: 'If "race" originates as a category that hierarchically privileges a ruling status and makes the Other(s) inferior, then for the English the group that was first to be shunted into this discursive derogation and thereafter invoked as almost a paradigm of inferiority was not the black "race" – but the Irish "race" '. Boose sees the English view of Ireland as one in which 'the derogation of the Irish as "a race apart" situates racial difference within cultural and religious categories rather than biologically empirical ones' (1994: 36).

Colonial readings of *The Tempest* venture well beyond Ireland. According to the Kenyan writer, Ngugi wa Thiong'o:

> The play is interesting in that it has all the images that are later to be reworked into a racist tradition particularly in popular European literature about the colonised people: the savage as a rapist, lazy, a lover of whisky, stupid, cannibalistic. But the main thing is that Shakespeare does give to Caliban the capacity or voice to say 'no'. Caliban is invested with energy. And remember that at the time, Europe has occupied only a little corner of the globe. (1993: 15)

Stephen Greenblatt says that 'self-fashioning occurs at the point of encounter between an authority and an alien [and] what is produced in this encounter partakes of both [. . .] and hence [. . .] any achieved identity always contains within itself the signs of its own subversion or loss' (1980: 9). The colonial reading is complicated insofar as the island is not the final destination of Prospero, or of his brother, but rather it provides a pretext for the working out of domestic disorder, and for the restoration of that order 'at home'. In that sense it is tempting to see it as merely pastoral, like the Forest of Arden, rather than necessarily exotic. Prospero himself is part Faustus, part King Lear, disaffected scholar and deposed ruler who finds a fresh force in nature, an Edgar in Ariel, an Edmund in Caliban.

But the colonial pretext is as important as the colonial context. After all, one benefit of Empire – or war – was the resolving or suspending of class tensions, and there is a sense in which *The Tempest* is a play about class – the discourse of masterlessness explored by Brown and Norbrook – and about the importance of applying theory, since Prospero was bookish without being politically astute till he reached Caliban's Island. Colonial ventures, like wars and crusades, offered ideal opportunities for the Renaissance state to divert the attention of its subjects.

The Tempest, with its peculiar confusion of places, ranging from the Mediterranean to the Caribbean, by way of the bogs of Ireland, has suggested itself as one of the most obvious locations of a concern with discovery and the encounter with the Other. One could see this either as a narrowing of perspective – compared to the old idea of the universal hero, translatable across cultures – or as an opening up of the text to more specific ideas of difference and identity, depending on one's critical position.

Race and representation have occupied much recent criticism, which has encouraged us to consider a black *Hamlet*, a Chinese *Twelfth Night*, an Irish *Tempest*, a Welsh and Scottish and Irish dimension to *1 Henry IV*, and a sonnet sequence in which the Dark Lady invokes a racialized romance. Jonathan Crewe, in '*Black Hamlet*: Psychoanalysis on Trial in South Africa' (2001), reads Wulf Sachs's 1937 study of that name – republished in 1947 and again in 1996 – as a failed attempt to impose a universalizing psychoanalytic model upon native African culture. In his work, Sachs, a leading South African psychoanalyst, had staged a dialogue between himself and a native healer-diviner whom he dubbed the 'black Hamlet'. Crewe argues that Sachs's bias, and with it the colonial mindset of Western psychoanalysis, reveals itself in the assimilationist assumptions of the exchange. Peter Erickson, in 'Can We Talk About Race in *Hamlet*?' (2002), explores the play's rhetoric of race, homing in, as does Patricia Parker, in '*Black Hamlet*: Battening on the Moor' (2003), on the passage where the prince compels his mother to compare her first and second husbands, demanding of her:

> Could you on this fair mountain leave to feed,
> And batten on this moor?   (3. 4. 65–66, p. 2143)

Where Erickson argues that *Hamlet* is preoccupied with whiteness as a sign of vulnerability, and that the questions of race it raises are also questions of nation, for Parker, 'Hamlet's opposition of "faire" and "Moore" iterates the polarizations of its culture, foregrounding its material "foils", in a context in which empire itself is ironized' (Erickson 2002; Parker 2003: 151). Gary Taylor has also shown the extent to which the play engages from its earliest performances as well as its opening lines with the question of the outsider. In *'Hamlet* in Africa 1607', Taylor presents extracts 'from the only surviving journals kept on the *Red Dragon* in 1607, en route from England to India and the Spice Islands on the Third Voyage of the East India Company' (2000: 211). Taylor's exploration of the earliest non-European performance of Shakespeare's most famous tragedy – off the coast of Sierra Leone – adds weight to the growing body of work envisaging *Hamlet*, that great play of self and psyche, as a play as sophisticatedly engaged with nation and race as *Henry V* or *Othello*.

Much of the new work on Shakespeare borrows freely from the old, picking up on hints dropped like handkerchiefs by earlier critics. Parker points out that although Dover Wilson as early as 1934 made the connection between Claudius and colour, 'it has not yet penetrated the consciousness of most critics, readers, and audiences of this most canonical of plays – from a corpus in which Moors are assumed to belong only to *Titus Andronicus, Antony and Cleopatra, The Merchant of Venice*, or *Othello'* (127). While Parker harks back to Dover Wilson, in 'Hamlet and the Scottish Succession?' (1994), Stuart Kurland borrows his title from a book published in 1921 by Lilian Winstanley. Where Winstanley had identified Hamlet with James VI, Kurland avoids such simplistic one-to-one correspondences, but takes seriously the claim that *Hamlet* is a play about the succession crisis whose historical context is the imminent succession of James, a Scottish king, to a new British throne. Kurland argues that the Scottish succession can be read as impinging on the play in a variety of ways. During the composition of *Hamlet* between 1599 and 1601 there were rumours James VI might take the English crown by force, with the help of his brother-in-law, Christian IV of Denmark. Kurland concludes that *Hamlet* can instructively be read in relation to the struggle surrounding the impending Union of Crowns between England and Scotland, so that 'the political world of the play is informed by the uncertainty engendered by James VI's maneuvers and threats to secure the English succession' (1994: 293). Andrew Hadfield pursues Kurland's argument further, revealing the extent to which a Scottish historical context can be established for a play increasingly regarded as one of Shakespeare's British plays, preoccupied with union and succession. Hadfield presents the case gingerly: 'Why Shakespeare would not have been able to write a play that dealt directly with the Scottish succession is rather easier to comprehend: Elizabeth had forbidden any discussion of the succession and by the last years of the sixteenth century the most likely successor to Elizabeth was James VI of Scotland' (2004: 93).

Race is also being read in the sonnets, and a new Other has stepped into the light in the shape of the 'dark lady'. Kim Hall (1998) explores 'whiteness' as a racial category, rather than as a supposed sign of innocence and purity. Marvin Hunt (1999) contrasts a little-known early seventeenth-century lyric tradition extolling the virtues of African women with the ways in which critics' discussions of the lady feature 'anxiety, revulsion, and covert desire' (369). Repeating a remark by Margreta de Grazia, Hunt points out that Shakespearean critical tradition 'has ever been slower to entertain the possibility that the poems express desire for a black woman than desire for a boy' (386; de Grazia 1994: 48). As with male-female sodomy, some acts and aspects are played down by editors and critics. It is a measure of the renewed interest in race that the dark lady has joined the list of Shakespeare's others, a list that grows with each opening up of the works to new readings.

Nor has *Twelfth Night* escaped the scoping exercise that has been finding out Otherness in unfamiliar places. Another instance of a footnote being raised into the body of an argument is the case of Shakespeare's use of the word 'Cataian' or 'Catayan'. Again, the evidence is noted by editors, but is thought tangential to the main action of the play. The scene in which the expression occurs is replete with gnomic allusions to race and nation, including Sir Andrew's praise for Feste's clowning:

> In sooth, thou wast in very gracious fooling last night, when thou spokest of Pigrogromitus, of the Vapians passing the equinoctial of Queubus.
> (2. 3. 19–21)

This elicits the enigmatic reply:

> My lady has a white hand, and the Myrmidons are no bottle-ale houses.
> (2. 3. 24–25)

Clearly, a good deal of clowning is going on here, but since the word 'clown' itself has a colonial context it is clowning of a particularly purposeful kind. The *OED* cites Fuller's *Worthies* II, 177: 'Clown from Colonus, one that plougheth the ground', but much earlier, in Holinshed's *Chronicles* (1577), Richard Stanyhurst observed that the Irish called the English settlers 'Collonnes of the Latin word *Coloni*, whereunto the clipt English worde, Clowne, seemeth to be aunswerable' (Maley 1997: 32). All the editorial dismissals of these lines as pure nonsense are rendered problematic once one begins to see the growing matrix of cross-cultural references in this play. Elsewhere, in *Troilus and Cressida*, we are reminded that Achilles is 'the Great Myrmidon' (1. 3. 371), leader of that mythical nation. The earlier editorial tradition that saw this whole passage as pure nonsense or just the drink talking is now being overtaken by a much more vigorous critical interest in the diverse cultural geography of Shakespeare's dramatic models.

When Maria rebukes him for 'caterwauling' and threatens him with ejection by Olivia's orders, Sir Toby replies:

> My lady's a Catayan, we are politicians, Malvolio's a Peg-o'-Ramsey, and
> 'Three merry men be we'. Am not I consanguineous? Am I not of her
> blood? Tilly-vally – 'lady'! There dwelt a man in Babylon, lady, lady'.
> (2. 3. 68–71, p. 1784)

Leaving aside the issue of caterwauling – which the *OED* defines as 'The cry of cats at rutting time; their rutting or heat', and 'Going after the opposite sex; lecherous motions or pursuits', clearly a loaded expression in a play where who's who is hard to see or hear – Sir Toby's seemingly inscrutable speech about blood and Babylon, has perplexed editors, who have noted that 'Catayan' was synonymous with 'trickster', or 'cheat', as well as being 'ethnocentric slang' for Chinese, as the Norton puts it (1784, n. 6).

The fraught relationship between 'Cathay' and 'China' is explored by Timothy Billings (2003). Billings takes issue with 'a transhistorical cultural essentialism' (2) that manages to reconcile the use of the same term by the Page in *The Merry Wives of Windsor* (2. 1. 128) to designate Nym a *'Chinese; scoundrel'* (as the Norton glosses it), with Sir Toby's usage to categorize his kinswoman. Furnishing the gloss with an undercoat, Billings notes the difficulty in finding a synonym for 'a foul, Sinophobic insult for Nym and a delightful, cheeky jest for Olivia' (3). Billings cites a contemporary account of the Cathayans – not to be confused with the Chinese – as ' "white kinde of people, w[ith]oute beardes, of small eyes" ' (4). He goes on to speak of 'the *Cataian* as a site of cultural fantasy', for editors and glossators alike (6). Like the reluctance to see sodomy as part of heteroeroticism, or to see the dark lady as ethnically other, so Billings identifies another tradition within Shakespearean editing among those unhappy with the contradictory glossing of Sir Toby's phrase: 'From time to time, especially when unsettled by the idea of a Chinese Olivia, annotators have proposed glosses that have nothing whatever to do with Chinese ethnicity or with Cathay' (9). For Billings, Cathay or 'Cataia' is 'an Elizabethan phantasm distinct from "China" ', and was bound up with failed privateering ventures, which makes Feste's travelogue twittering rather more germane (11). If we now have to add Sinophobia to the list of aversions that courses through Shakespeare studies, then it is safe to say that the field has been enriched. Peter Erickson aside, there have been few treatments of race in the histories, and few takers for the passage of supposed nonsense in *1 Henry IV* where Hal befuddles Francis:

Why, then, your brown bastard is your only drink! For look you, Francis,
your white canvas doublet will sully. In Barbary, sir, it cannot come
to so much. (2. 5. 68–70)

The Norton Shakespeare glosses Barbary as 'North African region from which
England acquired sugar' (1180, n. 4), making no mention of Iago's denigration
of Othello as 'a Barbary horse' (1. 1. 113), Desdemona's mother having 'a maid
called Barbary' (4. 3. 25), or Claudius wagering 'six Barbary horses' on
Hamlet's quarrel with Laertes (5. 2. 108). Greenblatt's essay, 'Invisible Bullets',
refers to Hal's 'few words of calculated obscurity', and 'deliberately mystify-
ing words' (1985a: 31, 32), but with Billings's reading of *Twelfth Night* in mind
it might be worth revisiting those lines.

Republicanism

Many critics have seen Shakespeare as both a 'royal propagandist' and advocate of empire (see introduction, this volume). However, an influential strand
of contemporary criticism suggests that Shakespeare was as preoccupied with
republican ideas as he was with royalty.

Usurpation is central to *Hamlet, The Tempest* and *1 Henry IV*. Horatio's questioning of the Ghost – 'What art thou that usurp'st this time of night' (1. 1. 44) –
establishes at that play's outset the theme of the dislodging of authority.
Andrew Hadfield takes the point further, seeing the play as preoccupied with
'whether to get rid of the incumbent monarch' (2003: 577). This is not to say
that Shakespeare's play pursues a republican line; rather it is to recognize that
the play's political complexity derives at least in part from both its immediate
political contexts and Shakespeare's immersion in the classical republican
writing he had already drawn on in his works. Hadfield points out that 'The
plot is [. . .] in essence a variation of the story of the killing of Tarquin, a
narrative of republican liberation that haunted Shakespeare's working life
and which was first used in *The Rape of Lucrece* (1594). There is no straightforward way out of the political impasse at Elsinore as there was in Rome. But
this may be a deliberate comment on the state of England in 1600' (2003: 577).

David Norbrook is another pioneering figure who has worked more
broadly on Renaissance republicanism. In his 1992 reading of *The Tempest*,
Norbrook fixes on the boatswain's refusal to answer Alonso's question,
echoed by Antonio, 'Where's the Master?' (1. 1. 8), except with a question of
his own: 'Do you not hear him?' (1. 1. 12). The storm is master now. And then
another, 'What cares these roarers for the name of king?' (1. 1. 15). Not a jot is
the answer. The roarers are the waves, but they might also be the workers, as
the boatswain prefaced his second question with the words 'You mar our
labour' (1. 1. 12). Norbrook sees in the play a willingness to explore political

perspectives antipathetic to monarchal rule, making the theatre a crucible of competing ideas: 'Despite their royal label, the King's Men owed most of their revenue to public performances; Shakespeare's plays were thus able to pit different discourses against each other with far greater freedom than courtly literature' (1992: 45).

Sexuality

Recent critical work concerned with questions of masculinity, effeminacy, the representation of women, patriarchy, cross-dressing and sexual politics has blurred genre boundaries as well as gender divisions (see Robson, this volume, Chapter 5). For example, although there was a time when gender was seen as an issue relevant chiefly to the comedies – bearing in mind the hierarchical approach that might want to rank the plays in terms of, first, tragedies, second, histories and third, comedies – it is now argued that questions of gender and sexuality are central to every treatment of national identity, and so it is hard to see how a full account of *Hamlet*, for example, could fail to take account of the gender politics of that play, especially in terms of the anxiety raised by the question of female succession. Anxiety about female rule was intense in the period, and John Knox's *First Blast of the Trumpet against the Monstrous Regiment of Women* (1558) was part of an assault on women rulers. What do you do when there's no male heir, a problem that faced Elizabethan England (see Hopkins, this volume, Chapter 8)? Moreover, if cross-dressing is an issue in the comedies where a boy dressed as a woman dresses as a man, then it must also be an issue in the other plays, where all the parts in the original productions were played by male actors. The work of Jonathan Goldberg (1992), Laura Levine (1994) and Steven Orgel (1989) forces us to rethink the boundaries of the various genres, and to dwell in particular on the way in which issues of gender and genre interact.

Arthur Marotti's essay, ' "Love is Not Love": Elizabethan Sonnet Sequences and the Social Order', for example, reads the Elizabethan sonnet sequence as being preoccupied chiefly not with sexual but social desires: 'Both historical precedent and contemporary usage sanctioned such poetry as a means of expressing personal ambition, and not simply that of the artistic kind. From the time of the troubadours, courtly authors in particular used love poetry as a way of metaphorizing their rivalry with social, economic, and political competitors' (1982: 398). Marotti cites Sir John Harington, who in 1591 characterized love rivals as 'those that be suters to one woman, as are competitors to one office' (1982: 399). The pun on 'office' and 'orifice' was a common one. Marotti's allegorical study argues that political ambition is represented through romantic aspiration.

Unable to speak openly about ambition, young male writers were instead speaking of unrequited love, by which they meant frustrated aspirations more generally. The case works better for public figures like Philip Sidney, whose sonnets resemble job applications or excerpts from a *curriculum vitae*, than for Shakespeare. Marotti's essay was contested by feminists and queer theorists for underplaying the importance of gender and sexuality. For feminists, Marotti's model meant women were damned twice, first by being marginalized and objectified, and then for thinking the sonnets were about them in the first place.

With regard to *Twelfth Night*, other critics complicate the picture of sexual politics further: Jonathan Crewe (1995) explores the variety of cultural habits of thinking about transvestism; Jami Ake (2003) discerns a lesbian poetics; Casey Charles (1997) applies Judith Butler's theory of gender-as-performance. Marotti subsumes sexual into social desire – the poems are more about social than sexual ambition. But critics like Keir Elam insist that the social and the sexual are united in a figure like Viola, who is both public and private, polite and theatrical, in a sense 'disembodied' and yet 'erotically corporal' (1996: 36).

The history of Shakespeare criticism shows each new generation of critics preoccupied with issues affecting their own time. If you go to a Shakespeare conference now you'll hear papers on Queer Shakespeare, Radical Shakespeare, Feminist Shakespeare, Deconstructive Shakespeare, Postcolonial Shakespeare, Postmodern Shakespeare, even Cyber Shakespeare. The margins have taken over the centre. This means that a lot of criticism that seemed subversive or radical in its day, thirty years ago, is the new orthodoxy. Let us remind ourselves that Nigel Lawson declared Shakespeare a Tory in the wake of a landslide victory for the Conservatives. Times have changed, and critical trends change with them.

Nigel Lawson, invoked by Margot Heinemann as an example of the commandeering of Shakespeare by a conservative political tradition, is less well known now than his daughter, TV chef Nigella, who provides some food for thought in a knowing aside about remembrance and bereavement. In her cookbook *Feast: Food That Celebrates Life*, Nigella focuses on comfort food in a section entitled 'Funeral Feast' when in the final recipe she gives the ingredients for Rosemary Remembrance Cake, in memory of her grandmother (2004: 458). Nigella's nod to Hamlet – 'There's rosemary, that's for remembrance' (4. 5. 173) – shows a greater awareness of cross-currents in Shakespeare studies than her father, for food and memory are emerging as central issues, as witness Joan Fitzpatrick's *Food in Shakespeare* (2007) and Peter Holland's edited collection *Shakespeare, Memory and Performance* (2006). The link between the Lawsons is a continuing awareness of Shakespeare's importance as a culturally central figure who speaks to more corners and constituencies of the realm than any other.

11 # Making Meanings: Shakespeare's Poetry for the Theatre

Ros King

Words and Sounds

There are more things in Shakespeare criticism and performance practice than can have been dreamt of by Shakespeare. Indeed, reading, performing and writing about art from the past needs to speak both emotionally and cognitively to a contemporary audience if it is to be more than a mere educational exercise or an indulgence in heritage nostalgia. It has to matter to us now, else why should we bother with it?

Many, perhaps most, current critics declare that it is in fact impossible to view the play from anything other than the present standpoint (see Hopkins, this volume, Chapter 8). We cannot know what Shakespeare thought. We are not even completely clear what he wrote. In Terence Hawkes's famous phrase, Shakespeare does not mean but we mean by Shakespeare. Of course, there have also been productions of plays such as *Henry V* (like Nicholas Hytner's for the National Theatre in London (2003)) which have presented the play as anti-war (and specifically anti-war-in-Iraq) by grimly presenting the speech that Henry makes before the walls of Harfleur, where he threatens to kill, rape and pillage the inhabitants of that town in order to force its surrender. It is a brutal speech and is usually cut from productions, such as Olivier's film, that seek to make Henry heroic.

Shakespeare's audience would have recognized that similar terrible acts had been taking place just across the channel as the Duke of Alva's army marched through the Low Countries, sacking captured towns which had not surrendered before siege (and sometimes those that had). Some of them may have taken part in that war, in the Duke of Leicester's army, sent by Elizabeth in support of the Dutch Protestants, and there were English mercenaries on the Spanish side (see King 2008; Fraser 2008). These atrocities, sanctioned by the law of war and by the Bible, took place on both sides, as they usually do. And Dutch artists, like Pieter Breughel, depicted them in paintings as the biblical massacre of the innocents, using the pity of a New Testament human story to refute what those with power claimed as divinely sanctioned law (Kunzle 2002). The use of the past to explore the present was an essential part of Renaissance culture, and the invention of a no-place, which never existed in either time or space, is a good way of exploring the present with a certain amount of impunity.

Shakespeare never sets a play in historically accurate time; even his history plays are anachronistic inventions that play with time, space, people and events. This metaphorical construction, combined with the flexibility and inventiveness of his language, raises many more questions than it answers, and has from the very beginning encouraged others to want to reinterpret and recreate his work. It is partly this quality that constitutes his enduring social and artistic value. But for these later treatments to work, adapters and performers need a nuanced understanding of how Shakespeare was using history and fantasy as a metaphor in the first place.

Memory and Performance History

We now expect each new production of Shakespeare to be exactly that – new – and no longer go to the theatre demanding to judge how well a particular actor performs a well-worn routine of stage business. An eighteenth-century Hamlet was supposed to turn as white as his neckerchief on first seeing the ghost; at the end of the nineteenth century, Sarah Bernhardt, one of a long line of female Hamlets, was roundly castigated in the press for introducing new business (rudely swinging her legs up to lie on a bench while talking to Polonius)[1] (see Hiscock/Longstaffe, this volume, Chapter 1). Her performance was deplored by the dramatist Elizabeth Robins as too much the 'scampish schoolboy' (1900: 909). Robins compares the characterization unfavourably with that of Edwin Booth, whom she saw in her youth: 'if I set down more of

Booth in detail than of Madame Bernhardt, it is because, although I saw her yesterday, and that other Hamlet years ago, the old performance is vivid still from end to end, and the new one only here and there' (914).

Robins's rationale for her strictures, like Bernhardt's own spirited defence of her innovations in the London *Times*, are couched in similar terms. Both claim to want a convincing reality in the performance itself, combined with faithfulness to Shakespeare. Both share the desire for honesty, dynamism and 'rightness' in theatre performance, but the performances under discussion clearly seemed very different at the time. Robins's account of Booth's poetic rendition of the role, however, suggests a performance that would most likely be as unconvincing to us now as Bernhardt's performance of Hamlet's final duel, currently showing on YouTube.[2]

The theatre history approach to the plays is a relatively new technique and is still being developed. (see Hampton-Reeves' Chapter 6 and Hopkins' Chapter 8, this volume) The most recent Arden and New Cambridge Shakespeare, for example, include details of performance in their critical commentaries and annotations. But merely extracting moments from a range of different performances, as has tended to happen, is no more than anecdotal. It does not demonstrate how that individual performance or production was conceived or received as a whole, nor does it give sufficient attention to the nature of the text being performed – that is the extent to which it has been altered or indeed rewritten for that production. Most important of all, despite twenty years of insistence that Shakespeare wrote for the stage, not the page, we have tended to ignore the *potential* for performance in these texts, whether in fact they have been performed that way or not (see also Cordner 2006).

In a short article in an internet round table on authorial intention, Cary Mazer suggests that the 'goal of the performance historian ... is to ask not *what* a particular theatre artist, in a particular time and place, *means* by Shakespeare, but *how* that artist means by Shakespeare, i.e. what the artist understands about how Shakespeare's scripts generate meaning and effect in performance'.[3] Such a project deals with a number of different points in history (that of the play, of the performance and other remembered performances, as well as our present), and it deals with a number of different states of the text (the earliest printed version[s], many of which display extensive variation, as well as later prompt book[s] for specific productions). Where available it will also draw on descriptions of stage effects, reviews and, occasionally, the diaries kept by performers. This comparative technique can begin to draw correlations between what was performed, how it was performed, why it was performed at that period and what the effect was then. It shows what has to be done to the text to create different meanings, and allows one to evaluate *how* meaning is constructed. None of this postulates authorial intention – what Shakespeare himself thought or meant, which will remain impossible to determine. But it does enable us to evaluate the different potential for meaning in different versions of the text.

Text and Performance

It is easy to notice when a Shakespearean text has been altered by being rewritten or added to (see Hiscock/Longstaffe, this volume, Chapter 1). But cuts can have as profound effects as additions on the meanings and context of the worlds that remain. Productions of *Othello* frequently cut the dialogue in which Desdemona plays up to her role as the commander's wife by countenancing, even encouraging and then equably reproving the bawdy jokes of her husband's trusted ensign (2. 1. 99–162). Such cutting denies us full access to the assured and spirited young woman who can talk as readily to the Venetian senate about the grand themes of love and war as she can to the common soldiery about domestic sexuality. Too many hapless Desdemonas have been shorn of their verbal and social skills through the cutting of that scene with Iago, often blamed for interfering in matters that do not concern them in the Cyprus scenes, and are thus left merely pathetic at the end. We rarely see Desdemonas onstage who are anything other than naïve, and that traditional image blinds literary critics – who like invariably ignore that scene of bawdy banter sometimes blaming the play for its supposedly misogynistic, victimizing treatment of its heroine (see Ziegler 2008). It is not the text but the cut that is misogynistic.

Shakespeare: Literary Author

The 1623 First Folio is one of the most celebrated and most studied books in the world. As rare books go, however, it is not particularly uncommon with about forty complete extant copies (and as many as 228 incomplete copies), and it is not particularly beautiful or well printed. It is also widely reproduced both on the internet and in printed facsimile. Most copies are now housed in universities or other public library collections, with seventy-nine in the Folger Library, Washington. The current market value of any *individual* copy (up to £3.5 million) and the brouhaha that erupts when one comes on sale is thus out of proportion either to its intrinsic value as a *book*, or its ability to contribute to our knowledge and understanding of the *plays* whose printed representations it contains. Rather, its value is produced by a fetishizing of Shakespeare as a moral force that teaches us how to live.

Some of those wishing to debunk the idea of a morally improving, establishment Shakespeare therefore fell with enthusiasm on a perhaps infelicitous term 'authorial instability', coined by the textual scholar Ernst Honigmann, to describe the process whereby an author, copying his own work, may sometimes introduce small variations in the choice of word which are artistic-ally neither better nor worse than those he had chosen previously. The term instability was taken up by those who wished to correct the notion of Shakespeare as unique genius by insisting that drama is a 'collaborative' activity and the texts that have come down to us the result of 'collaboration' between printer, actor, book keeper, scribe and any of a multitude of peo-ple who may have had some kind of influence over the printed text or the manuscript from which it was copied.

Publishing Shakespeare, Performing Shakespeare

Lukas Erne's recent book *Shakespeare as Literary Dramatist* (2003) is an attempt to redress the balance. He argues that the substantial differences between the texts of some of the plays in the Folio and their earlier manifestations in single-play editions can be accounted for by the argument that most Shakespeare plays are too long to be performed in the 2–3 hours 'traffic of the stage'. Shakespeare, he says, knew that the company would cut his plays down to size and deliberately wrote more than they would want, because he was aiming at publication in print. Successful productions by university-based professional companies on both sides of the Atlantic demonstrate that what determines audience understanding and willing endurance is the pace of delivery.[4] Shakespeare's verse is very much more comprehensible when taken at a pace that allows audiences to grasp the shape of whole speeches. This has been known for a long time, although it is rarely practised. Review-ing Harley Granville-Barker's production of *The Winter's Tale* in 1912, John Palmer observed that Leontes 'delivered some of his speeches very rapidly, because they were speeches which are unintelligible if they are delivered slowly' (*Saturday Review*, 23 November 1912).

The cultural value attached to Shakespeare in the twentieth century, however, encouraged the assumption that sixteenth- and early-seventeenth-century publishers were fighting each other and the theatre companies for the right to print play-texts. Nevertheless, an important essay by Peter Blayney has convincingly argued that this is a myth (Blayney 1997). By calculating the economic costs of book production, Blayney demonstrates that no-one got rich publishing play-texts, and suggests that it was the acting companies that stood to benefit from publication since the appearance of the printed book would provide valuable free advertising for any revival of a play that was a few years old. Judging by the number of reprints of play editions, he also shows that plays by Shakespeare were only the sixth and seventh most popu-lar in print. The top places go to two closet and academic dramas which were never aired on the public stage, and also to three plays, which seem to have had an unusually strong hold on the public stage over many years: *Mucedorus*;

Dr Faustus; and *The Spanish Tragedy* (Blayney 1997: 388). Despite this, Erne's book is heavily dependent on that article and quotes from it liberally. He gathers a comprehensive collection of the albeit scanty extant evidence, yet even while acknowledging that less than half of Shakespeare's plays were published in his lifetime, he states repeatedly and emphatically that Shakespeare wrote specifically for publication in print. The evidence just does not support that assertion.

Perhaps the major problem with Erne's thesis is the fact that ordinary readers find play-texts difficult to read. Modern readers ascribe that difficulty to the age of the language and the complexity of the poetry; they frequently express amazement that they can understand the plays perfectly well when they see them performed in the theatre or on video, and, sometimes, if they read them out loud. Readers also remark on the lack of stage directions in Shakespeare, which they find makes it difficult to picture what is going on.[5] The remainder of this chapter will be devoted to demonstrating that Shakespeare's stage directions are in fact embedded in the dialogue to a far greater extent than is normally appreciated even by critics. It is not so much the language that is the problem, but the shortcomings of the processes of silent reading when dealing with this particular kind of text.

The title page of *Damon and Pythias* (1571), one of the earliest of Elizabethan printed plays, gives a clue as to what might have been happening. It appears that the intended readership for the printed edition of that play was not the single, silently reading individual of twenty-first-century experience, but the group. It states both the occasion of its intended first performance and its function as a printed book: 'Newly imprinted, as the same was shewed before the Queenes Maiestie, by the Children of her Graces Chappell, except the Prologue that is somewhat altered for the proper use of them that hereafter shall have occasion to plaie it, either in private, or open audience.' In other words, it was published with the expectation that it would be *performed*, perhaps in amateur theatricals at home, or perhaps in the school classroom, since participation in theatrical performance, whether in Latin or in English, was an expected part of a sixteenth-century humanist education. This then may also be the reason why so many of Shakespeare's plays chosen for publication in print are improving histories or those with classical connections.

Shakespeare: Performance Poet

Coriolanus is famous for possessing one of the very few performative stage directions in the whole of Shakespeare: '*He holds her by the hand, silent*' (5. 3. 183). It is an agonizing moment, and not only because of the tense emotion between mother and son at this point. She has asked him in the name of family and Roman loyalty to call off his attack on Rome. The silence allows memories of all the conflicting loyalties that have formed Coriolanus's relationship with his native city and indeed with his mother up to this moment. It also anticipates the end, letting us understand that he knows what will happen to him if he now betrays his new allies, the Volsces. They are not alone on stage; they are surrounded by other watching, waiting, silent groups of people, each of whom has a different agenda. Coriolanus's wife, son and the family friend Valeria on the one hand presumably see only the family ties and the prospect of their own deaths if their embassy fails. Aufidius and the Volsces he leads, on the other hand, must be looking at the divided loyalty of this turncoat in their midst, and considering how they will deal with him when he turns again. The longer this silence is held, the more time an audience has to register these conflicting imperatives, and to develop the necessary empathy for a character who has been far from sympathetic for most of the play. It is not a moment that could be engineered through dialogue.

This stage direction has commonly been regarded as unique although there are others: '*Stand forth Demetrius*' and '*Stand forth Lysander*' in *A Midsummer Night's Dream* (1. 1. 24–26) and '*Silence*' as Hermione walks in to her trial in *The Winter's Tale* (3. 2. 10). All three appear in the Folio text in italics, ranged to the right of the column. As stage directions, they have great potential for performance: humorous in *Dream*; and a profound expression of unease in *The Winter's Tale*. But in modern editions they are usually rendered as verbal commands (assigned to Egeus and to a court official respectively), and the effect is invariably stilted.

In *Coriolanus*, this moment has been preceded by a speech in which two very different techniques have been used to write both silence and action into the words.

> My wife comes foremost, then the honoured mould
> Wherein this trunk was framed, and in her hand
> The grandchild to her blood. But out affection,
> All bond and privilege of nature break;
> Let it be virtuous to be obstinate.
> What is that curtsey worth? Or those dove's eyes
> Which can make gods forsworn? I melt, and am not
> Of stronger earth than others: my mother bows
> As if Olympus to a mole hill should
> In supplication nod: and my young boy
> Hath an aspect of intercession, which
> Great Nature cries, 'Deny not'. Let the Volsces
> Plough Rome, and harrow Italy; I'll never
> Be such a gosling to obey instinct: but stand

As if a man were author of himself,
And knew no other kin.
    (*Coriolanus*, F text, with modernized spelling, 5. 3. 22–37)

Coriolanus observes as his wife walks into view, followed by his mother holding the hand of the boy he denotes not as his son, but as her grandson. He describes a succession of actions: his wife curtsies; her gentle eyes make him 'melt'. He surprises himself by this. He is not of 'stronger earth' than others after all. His mother bows to him, her aristocratic bearing and his lifelong feelings of not being good enough expressed in 'As if Olympus to a Mole-hill, should / In supplication nod'; his little boy, perhaps just because he is a child, and perhaps because as in some productions he lifts up his arms in supplication, exerts a pressure on him 'which great Nature' cries, 'Deny not'. Those trained to obey the line lengths in the poetry, might also notice the way in which the final word in so many of these lines carries a strong stress, demanding to be lingered over, even while the sense pushes on into the next line. The long syllables and consecutive stresses of 'Plough Rome' are counterpoised by the sharp stresses on the first syllables of the two words 'harrow Italy', completely disrupting the metre, while the surprising idea that he could liken himself to a gosling (even though it was geese that defended the Roman capitol) combines with the explosive sound of the word, and in this case readily lends itself to the expression of exasperation. It is intensely emotional; nevertheless he composes himself on the stressed word 'stand' at the end of the line, and the following line and a half is, for the first time in this speech since 'But out affection', in regular iambs.

But when verse lines are shared between characters, other techniques in the writing and presentation of dialogue for actors come into play, which we have only recently begun to appreciate. Experienced actors would realize that paying attention to the way in which an accomplished writer for the theatre arranges words in line lengths that variously reinforce and intercut patterns of both rhetoric and rhythm would help them to create a performance (see Tucker 2001, which is based on his workshops and experimental productions with the Original Shakespeare Company; also Palfrey and Stern 2007).

In the folio text the lineation is as follows:

	As if a man were author of himself, and knew no other kin.
Virgilia	My lord and husband.
Coriolanus	These eyes are not the same I wore in Rome.
Virgilia	The sorrow that delivers us thus changed
	Makes you think so.
Coriolanus	Like a dull actor now, I have forgot my part,
	And I am our, even to a full disgrace. Best of my Flesh

> Forgive my tyranny: but do not say
> For that forgive our Romans. (F text, TLN 3385–93; 5. 3. 35–44)

A good actor will hear echoes and counterparts to his own lines in the lines of another. Virgilia's cue word is 'kin', and her greeting 'My lord and husband' matches the meaning of that word and continues the metre seamlessly. Ironically, she thus denies Coriolanus's denial of kinship. His regular 'These eyes are not the same I wore in Rome' is secretly true, in that he has just been weeping, but overtly it is an attempt to try to convince her he no longer cares. Her response picks up his true meaning in the word 'sorrow' while concurring with one aspect of his overt meaning: they too are 'changed'. Metrically her first line here again matches his, but the subsequent half line turns that on its head. 'Makes you think so' reverses the stress pattern and also tells him he is wrong. Virgilia's line is metrically incomplete, but he is non-plussed and can think of nothing to say. There has to be a pause here, both because the sense of what he says next demands it – he is like an actor who has forgotten his lines – and because of the rhythmic form those words create. The rhythm is not iambic; indeed it is not even metrical. In the Folio he continues for another eleven non-metrical syllables, scrabbling around, perhaps gesturing, as bad actors do when they dry. When he composes himself again, however, he first picks up on Virgilia's stress/unstress rhythm, 'Best of my flesh', thus effectively completing her unfinished half line of verse, and overriding the non-metrical hiatus in between, before reverting to regular iambics.

This wonderfully theatrical prosody which suggests tone of voice, pace, pause and gesture is invariably smoothed out in modern editions:

Virgilia	The sorrow that delivers us thus changed
	Makes you think so.
Coriolanus	Like a dull actor now
	I have forgot my part, and I am out
	Even to a full disgrace. [*Rising*] Best of my flesh . . . (5. 3. 39–42)

How even, dull, and incomprehensible that sounds in comparison.

As an actor and performer himself, Shakespeare would have known how important it is for the performer to be allowed, indeed encouraged, to put his own stamp on the work. A good play-text needs to excite (not corral) the imagination of its first end user, the actor. Of course Shakespeare wrote to be read: reading is a necessary preliminary to speaking and performing his work. As a writer he needed to ensure that his plays could be vividly interpreted by actors, even when he was not there to instruct them, and to function as a springboard for the performative imagination.

Glossary of Critical and Theoretical Terminology

Peter Sillitoe

Absolutism: A continental form of kingship in which the 'absolute will' of the monarch takes precedence over all other forms of authority. In criticism surrounding early modern England, this is often wrongly associated with James I and, more correctly, associated with Charles I's reign.

Accent: The stressed syllables in verse, such as in Shakespeare's use of IAMBIC PENTAMETER.

Allegory: The term that applies to a metaphoric reading of characters in a work of art, as the reader is encouraged to 'read allegorically'. For instance, in Edmund Spenser's *Fairie Queene* the portrayal of many characters can be read as gesturing towards other characters or historical persons. Thus, Spenser's portrayal of Gloriana, the Faerie Queene, can be viewed through historical allegory as mirroring and suggesting Elizabeth I. Other types of allegory include moral, political and biblical/religious readings.

Anachronism: Wrongly assigning an object, practice, language use, costume etc. to an historical period where it does not belong.

Anapaest: A metrical foot, featuring two unstressed syllables and a final stressed syllable.

Aside: Part of a theatrical character's speech that is designed to be heard by the audience, but not the other characters on stage. Owing to this, the aside is often seen to privilege the audience, as witnessed at the opening of Shakespeare's *Richard III*. This differs, however, from the DIRECT ADDRESS to the audience.

Atheism: Believing that there is no god (from the Greek word meaning 'godlessness'). The connotations of this in Shakespeare's time were profoundly negative, and it was most often used as a catch-all term for immoral behaviour in general.

Bear-Baiting: The spectator sport of setting dogs on a chained bear, and betting on the results. In London this took place in dedicated venues such as the Bear Garden on the South Bank, which were centred on a roughly circular arena surrounded on all sides by seating. The shape was very similar to some of the open-air theatres, and indeed the Hope theatre (which was built on the site of the demolished Bear Garden in 1613) was also licensed for bear-baiting.

Blank Verse: Unrhymed IAMBIC PENTAMETER as used by Shakespeare and his fellow playwrights (see 'iambic pentameter').

Bombast: Heightened, but also overblown, use of language by a character on stage usually employed to show anger and/or rhetorical violence.

Book of Common Prayer: A standardized collection of prayers from the period of the English Reformation (see REFORMATION). The book was published in the mid-sixteenth century and so became symbolic for the PROTESTANT faith throughout the early modern age.

Caesura: A pause or halt in a line of poetry.

Catholicism/Roman Catholicism: The dominant Christian faith in Europe until the REFORMATION and the birth of PROTESTANTISM. The belief is marked by a commitment to the Virgin Mary and the divinely-inspired power of the Pope as the head of the Roman Church. In Shakespeare's lifetime, England was isolated from mainland European powers, such as Spain, in terms of a preference for the Protestant faith over Catholicism.

Character: The actual persona assumed by an actor during the performance. Thus, we might discuss 'Prince Hamlet', or 'the actor's portrayal of the character of Prince Hamlet'.

Chronicle: See HISTORY.

Church of England: The official English Protestant church as founded by its subsequent head, Henry VIII in 1534, when the king broke way from the Roman Catholic Church (see PROTESTANTISM and CATHOLICISM).

Clown: The title often given to comedic figures in Shakespearean drama, including Touchstone in *As You Like It*. However, the character might offer perceptive guidance to monarchs and courtly figures (see FOOL).

Co-authorship: A critical term that signifies dual authorship of a Renaissance text. For instance, there is now strong evidence that Shakespeare collaborated with George Peele on *Titus Andronicus*. Indeed, many scholarly studies are now increasingly interested in Shakespeare's literary position as a co-author in early modern London.

Conceit: The author's use of a combination of metaphors and/or similes in order to construct a verbal picture during an entire poem or section of verse in poetry and drama. Usually taken to be clever and witty as a rather 'learned' literary device.

Conversion: The act of undergoing a religious conversion, from the Catholic faith to the Protestant faith or vice versa.

Cross-Dressing: On the Shakespearean all-male stage, boy actors would be required to cross-dress in order to play the female roles, owing to the barring of female actors on the public stage until 1660.

Cultural Materialism: British-based version of NEW HISTORICISM (see below) as exemplified by the politically inflected work of Jonathan Dollimore and Alan Sinfield.

Direct Address: When a character addresses the audience, thus bridging the gap between actor and spectator, illusion and reality.

Editor: The editor of a (Shakespearean) text literally 'edits' the available material. In the past, Shakespearean editors have claimed that they were aiming to produce a version of the text as close as possible to the author's original idea of the script.

Effeminacy: The term used to describe the possession of stereotypically 'feminine' characteristics by a male, often with negative connotations. However, in Renaissance England the label was often applied to men who displayed a fondness for the supposedly feminine vice of pleasure-seeking and recreational gratification.

Elizabethan: Refers to cultural events during the reign of Queen Elizabeth I (1558–1603).

Empire: This signifies the expansion of one country at the expense of others and is therefore usually linked with the early modern colonialism, even though there was no English empire to speak of in the period. The phrase also has connotations of Roman classicism and was therefore important to James I and his failed project of the union of England with Scotland.

Enlightenment: The cultural, intellectual and artistic movement of the eighteenth century which included a renewed and re-energized interest in classicism, particularly in architecture and literature, as well as a flourishing of scientific and intellectual pursuit and debate. This European-based movement boasts key figures such as David Hume and Isaac Newton.

Ethnicity: Suggests a person's ethnic and cultural grouping and her or his racial identity. For instance, we might refer to Othello's ethnicity when compared to those around him in the play.

Exempla: Exempla is the plural form of the Latin word 'exemplum', which means 'example'. It is usually used of a short story intended to make a moral point.

Feminism: Gender-based approach to the study of literature and its cultural contexts as exemplified in the work of Catherine Belsey.

First Folio: The first printing of Shakespeare's collected works, published posthumously in FOLIO format in 1623. Texts of Shakespeare's plays taken from the First Folio are often referred to as F texts.

Flight of the Earls: See also the NINE YEARS WAR IN IRELAND (below). In 1607, the defeated Irish earls, Hugh O'Neill of Tyrone and Rory O'Donnell of Tyrconnell, fled Ireland for the continent in order to gain support from Spain against the English, though this was eventually not possible.

Folio: A printed work consisting of one fold of the paper used.

Fool: An often comedic figure in Shakespearean and Renaissance drama (see also CLOWN). However, the fool is occasionally used as a figure of sage and astute counsel and wisdom, particularly in *King Lear*.

Foul Papers: A working draft of the author's finished version of a play.

Grammar: Refers to sentence construction in the modern sense, but early modern usage implies rhetorical persuasion and even classical learning and humanism.

Guicciardini: Highly influential political thinker from the Italian Renaissance and one of the first major historians in the modern sense. See also MACHIAVELLI.

Guild: A collective of people associated with a particular craft or trade, often connected with London in the early modern period.

Hegemony: This refers to the authority and dominance of one group of people over many others. For instance, it might be argued that the Protestant faith in Renaissance England controlled those that followed the Catholic faith, or that an aristocratic elite enjoyed what they perceived as a political and cultural supremacy over the rest of the nation.

Historicism: A brand of intellectual inquiry defined by a rigorous commitment to historical and contextual cultural investigation. In literary studies, the practising critic might attempt to 'contextualize' a Shakespearean text in terms of its historical background and transmission. See also 'new historicism'.

Huguenot: French Protestants from the new Reformed Church of Calvin in the early modern period who were associated with strong feelings of anti-Catholicism.

Humanism: The Christian and educational movement known as Renaissance and/ or sixteenth-century humanism refers to the growth of interest in classical learning alongside Christian belief in the full, unique potential of all human beings. Key figures include Erasmus and Thomas More at the court of Henry VIII.

Iamb/Iambic: A metrical foot featuring an unstressed syllable followed by a stressed syllable.

Iambic Pentameter: Poetic metre of five iambic feet. Often used by Shakespeare and his contemporaries.

Image/Imagery: Language used by the playwright to construct a verbal picture in the mind of the audience and/or reader.

Internet Shakespeare Editions: An internet website that provides digital reproductions of Shakespearean texts in their original printed forms, including QUARTO and FOLIO versions.

Islam/Islamic: Muslim religion usually associated with the Ottoman Empire in Renaissance literary discourse. See also OTHERS.

Jacobean: Refers to cultural events during the reign of King James I.

Joint-Stock: See also 'guild'. Similar to the guilds of Renaissance London, but the joint-stock companies consisted of shareholders and are viewed as forerunners of capitalist enterprise and mercantile trade.

Jonson, Ben: Along with Shakespeare and Marlowe, probably one of the best-known Renaissance playwrights. Jonson wrote and published poetry as well as plays for the public theatre, including the Roman tragedy *Sejanus* (1603) and the city comedy *Volpone* (1606). However, Jonson is associated with the Jacobean court more than any other dramatist, as he wrote masques for the court at Whitehall Palace and beyond, including *The Masque of Blackness* (1605) for Queen Anna. Jonson's career spanned the late Elizabethan period through to the reign of Charles I, and he published, along the way, his collected *Works* in 1616.

Machiavelli, Niccolo: Enormously influential Italian political thinker associated with statecraft through his important 1513 text *The Prince*, a work of political theory. Machiavelli famously urged rulers to dominate through fear and violence, though his message was often exaggerated and taken out of context by English Renaissance writers. Many dramatic villains may be seen as stereotypical 'stage Machiavels', including Shakespeare's Richard III and Iago.

Materialism: An influential aspect of Marxism that prioritizes the physical and material forms of existence over spiritual thought. For instance, a materialist reading of a Shakespeare play might foreground the depiction of industrial and/or labour forces in the text. See also CULTURAL MATERIALISM.

Metadrama/Metatheatre: A mode of drama which compels audiences to reflect the mechanics of play-making and performance. An example of this is a 'play within a play' scene in a text such as the famous 'Mousetrap' in *Hamlet*. In such a scenario, the real audience will be watching an onstage audience of actors 'watching' a play.

Middleton, Thomas: Highly influential Renaissance dramatist, known particularly for his Jacobean tragedies and city comedies. Middleton often collaborated with other playwrights, particularly William Rowley, and, almost certainly, Shakespeare. His best-known plays include the controversial *A Game at Chess* (1624) and the *Revenger's Tragedy* (1606), though the authorship of the earlier play has often been questioned. Like Ben JONSON (see above), Middleton also wrote Jacobean masques and civic entertainments for the city of London.

Metaphor: A figurative trope in which two things are compared that would usually be seen to have little in common with the other (such as, for instance, 'sun' and 'king').

Monarchical: Refers to the dominance of a king or queen. For instance, 'monarchical discourse' as opposed to 'republican discourse'.

Morrano: Spanish Jews forced to conceal their cultural identity in the period.

Mystery Cycles/Mystery Plays: Highly didactic religious plays performed through the medieval period until the 1560s. Surviving examples include those from York, Coventry, Wakefield and Chester. Such plays fell out of favour during and after the REFORMATION, though they were performed during the early part of Shakespeare's life. Along with the morality tradition, this genre was influential on early Elizabethan public theatre, including the work of Marlowe.

New Historicism: Critical theory that places the literary text in a deep-rooted historical narrative drawing upon the ideas of the cultural theorist Michel Foucault. Best exemplified by the work of Stephen Greenblatt and Stephen Orgel.

Nine Years War in Ireland (1594–1603): The conflict between the native Irish, guided by Hugh O'Neill, and the Elizabethan settlers and soldiers. See also FLIGHT OF THE EARLS (above) for information on the Irish defeat and the resulting problems.

Others: A relatively recent critical term that suggests the opposite of the 'self'. For instance, an Elizabethan traveller might be the 'self' to the colonized 'other' in an American settlement. Similarly, critics often refer to the period's fascination with the 'self/other dichotomy'.

Patriarchy: Refers to any male-dominated society in which equality between the sexes is not prioritized. Thus, the rule of Queen Elizabeth I may be seen to have problematized the period's patriarchal codes.

Plantation: A settlement on foreign soil in which the members have to farm crops for sustenance. In the early modern period there were various American plantations, including the first, Jamestown.

Postcolonialism: Critical and cultural theory influenced by the work of Edward Said, particularly his volume *Orientalism* (1978). Often applied to Shakespeare's *Othello*, and, particularly, *The Tempest*. The use of this theory would typically include an examination of early modern England and/or Europe and an encounter with the 'New World' such as the Americas.

219

Proscenium Arch: The front section of a theatre where part of the architecture forms an arch across and above the location of theatrical activity, that being the physical stage which the actors occupy. As such, this approach to theatre building is the most widely used form of staging.

Prosody: Refers to the study of verse and metre. In Renaissance England a number of works were published that discussed the theme, including George Puttenham's influential *The Arte of English Poesie* (1589).

Protestant/Protestantism: The Christian faith that broke away from Catholicism in the sixteenth century during the Reformation. Key figures include Martin Luther and John Calvin. See also 'REFORMATION', 'CATHOLICISM' and 'BOOK OF COMMON PRAYER'.

Psychoanalytic Theory: Critical theory that is often applied to works such as *Hamlet* and is usually based on the work of Sigmund Freud and, particularly, his *Interpretation of Dreams* (1900). This critical methodology will tend to examine the psychological 'character' of a literary creation, such as the complex intellectualism of Prince Hamlet in Shakespeare's play.

Purgatory: In Catholic belief, an otherworld in which the soul of the recently deceased awaits a placement in heaven or hell.

Puritan/Puritanism: The Puritans were the most extreme group of Protestants (see PROTESTANT/PROTESTANTISM). The movement steered away from the ceremony of the Church of England and so became the most extreme Protestant alternative to Catholicism.

Quarto: A cheaper version of a printed book or pamphlet, as the paper is folded twice, creating a smaller size. The texts of those of Shakespeare's plays first published in this size are often referred to as Q1, Q2 etc.

Queer Theory: Critical theory that builds on the work of theorists such as Eve Kosofsky Sedgwick and Judith Butler, as well as the cultural historian Alan Bray and various literary critics, including the work of Jonathan Goldberg. This critical methodology attempts to uncover expectations surrounding gender performance and normative/non-normative representations of sexuality from the literary text and might be fruitfully applied, for instance, to Shakespeare's *As You Like It*.

Recusancy: The term applied to secret Catholics (see CATHOLICISM) in England who would not convert to PROTESTANTISM and the CHURCH OF ENGLAND during the Renaissance period.

Reformation: The religious changes brought about by the move from CATHOLICISM to PROTESTANTISM during the reigns of Henry VIII and Edward VI. The Catholic Mary I brought about a Catholic Counter-Reformation (1553–58) before Elizabeth I restored the Protestant religion.

Republican: Cultural and political viewpoint that abandons the need for a king or queen as the head of state. Best exemplified by the period after the civil wars in England (1649–60) before the restoration of the monarchy.

Revenge Tragedy: Popular Elizabethan and Jacobean genre influenced by Senecan drama. Among the first surviving examples in Elizabethan drama is Thomas Kyd's *Spanish Tragedy* (c. 1588–92). Shakespeare produced two plays of this nature, the early *Titus Andronicus* (c. 1592) and the more complex *Hamlet* (c. 1600–01).

Self-Fashioning: A term first used by the 'new historicist' critic Stephen Greenblatt (see above) in his 1980 monograph, *Renaissance Self-Fashioning*. Owing to the influence of this critical work, 'self-fashioning' has become an approved term in Renaissance scholarship. The expression refers to moments of self-creation and assertion by individual writers and literary characters.

Sententiae: This is the plural of 'sententia', which means 'judgement' in Latin. It refers to a short saying carrying a clear message (and so covers proverbs, epigrams and quotations). Polonius's 'Neither a borrower nor a lender be' is a sententia – and, indeed, was highlighted for the reader's special attention in the first quarto of *Hamlet* (none of Hamlet's were). Another form of sententia in plays is the use of a couplet at the end of a long speech or a scene.

Soliloquy: A lengthy, formal speech in verse, usually spoken by an important character in a play, and often by the central protagonist. For instance, Hamlet's 'To be, or not to be . . .' speech in Shakespeare's tragedy. Often, the character is alone on stage as the audience is given a unique glimpse of his or her thoughts and feelings.

Sonnet: Poetic form of 14 lines, often dealing with the issues of love and success at court. Shakespeare's sequence of *Sonnets* was published in 1609 though probably written (at least in part) in the early 1590s. Other sonneteers include Edmund Spenser and Philip Sidney.

Sovereignty: The idea that the monarch or 'sovereign' possesses power over his or her subordinate subjects, so that decisions can be made on behalf of the people and the realm by that one person.

Spanish Armada: The failed attempt at the invasion of England by the Catholic Philip II of Spain in 1588.

Spondee: This refers to two stressed syllables in a row in a line of poetry.

Stylometry: A mode of inquiry that often seeks to identify the authorship of a literary text, owing to a supposedly distinctive literary style.

Subjectivity: A theoretically-loaded term that applies to a person's selfhood and/ or interiority. In criticism, many studies have seen *Hamlet* as the birth of a modern subjectivity or 'subjective self', and the term came to prominence through psychoanalytical criticism, and, particularly, American New Historicism and British Cultural Materialism in the 1980s.

Succession: Any king or queen must have a 'successor' in order to continue the monarchical governance of a realm. Thus, early modern society was constantly interested in debates about the 'succession', particularly towards the end of Elizabeth's reign, as the childless queen had not named an heir.

Tragi-Comedy: A generic mixture of tragedy and comedy, and, possibly, the third major genre in Renaissance theatre, a Shakespearean example being *Measure for Measure*. However, this is often a problematic term as the 'First Folio' of Shakespeare's works (1623) only divides plays into comedies, histories and tragedies. However, various critics have tended to see some plays as too 'light' for tragedy, yet too serious for comedy, with potential tragedy hovering over much of *Measure for Measure*. Because a play such as this does not become wholly tragic, the label tragi-comedy is often used as a useful go-between.

Trans-Gender: Refers to a male or female who does not conform to a society's cultural expectations of his or her gender, in terms of behaviour, dress and other life choices.

Transgression: The term applied to a person's actions when that act breaks either the official laws of a state or a cultural expectation that is viewed as important and supposedly correct. Thus, we might speak of Lady Macbeth's 'gender transgression' or King Edward's 'sexual transgression' in Marlowe's *Edward II* (1592).

Transsexuality: This indicates the conflicted sexual status of an individual when that person's own interpretation of his or her gender differs from the biological gender of the physical body.

Transvestism: Refers to the act of cross-dressing in the clothes of the opposite sex. Therefore, the all-male, cross-dressing early modern stage was also a site of constant transvestism.

Trochee: In this metrical feature, the iamb is reversed (see IAMB/IAMBIC). Thus the poetic foot consists of a stressed syllable and then an unstressed syllable.

Ulster Plantation: Refers to the establishment in 1609 of a number of settlers from mainland Britain, effectively forming an English and Protestant colonial community in Catholic Ireland, though the enterprise enjoyed little success.

Union of Crowns: In 1603 Queen Elizabeth I died, so becoming the last of the Tudor monarchs. King James VI of Scotland thus became James I of England as the crowns were unified under one monarch. However, in reality Scotland and England continued to be thought of as two kingdoms that just happened to share the same head of state.

Usurpation: A king, queen or any ruler might have her or his rule challenged by a 'usurping' enemy who wishes to displace that monarch and take the crown and accompanying power for his or herself.

Utopia: A classical concept that imagines the perfect, ideal world or society. Thomas More's *Utopia* from the early sixteenth century was the major literary version of the idea in the Renaissance.

Verse: Poetic text with a recognized structure of non-stresses and stresses/accents, as used in Shakespearean theatre in contrast with PROSE. In Renaissance theatre, verse is usually spoken by the 'higher' aristocratic and monarchical characters. Famous examples include Hamlet and King Richard II.

Word-Play: A technique often used by Shakespeare and his contemporaries in which the rhetorical construction of an expression plays on the actual meaning being signified.

Appendix: Shakespeare: Teaching, Curriculum and Learning

David Webb

Chapter Overview

Core Topics
Ways of Teaching

This chapter is available online at
www.continuumbooks.com/resources/9780826495785

Notes on the Contributors

Gabriel Egan is a Reader in Shakespeare Studies at Loughborough University and a co-editor of the journals *Shakespeare* and *Theatre Notebook*. His books include *Shakespeare and Marx* (2004; Turkish translation 2006), *Green Shakespeare* (2006), and the *Edinburgh Critical Guide to Shakespeare* (2007). He writes the 'Shakespeare: Editions and Textual Studies' section for the *Year's Work in English Studies* and is currently working on a book about the theory and practice of editing Shakespeare in the twentieth century.

William Engel is an Associate Professor of English at The University of the South in Sewanee, Tennessee. In addition to contributing chapters in collections such as *The Shakespeare Yearbook* (2007), he is the author of several books on intellectual history, including *Mapping Mortality: The Persistence of Memory and Melancholy in Early Modern England* (University of Massachusetts Press, 1995), *Death and Drama in Renaissance England* (Oxford University Press, 2002), and *Chiastic Designs in English Literature from Sidney to Shakespeare* (Ashgate, 2009).

Robert C. Evans, who has taught at Auburn University, Montgomery since 1982, received his PhD from Princeton University in 1984. At AUM he has been selected as Distinguished Research Professor, Distinguished Teaching Professor and University Alumni Professor. The recipient of grants from the ACLS, the NEH, the Mellon Foundation and the UCLA Center for Renaissance Studies and from the Beinecke, Folger, Huntington and Newberry Libraries, he has also won various teaching awards. He is the author of numerous articles and the author or editor of over twenty books.

Stuart Hampton-Reeves is a Professor of Research-informed Teaching at the University of Central Lancashire. He is the author of *The Shakespeare Handbooks: Measure for Measure* (Palgrave, 2007) and, with Carol Chillington Rutter, *Shakespeare in Performance: the 'Henry VI' Plays* (Manchester University Press, 2007).

Andrew Hiscock is a Professor of English at Bangor University, Wales. He has published widely on early modern literature and his most recent monograph is entitled *The Uses of this World: Thinking Space in Shakespeare, Marlowe, Cary and Jonson*. He is series co-editor for the *Continuum Renaissance Drama*, edited the MHRA's *2008 Yearbook of English Studies* devoted to Tudor literature and co-edited Palgrave's *Teaching Shakespeare and Early Modern Dramatists*. He is also Co-Editor for the journal *English* (OUP).

Lisa Hopkins is a Professor of English at Sheffield Hallam University and co-editor of *Shakespeare*, the journal of the British Shakespeare Association. Her publications include *The Cultural Uses of the Caesars on the English Renaissance Stage* (Ashgate, 2008), *Shakespeare on the Edge: Border-crossing in the Tragedies and the Henriad* (Ashgate, 2005) and *Beginning Shakespeare* (Manchester University Press, 2005).

Ros King is a Professor of English Studies at the University of Southampton, as well as a theatre director and dramaturge. She is the editor of a range of Shakespearean and pre-Shakespearean play texts, and co-editor of the collection of essays, *Shakespeare and War*. Her other books include *The Works of Richard Edwards: Politics, Poetry and Performance in Sixteenth-Century England, Cymbeline: Constructions of Britain,* and *The Winter's Tale.*

Stephen Longstaffe is a Senior Lecturer in English at the University of Cumbria. He has published an edition of the Elizabethan history play *The Life and Death of Jack Straw* and on topics including Marlowe in performance, Bakhtin and Shakespeare, editing Shakespeare, clowning, and various aspects of early modern radical traditions. He is currently working again on clowning and the politics of early modern performance, and in his spare time plays around with his local comedy/drama improvisation group.

Willy Maley is a Professor of Renaissance Studies at Glasgow University. He is author of *A Spenser Chronology* (1994), *Salvaging Spenser* (1997), and *Nation, State and Empire in English Renaissance Literature* (2003), and editor of *Representing Ireland: Literature and the Origins of Conflict, 1534–1660* (1993), *Postcolonial Criticism* (1997), *A View of the Present State of Ireland* (1997), *British Identities and English Renaissance Literature* (2002), *Shakespeare and Scotland* (2004), and *Spheres of Influence: Intellectual and Cultural Publics from Shakespeare to Habermas* (2007).

Kirk Melnikoff is an Assistant Professor of English at the University of North Carolina at Charlotte. His essays have appeared in *Mosaic, Studies in Philology* and *The Library*, and he is editor of *Writing Robert Greene: Essays on England's First Notorious Professional Writer*. He is currently finishing a book project on Elizabethan publishing practices.

Mark Robson teaches at the University of Nottingham. He is the author of *Stephen Greenblatt* (2007) and *The Sense of Early Modern Writing: Rhetoric, Poetics, Aesthetics* (2006), co-author of *Language in Theory* (2005), editor of Hester Pulter, *Poems* (forthcoming) and *Jacques Ranciere: Aesthetics, Politics, Philosophy* (2005) and co-editor of *The Limits of Death: Between Philosophy and Psychoanalysis* (2000). He is currently completing (with James Loxley), *Shakespeare, Jonson, and the Claims of the Performative* (forthcoming).

Peter Sillitoe studied English literature at the Bangor University, Wales, before completing a PhD on Renaissance court entertainments at the University of Sheffield. He has taught at Sheffield, De Montfort, and Wolverhampton universities and is currently completing a monograph entitled *Defining Elite Space in Early Stuart England*.

Adrian Streete is a Lecturer in English at Queen's University Belfast. He is the co-editor of *Refiguring Mimesis: Representation in Early Modern Literature* (University of Hertfordshire Press, 2005) and has published essays in journals such as *The Review of English Studies, Textual Practice* and *Literature and History*. His book *Protestantism and Drama in Early Modern England* is forthcoming with Cambridge University Press.

David Webb is currently teaching for the Open University and is involved in research projects in the Department of Education, Oxford University. He taught Renaissance literature and was responsible for English for intending primary and secondary teachers at St Martin's College, Lancaster (now the University of Cumbria). He has published on Marlowe, Shakespeare and educational topics, and was winner of the Calvin Hoffman prize for publication on Marlowe.

Notes

Chapter 2
1   The author wishes to express his gratitude to W. B. Patterson for offering helpful suggestions on this essay.

Chapter 9
1   You can take a 'virtual tour' of the interior of the Globe at http://www.shakespeares-globe.org/virtualtour/stage/.

Chapter 11
1   The production, in a French prose translation, was performed in London at the Adelphi in June 1899.
2   http://uk.youtube.com/watch?v=7jiAs5gG1AA, accessed 1 September 2008.
3   Shaksper, 11 June 2008; http://www.shaksper.net/archives/2008/0349.html.
4   Productions by Tower Shakespeare Company in London in the 1980s, and Shenandoah Shakespeare Express, touring campuses in the US have performed uncut Folio text versions of even the longest plays in approximately three hours; see also the almost entirely uncut production of *Cymbeline* by Shakespeare Santa Cruz (2000); discussed by King (2005: 173–80) and Orgel (2001).
5   Copious descriptive stage directions are found in the works of Henrik Ibsen and George Bernard Shaw, but this was an innovation forced on those playwrights who had found it difficult to get their plays performed for reasons of censorship and had prepared their texts specifically for the *reading* public.

Annotated Bibliography

Robert C. Evans

The following bibliography, which of course can only skim the surface of valuable scholarship on Shakespeare, attempts to focus (a) on classic studies; (b) on recent overviews and on comprehensive guides; (c) on multi-author collections offering a variety of critical perspectives; (d) on critical controversies; and (e) on works likely to be especially helpful to newer students of Shakespeare. The bibliography is broken into the following sub-sections: (1) one-volume editions; (2) multi-volume editions; (3) reference works; (4) biographies; (5) history of criticism; (6) criticism: important general studies; (7) performance on stage and film; (8) the plays: comedies; (9) the plays: histories; (10) the plays: romances and other late plays; (11) the plays: tragedies; (12) the poems.

Editions: One-volume Versions

Shakespeare, W. (1996), *The Riverside Shakespeare* (2nd edn), ed. G. B. Evans. New York: Houghton Mifflin. Includes essays on modern criticism and on the plays in performance.

—— (2001), *Arden Shakespeare: Complete Works* (revised edn), ed. D. S. Kastan, R. Proudfoot and A. Thompson. London: Arden/Thomson Learning. Emphasizes historical attitudes towards the works, Shakespeare's life and reading and the ways his plays were originally performed.

—— (2004), *Complete Works of William Shakespeare* (5th edn), ed. D. Bevington. New York: Pearson Longman. Emphasizes historical data, language, cultural contexts and interpretive issues.

—— (2005), *The Oxford Shakespeare: The Complete Works* (2nd edn), ed. S. Wells, G. Taylor, J. Jowett and W. Montgomery. Oxford: Oxford University Press. Controversial but highly influential edition emphasizing textual dilemmas.

—— (2008), *The Norton Shakespeare: Based on the Oxford Edition* (2nd edn), ed. S. Greenblatt, W. Cohen, J. E. Howard and K. E. Maus. New York: W. W. Norton. Emphasizes Shakespeare's world, theatrical environment, life and art and textual issues.

Editions: Multi-volume Versions

Shakespeare, W. (1982–), *The Oxford Shakespeare*, ed. S. Wells. Oxford: Oxford University Press. Each volume offers a detailed introduction, a rigorously edited text, copious notes and, often, various helpful appendices. Wells edits the series; individual volumes are edited by particular experts. See also the Oxford School Shakespeare series, which emphasizes ways to engage students.

—— (1984–), *New Cambridge Shakespeare,* ed. B. Gibbons. Cambridge: Cambridge University Press. Thorough introductions and notes; emphasizes theatrical issues. See also *The New Cambridge Shakespeare Quartos* as well the Cambridge School Shakespeare series (general editor: Rex Gibson), which emphasizes ways to teach the plays.

—— (1992–2006), *New Folger Library Shakespeare,* ed. B. Mowat and P. Werstine, P. 31 vols. New York: Washington Square Press. Notes and splendid illustrations appear on pages facing the texts. Each volume presents detailed plot summaries, copious textual notes, annotated lists of secondary sources and an essay offering a 'Modern Perspective'.

—— (1995–), *The Arden Shakespeare* (3rd series), ed. R. Proudfoot, D. S. Kastan and A. Thompson. Volumes offer meticulously edited texts, substantial introductions, helpful appendices and voluminous notes.

Reference Works

Andrews, J. F. (ed.) (1985), *Shakespeare: His World, His Work, His Influence.* 3 vols. New York: Scribner's sixty essays on numerous topics.

Baldwin, T. W. (1944), *William Shakespere's Small Latine and Lesse Greeke.* 2 vols. Urbana: University of Illinois Press. Exhaustive study of Shakespeare's likely education, including extensive discussion of required books.

Bentley, G. E. (1941–68), *The Jacobean and Caroline Stage.* 7 vols. Oxford: Clarendon Press. Data on nearly every aspect of the theatrical world.

Bergeron, D. and de Sousa, G. U. (1995), *Shakespeare: A Study and Research Guide* (3rd edn). Lawrence: University Press of Kansas. An exceptionally helpful guide covering criticism, reference materials and editions. Extremely useful for beginning students.

Berman, R. (1973), *A Reader's Guide to Shakespeare's Plays* (revised edn). Glenview: Scott, Foresman. Dated but still useful.

Bullough, G. (ed.) (1957–75), *Narrative and Dramatic Sources of Shakespeare.* 8 vols. London: Routledge and Kegan Paul. Extremely useful; discusses and reprints major sources.

Campbell, O. J. and Quinn, E. G. (1966), *The Reader's Encyclopedia of Shakespeare.* New York: Thomas Y. Crowell. Huge, if somewhat dated; especially valuable for its excerpts from important critics.

Chambers, E. K. (1923), *The Elizabethan Stage.* 4 vols. Oxford: Clarendon Press. A standard work emphasizing facts, figures and documents.

Champion, L. S. (1993), *Essential Shakespeare: An Annotated Bibliography of Major Modern Studies* (2nd edn). New York: G. K. Hall. An indispensable overview.

Charney, M. (1993), *All of Shakespeare.* Columbia: Columbia University Press. Comprehensive coverage and sensible interpretations; a good introduction.

de Grazia, M. and Wells, S. (eds) (2001), *The Cambridge Companion to Shakespeare.* Cambridge: Cambridge University Press. Includes chronologies plus discussions of such topics as Shakespeare's life; the reproduction of his texts; his reading; his use of language; his poems; generic issues; theatrical conditions; life in London; gender and sexuality; outsiders in Elizabethan England;

Shakespeare and history; the plays' theatrical history; films; relations between page and stage; Shakespeare's worldwide impact; the history of Shakespeare criticism and important reference books.

Dobson, M. and Wells, S. (eds) (2005), *Oxford Companion to Shakespeare* (new edn). Touches on nearly all things Shakespearean.

Donker, M. and Muldrow, G. M. (1982), *Dictionary of Literary-Rhetorical Conventions of the English Renaissance*. Discusses numerous kinds of writing of the era.

Harbage, A. (1963), *William Shakespeare: A Reader's Guide*. New York: Noonday Press. [Also published as *A Reader's Guide to William Shakespeare*.] Provides sensible close readings; especially valuable for beginners.

Kastan, D. S. (ed.) (1999), *A Companion to Shakespeare*. Oxford: Blackwell. Covers such topics as Shakespeare's culture; Shakespeare the man; Shakespeare's England and London; religious identities; the family and household; political thought and culture; readers and reading; reading the bible, the classics, history and vernacular literature; playwrighting; the English language; dramatic verse; rhetorical culture; genre; the economics of playing; Shakespeare's acting companies; his repertory; his playhouses; licensing and censorship; Shakespeare in print, 1593–1640; manuscript playbooks; the craft of printing; the book-trade; press censorship; and Shakespeare: the myth.

Kölin, P. C. (1991), *Shakespeare and Feminist Criticism: An Annotated Bibliography and Commentary*. New York: Garland. Covers the years 1975–1988.

McDonald, R. (2001), *The Bedford Companion to Shakespeare: An Introduction with Documents* (2nd edn). Boston: Bedford/St Martin's. An exceptionally helpful overview, with chapters on the life and the authorship controversy; dramatic language; theatre and dramatic genres; performance, playhouses and players; textual issues; Shakespeare's reading; life in Shakespeare's England; gender issues and social structure; politics and religion; and the history of performances. Contains numerous excerpts from primary documents as well as many illustrations.

Quinn, E. G., Ruoff, J. and Grennen, J. (1973), *The Major Shakespearean Tragedies: A Critical Bibliography*. New York: Free Press. Dated but still valuable.

Rivers, I. (1994), *Classical and Christian Ideas in English Renaissance Poetry: A Student's Guide*. London: Routledge. Intelligently organized chapters deal with the golden age and the Garden of Eden; the pagan gods; Platonism and neo-Platonism; stoicism; views of history; cosmology; Reformation and Counter-Reformation; Protestant theology; humanism; biblical exegesis and typology; theories of poetry; allegory; and numerology.

Shaughnessy, R. (ed.) (2007), *The Cambridge Companion to Shakespeare and Popular Culture*. Cambridge: Cambridge University Press. Topics include relations between popular entertainment and literature; Shakespeare abbreviated; Shakespearean stars; Shakespeare illustrated; Shakespeare: myth and biographical fiction; narration and staging in *Hamlet* and its after-novels; Shakespeare serialized; musical Shakespeares; radio adaptations and performances; Shakespeare and tourism; performing Shakespeare in digital culture; and Shakespeare's popular face: from playbill to poster.

Biographies

Chambers, E. K. (1930), *William Shakespeare: A Study of Facts and Problems*. 2 vols. Oxford: Clarendon Press. Classic early biography; the second volume brims with contemporary documents and data, including early references to Shakespeare and evidence concerning the development of his reputation into the mid-nineteenth century.

Honan, P. (1998), *Shakespeare: A Life*. Oxford: Oxford University Press. A sane, thorough study that emphasizes Shakespeare's life as a theatrical professional. Acknowledges the limits of our knowledge and deals sensibly with the standard controversies.

Schoenbaum, S. (1975), *William Shakespeare: A Documentary Life*. New York: Oxford University Press. Includes and discusses photographic reproductions of more than 200 documents.

—— (1981), *William Shakespeare: Records and Images*. New York: Oxford University Press. Adds more than 150 further documents to those included in Schoenbaum's 1975 volume.

—— (1991), *Shakespeare's Lives* (new edn). Oxford: Clarendon. Traces the biographical tradition and discusses claims that various other persons may have been the 'real' authors of Shakespeare's works.

History of Criticism

Eastman, A. M. (ed.) (1968), *A Short History of Shakespearean Criticism*. New York: Random House. A standard overview with extensive excerpts.

Ralli, A. (1932), *A History of Shakespeare Criticism*. 2 vols. Oxford: Oxford University Press. A massive compendium moving from the seventeenth to the early twentieth centuries and featuring British, French and German thinkers.

Taylor, G. (1991), *Reinventing Shakespeare: A Cultural History from the Restoration to the Present*. Explores the ways Shakespeare's reputation has been affected by differing historical conditions.

Taylor, M. (2001), *Shakespeare Criticism in the Twentieth Century*. Oxford: Oxford University Press. Topics include the era of F. H. Bradley, the rise of formalism, theatrical approaches, historical approaches and approaches stressing marginal groups and marginal perspectives.

Vickers, B. (1974–81), *Shakespeare: The Critical Heritage*. 6 vols. London: Routledge and Keegan Paul. Offers excerpts from commentary published between 1623 and 1801.

Criticism: Important General Studies

Battenhouse, R. (ed.) (1994), *Shakespeare's Christian Dimension: An Anthology of Commentary*. Bloomington: Indiana University Press. A huge collection arguing for the importance of Christian backgrounds and meanings.

Bradshaw, G. (1993), *Misrepresentations: Shakespeare and the Materialists*. Ithaca: Cornell University Press. Skeptical responses to 'new historicist' and 'cultural materialist' approaches.

Calderwood, J. (1971), *Shakespearean Metradrama*. Minneapolis: University of Minnesota Press. Focusing on five works, suggests how they reflect on drama itself as a central topic.

Callaghan, D. (ed.) (2001), *A Feminist Companion to Shakespeare*. Oxford: Blackwell. Topics include the history of feminist Shakespeare criticism; text and language; social economies; race and colonialism; performing sexuality; and religion.

Clemen, W. H. (1951), *The Development of Shakespeare's Imagery*. Cambridge: Harvard University Press. A classic study.

—— (1964), *Shakespeare's Soliloquies*. Cambridge: Cambridge University Press. Still a standard work.

Dollimore, J. and Sinfield, A. (eds) (1985), *Political Shakespeare: New Essays in Cultural Materialism*. Ithaca: Cornell University Press. An influential collection of leftist essays. 2nd revised edition (1994).

Drakakis, J. (ed.) (1985), *Alternative Shakespeares*. London: Methuen. Challenges older views by offering a variety of recent, politically-oriented perspectives. 2nd edition (2002).

Dusinberre, J. (1975), *Shakespeare and the Nature of Women*. London: Macmillan. Suggests that Puritan ideas helped shape Shakespeare's sympathetic portrayal of women.

Erne, L. (2003), *Shakespeare as Literary Dramatist*. Cambridge: Cambridge University Press. Argues that Shakespeare often wrote his plays to be read as well as performed, contends that longer 'literary' versions were often trimmed for performance.

French, M. (1981), *Shakespeare's Division of Experience*. New York: Summit. Suggests the ways masculine and feminine tendencies are emphasized to different degrees in the comedies, tragedies and romances.

Frye, R. M. (1963), *Shakespeare and Christian Doctrine*. Princeton: Princeton University Press. Warns against excessively doctrinaire readings of the plays.

Goddard, H. C. (1951), *The Meaning of Shakepeare*. 2 vols. Chicago: University of Chicago Press. Detailed readings of numerous plays.

Greenblatt, S. (1980), *Renaissance Self-Fashioning: From More to Shakespeare*. Chicago: University of Chicago Press. Extremely influential 'new historicist' text; emphasizes how subversive impulses are both generated and contained.

—— (1988), *Shakespearean Negotiations: The Circulation of Social Energy in Renaissance England*. Berkeley: University of California Press. Influential but controversial essays.

Gurr, A. (2004), *Playgoing in Shakespeare's London* (3rd edn). Cambridge: Cambridge University Press. Suggests that various kinds of people – not predominantly either commoners or the privileged – attended plays.

Hall, K. F. (1996), *Things of Darkness: Economies of Race and Gender in Early Modern England*. Ithaca: Cornell University Press. Influential study of two topics greatly emphasized by recent critics.

Jardine, L. (1983), *Still Harping on Daughters: Women and Drama in the Age of Shakespeare*. Sussex: Harvester. Emphasizes oppressive forces.

Kott, J. (1964), *Shakespeare Our Contemporary*. Garden City: Doubleday. Argues for the relevance of Shakespeare to modern culture.

Levin, R. L. (2003), *Looking for an Argument: Critical Encounters with the New Approaches to Shakespeare and His Contemporaries*. Madison: Fairleigh Dickinson University Press. Sceptical responses to recent methods and interpretations.

Murphy, A. (ed.) (2007), *A Concise Companion to Shakespeare and the Text*. Twelve essays on histories of the books, theories of editing and practicalities.

Neely, C. T. (1985), *Broken Nuptials in Shakespeare's Plays*. New Haven: Yale University Press. Discusses marriage in plays from various genres.

Orgel, S. (1996), *Impersonations: The Performance of Gender in Shakespeare's England*. Cambridge: Cambridge University Press. An influential critic considers such matters as cross-dressing and boy-actors playing female roles.

Parker, P. and Hartman, G. (eds) (1985), *Shakespeare and the Question of Theory*. London: Methuen. Emphasizes recent linguistic, political and feminist perspectives.

Paster, G. K. (1993), *The Body Embarrassed: Drama and the Disciplines of Shame in Early Modern England*. Ithaca: Cornell University Press. Emphasizes the importance of contemporary 'humours' theory.

Pechter, E. (1995), *What Was Shakespeare?: Renaissance Plays and Changing Critical Practice*. Ithaca: Cornell University Press. Confronts and comments on the dizzying variety of approaches that have arisen in recent decades.

Rabkin, N. (1967), *Shakespeare and the Common Understanding*. New York: Free Press. Emphasizes the paradoxical nature of the plays.

—— (1981), *Shakespeare and the Problem of Meaning*. Chicago: University of Chicago Press. Emphasizes the complexities and contradictions the plays embody.

Righter [Barton], A. (1962), *Shakespeare and the Idea of Play*. London: Chatto and Windus. Relates the plays to both earlier and Elizabethan ideas about theatre.

Skura, M. (1993), *Shakespeare the Actor and the Purposes of Playing*. Chicago: University of Chicago Press. Explores depictions of acting in various plays and the ways Shakespeare's experiences as an actor may have helped shape his texts.

Spurgeon, C. F. E. (1935), *Shakespeare's Imagery and What It Tells Us*. Cambridge: Cambridge University Press. A pioneering study.

Styan, J. L. (1967), *Shakespeare's Stagecraft*. Cambridge: Cambridge University Press. Influential early study of the plays as works for the theatre.

Tillyard, E. M. W. (1943), *The Elizabethan World Picture*. London: Chatto and Windus. Brief but highly influential overview emphasizing order and orthodoxy; frequently attacked by more recent critics.

Vickers, B. (1968), *The Artistry of Shakespeare's Prose*. London: Methuen. Examines different uses of prose in the comedies and tragedies and in different periods of Shakespeare's career.

—— (1993), *Appropriating Shakespeare: Contemporary Critical Quarrels*. Criticizes short-comings of recent approaches, especially deconstruction, new historicism, feminism and Marxism as well as psychological and Christian perspectives.

Wayne, V. (ed.) (1991), *The Matter of Difference: Materialist Feminist Criticism of Shakespeare*. Ithaca: Cornell University Press. Essays emphasizing the political dimensions of feminism.

Performance on Stage and Film

Granville-Barker, H. (1946), *Prefaces to Shakesepeare*. 4 vols. Princeton: Princeton University Press. Classic theatre-oriented studies by a noted director.

Gurr, A. (1992), *The Shakespearean Stage, 1574–1642* (3rd edn). Cambridge: Cambridge University Press. A standard study.

Henderson, D. (ed.) (2005), *A Concise Companion to Shakespeare on Film*. Oxford: Blackwell. Twelve essays on various topics.

Hodgdon, B. and Worthen, W. (eds) (2005), *A Companion to Shakespeare and Performance*. Oxford: Blackwell. Performance is discussed in terms of writing, histories, cultural technologies and teaching.

Jackson, R. (ed.) (2007), *The Cambridge Companion to Shakespeare on Film*. Cambridge: Cambridge University Press. Topics include the marketplace; from play-script to screenplay; video; screen history: *Richard III*; *Hamlet*; Macbeth; *King Lear*; the comedies; the histories; the tragedies of love; various directors; women; national and racial stereotypes; the supernatural; and Shakespeare's cinematic offshoots.

Wells, S. and Stanton, S. (eds) (2002), *The Cambridge Companion to Shakespeare on Stage*. Topics include Renaissance stagings; later adaptations; Romantic Shakespeare; pictorial Shakespeare; reconstructive Shakespeare; twentieth-century performances; tragic and comic actors; women and performance; touring Shakespeare; modern political stagings; and Shakespeare in North America, Asia and Africa.

The Plays: Comedies

Barber, C. L. (1959), *Shakespeare's Festive Comedy*. Princeton: Princeton University Press. Relates the plays to celebratory traditions.

Berry, R. (1972), *Shakespeare's Comedy: Explorations in Form*. Princeton: Princeton University Press. Emphasizes appearance vs reality.

Brown, J. R. (1962), *Shakespeare and His Comedies* (2nd edn). London: Methuen. Emphasizes different treatments of love.

Carroll, W. C. (1985), *The Metamorphoses of Shakespearean Comedy*. Princeton: Princeton University Press. Explores various kinds of change.

Champion, L. S. (1970), *The Evolution of Shakespeare's Comedy: A Study in Dramatic Perspective*. Cambridge: Harvard University Press. Especially valuable for summarizing and assessing previous criticism.

Charlton, H. B. (1938), *Shakespearean Comedy*. London: Methuen. An influential early study.

Dutton, R. and Howard, J. (2003), *A Companion to Shakespeare's Works, Volume III: The Comedies*. Oxford: Blackwell. Topics include stage comedy; festive comedies; social discipline; class; social relations; cross-dressing; homoerotics; material life; comic geographies; rhetoric and comic personation; Falstaff; film and genre; and individual plays.

Evans, B. (1960), *Shakespeare's Comedies*. Oxford: Clarendon Press. Emphasizes the theme of ignorance vs knowledge.

Frye, N. (1965), *A Natural Perspective: The Development of Shakespearean Comedy and Romance*. New York: Columbia University Press. Emphasizes the importance of reconciliations, often in marriage.

Hassell, R. C., Jr (1980), *Faith and Folly in Shakespeare's Romantic Comedies*. Athens: University of Georgia Press. Relates the plays to Christian ideas about foolishness.

Hunter, R. G. (1965), *Shakespeare and the Comedy of Forgiveness*. New York: Columbia University Press. Relates a half-dozen plays to ideals of Christian charity.

Huston, J. D. (1981), *Shakespeare's Comedies of Play*. New York: Columbia University Press. Emphasizes playfulness and playing.

Kirsch, A. C. (1981), *Shakespeare and the Experience of Love*. Cambridge: Cambridge University Press. Employs both religious and psychoanalytical approaches.

Leggatt, A. (ed.) (2002), *The Cambridge Companion to Shakespearean Comedy*. Cambridge: Cambridge University Press. Topics include traditional theories of comedy; Roman comedy; Italian stories on the stage; Elizabethan comedy; popular festivity; Shakespeare's forms of confusion; love and courtship; laughing at 'others'; comedy and sex; language and comedy; sexual disguise and the theatre of gender; matters of state; and the experiment of romance.

—— (1973), *Shakespeare's Comedy of Love*. London: Methuen. Discusses the distinctiveness of each play by relating it to standard patterns.

McFarland, T. (1972), *Shakespeare's Pastoral Comedy*. Chapel Hill: University of North Carolina Press. Relates a handful of plays to ideals of rural life.

Nevo, R. (1980), *Comic Transformations in Shakespeare*. Examines the ways Shakespeare transforms earlier traditions of comedy.

Phialas, P. G. (1966), *Shakespeare's Romantic Comedies: The Development of Their Form and Meaning*. Emphasizes the central theme of love.

Salingar, L. (1976), *Shakespeare and the Traditions of Comedy*. Cambridge: Cambridge University Press. Connects the plays to classical, medieval and Renaissance precedents.

Smith, E. (2003), *Shakespeare's Comedies: A Guide to Criticism*. Oxford: Blackwell. Part I covers 1590–1914; Part II stresses the twentieth-century studies.

Waller, G. (ed.) (1991), *Shakespeare's Comedies*. London: Longman. Emphasizes recent critical trends, especially Freudianism, feminism and new historicism.

Wheeler, R. P. (1981), *Shakespeare's Development and the Problem Comedies: Turn and Counter-Turn*. Berkeley: University of California Press. Relates these plays to the earlier and later comic works.

Wilson, J. D. (1962), *Shakespeare's Happy Comedies*. Evanston: Northwestern University Press. Emphasizes the joyful, non-satiric aspects of various plays.

The Plays: History Plays

Campbell, L. B. (1947), *Shakespeare's 'Histories': Mirrors of Elizabethan Policy*. San Marino: Huntington Library. Sees the plays as responses to specific Elizabethan issues and connects them to history-writing of that period.

Champion, L. S. (1980), *Perspective in Shakespeare's English History Plays*. Athens: University of Georgia Press. Emphasizes how points of view control audience response; valuable for its overview of previous criticism.

Chernaik, W. (2007), *The Cambridge Introduction to Shakespeare's History Plays*. Cambridge: Cambridge University Press. Topics include the uses of history and the wars of the critics. Discussions of individual plays emphasize their distinctive features and also stage and screen performances.

Dutton, R. and Howard, J. (eds) (2003), *A Companion to Shakespeare's Works, Volume II: The Histories*. Oxford: Blackwell. Topics include Elizabethan history-writing, history-plays and dramatists of history; censorship; nation formation; Irish contexts; theories of kingship; recent films; riot and rebellion; masculinity, effeminacy and homoerotics; French marriages and the Protestant nation; the first and second tetralogies in performance; and studies of the individual plays.

Hattaway, M. (ed.) (2003), *Cambridge Companion to Shakespeare's History Plays*. Cambridge: Cambridge University Press. Topics include Shakespearean and other early modern history plays; pageants and masques; Elizabethan historiography and Shakespeare's sources; women's roles; relevant royal dynasties; discussions of specific plays; Shakespeare's ancient Rome; his other historical plays; and theatrical productions.

Leggatt, A. (1988), *Shakespeare's Political Drama: The History Plays and the Roman Plays*. London: Routledge. Detailed readings of eleven plays, focusing on tensions between realities and ideals and the need for rules to create scripts and act roles.

Rackin, P. (1990), *Stages of History: Shakespeare's English Chronicles*. London: Routledge. Emphasizes the silenced voices of women and common folk.

Reese, M. M. (1961), *The Cease of Majesty*. London: Edward Arnold. Relates the plays to previous dramas and to preceding works of history; also links them to Elizabethan issues.

Ribner, I. (1965), *The English History Play in the Age of Shakespeare* (revised edn). London: Methuen. Synthesizing and responding to earlier scholarship, this work emphasizes the influence of previous kinds of plays about history and the different purposes they could serve.

Saccio, P. (1977), *Shakespeare's English Kings: History, Chronicle, and Drama*. London: Oxford University Press. Provides reliable historical information, discusses how the various reigns were viewed by Shakespeare's predecessors, and indicates how Shakespeare himself shaped and altered previous facts and interpretations. A standard reference source.

Smith, E. (2003), *Shakespeare's Histories: A Guide to Criticism*. Oxford: Blackwell. Topics covered include the developing critical tradition; genre; language; gender and sexuality; history and politics; and performance.

Tillyard, E. M. W. (1944), *Shakespeare's History Plays*. London: Macmillan. Argues that the plays form an English epic in which order (culminating in the Tudor dynasty) evolved out of preceding disorder thanks to divine providence. A highly influential early study that has been significantly challenged by more recent scholars.

Traversi, D. A. (1957), *Shakespeare: From 'Richard II' to 'Henry V'*. Stanford: Stanford University Press. Examines traits of the kings and kingship.

The Plays: Romances and Other Late Plays

Dutton, R. and Howard, J. (eds) (2003), *A Companion to Shakespeare's Works, Volume IV: The Poems, Problem Comedies, Late Plays*. Oxford: Blackwell. Topics include the sonnets and sexuality; Ovid's impact on *Venus and Adonis*; the problem plays and the drama of Shakespeare's time; scatology and satire; early modern marriage; varieties of collaboration; generic issues; Shakespeare and Beaumont and Fletcher; place and space in three late plays; politics and the technology of spectacle; and explorations of individual works.

Felperin, H. (1972), *Shakespearean Romance*. Princeton: Princeton University Press. Examines the influence of classical and medieval precedents on the romance genre.

Foakes, R. A. (1971), *Shakespeare: The Dark Comedies to the Last Plays: From Satire to Celebration*. Charlottesville: University of Virginia Press. Emphasizes performance issues and changes in characterization.

Frye, N. (1965). *A Natural Perspective: The Development of Shakespearean Comedy and Romance*. New York: Columbia University Press. Stresses mythic patterns of rebirth and renewal.

Hartwig, J. (c. 1972), *Shakespeare's Tragicomic Vision*. Baton Rouge: Louisiana State University Press. Emphasizes the complex responses these plays provoke and their common elements of plot.

Kay, C. M. and Jacobs, H. E. (eds) (1978), *Shakesepeare's Romances Reconsidered*. Lincoln: University of Nebraska Press. Contains eleven essays, a critical overview and a lengthy bibliography.

Knight, G. W. (1947), *The Crown of Life: Essays in Interpretation of Shakespeare's Last Plays*. London: Oxford University Press. Emphasizes the plays' visionary qualities and their real artistic success.

Tillyard, E. M. W. (1938), *Shakespeare's Last Plays*. Focuses on three plays, linking them to related kinds of writing (particularly tragedy).

Traversi, D. A. (1954), *Shakespeare: The Last Phase*. New York: Harcourt, Brace. Stresses patterns of reconciliation.

Yates, F. A. (1975), *Shakespeare's Last Plays: A New Approach*. London: Routledge. Connects the plays to developments in the royal family.

The Plays: Tragedies

Battenhouse, R. W. (1969), *Shakespearean Tragedy: Its Art and Its Christian Premises*. Bloomington: Indiana University Press. Argues that the religious dimension is crucial.

Bell, M. (2002), *Shakespeare's Tragic Skepticism*. New Haven: Yale University Press. Emphasizes the conflicts and contradictions within the plays that reflect Shakespeare's doubts about our ability to know with certainty.

Bradley, A. C. (1904), *Shakespearean Tragedy*. New York: St Martin's. Highly influential studying emphasizing the personalities of the tragic characters.

Brown, J. R. (2001), *Shakespeare: The Tragedies*. New York: Palgrave. Topics include popular tragedies, historical tragedies, histories and heroes; unsettling the audience; sources, contexts and stage actions in *Hamlet*; sexuality and difference; power and the imagination; and power and uncertainty.

Campbell, L. B. (1930), *Shakespeare's Heroes: Slaves of Passion*. Cambridge: Cambridge University Press. Argues that each of the major tragic heroes is irrational (and thus immoral) in some distinct way.

Champion, L. S. (1976), *Shakespeare's Tragic Perspective*. Athens: University of Georgia Press. Especially valuable as a guide to earlier criticism.

Dillon, J. (2007), *The Cambridge Introduction to Shakespeare's Tragedies*. Cambridge: Cambridge University Press. Topics include defining 'Shakespearean tragedy'; traits of the tragic hero; whether some plays are more tragic than others; and the individual dramas.

Dollimore, J. (2004), *Radical Tragedy: Religion, Ideology and Power in the Drama of Shakespeare and His Contemporaries* (3rd edn). Durham: Duke University Press. Influential 'subversive' reading; sees the plays as unorthodox and skeptical.

Dutton, R. and Howard, J. (eds) (2003), *A Companion to Shakespeare's Works, Volume I: The Tragedies*. Oxford: Blackwell. Topics include the idea of tragedy; tragedies of Shakespeare's contemporaries; emotions; divided subjects; disjointed times; tragedies of love; changing conceptions of Hamlet; multiple-text tragedies; religious issues; geography; classic films; contemporary films and individual plays.

Farnham, W. (1950), *Shakespeare's Tragic Frontier: The World of His Final Tragedies*. Berkeley: University of California Press. Stresses the paradoxical nature of the flawed but noble tragic heroes.

Felperin, H. (1977), *Shakespearean Representation: Mimesis and Modernity in Elizabethan Tragedy*. Princeton: Princeton University Press. Discusses how Shakespeare's use of dramatic traditions helped him makes his plays seem fresh and realistic.

Frye, N. (1967), *Fools of Time: Studies in Shakespearean Tragedy*. Toronto: University of Toronto Press. Emphasizes tragedies of order, passion and isolation.

Garner, S. N. and Sprengnether, M. (eds) (1996). Bloomington: Indiana University Press. Topics include history and tragedy; madness and gender; maternal power; various studies of *Othello*; liberal humanism; and Shakespeare's contemporary relevance.

Goldman, M. (1985), *Acting and Action in Shakespearean Tragedy*. Princeton: Princeton University Press. Argues that each play's great tragic role has its defining set of acting challenges and rewards.

Holloway, J. (1961), *The Story of the Night: Studies in Shakespeare's Major Tragedies*. Lincoln: University of Nebraska Press. Emphasizes how the protagonists are expelled and scape-goated.

Hunter, R. G. (1976), *Shakespeare and the Mystery of God's Judgments*. Athens: University of Georgia Press. Emphasizes religious controversies of the time.

Knight, G. W. (1949), *The Wheel of Fire: Interpretations of Shakespearian Tragedy* (revised edn). Oxford: Oxford University Press, 1949. Emphasizes imagery, symbolism and atmosphere and focuses especially on matters of time and space.

Lawlor, J. (1960), *The Tragic Sense in Shakespeare*. London: Chatto and Windus. Emphasizes the dilemmas the protagonists face and the revelations the plays provide.

Mack, M. (1993), *Everybody's Shakespeare: Reflections Chiefly on the Tragedies*. Lincoln: University of Nebraska Press. New and collected essays by a major scholar.

McEachern, C. (ed.) (2002), *The Cambridge Companion to Shakespearean Tragedy*. Cambridge: Cambridge University Press. Topics include defining Shakespearean tragedy; the language of tragedy; tragedy in Shakespeare's career; Shakespearean tragedy printed and performed; religion and Shakespearean tragedy; tragedy and political authority; gender and family; the tragic subject and its passions; tragedies of revenge and ambition; tragedies of love; Shakespeare's classical tragedies; the tragedies' critical reception; and *Antony and Cleopatra* in the theatre.

McElroy, B. (1973), *Shakespeare's Mature Tragedies*. Princeton: Princeton University Press. Emphasizes the psychological traits and experiences the protagonists share.

Muir, K. (1972), *Shakespeare's Tragic Sequence*. London: Hutchinson. Resists efforts to provide homogeneous interpretations; emphasizes each play's distinctiveness.

Ribner, I. (1960), *Patterns in Shakespearian Tragedy*. London: Methuen. Emphasizes patterns of ethical evolution.

Snyder, S. (1979), *The Comic Matrix of Shaksepeare's Tragedies: 'Romeo and Juliet', 'Othello,' 'Hamlet', and 'King Lear'*. Princeton: Princeton University Press. Traces changes in how Shakespeare explores comic and tragic impulses in these plays and examines how their comic elements intensify their tragic designs.

Traversi, D. A. (1963), *Shakespeare: The Roman Plays*. Stanford: Stanford University Press. Traces Shakespeare's evolving tragic outlook.

Young, D. (1990), *The Action to the Word: Structure and Style in Shakespearean Tragedy*. New Haven: Yale University Press. Emphasizes productive tension between the plays' dramatic action and their expressive language.

The Poems

Booth, S. (ed.) (1977), *Shakespeare's Sonnets: Edited with Analytic Commentary*. New Haven: Yale University Press. Contains extraordinarily detailed annotations.

Cheney, P. (ed.) (2007), *The Cambridge Companion to Shakespeare's Poetry*. Cambridge: Cambridge University Press. Includes chapters on the separate narrative poems and on the sonnets. Topics also include Shakespeare's poetry in the twenty-first century; Shakespeare and the development of English poetry; rhetoric, style and poetic form; print and manuscript; poetry, politics and religion; love, beauty and sexuality; classicism; poetry in the plays; poetry and performance; and matters of reception and influence.

Hubler, E. (1952), *The Sense of Shakespeare's Sonnets*. Princeton: Princeton University Press. Classic discussion of techniques and themes, including love, friendship, poetry, morality and change.

Landry, H. (1963), *Interpretations in Shakespeare's Sonnets*. Berkeley: University of California Press. Discusses themes, ordering and techniques.

Leishman, J. B. (1961), *Themes and Variations in Shakespeare's Sonnets*. London: Hutchinson. Relates the poems to earlier works by classical writers and Renaissance authors on the continent and in England.

Schoenfeldt, M. (ed.) (2006), *A Companion to Shakespeare's Sonnets*. Oxford: Blackwell. Topics include sonnet form and sonnet sequence; predecessors; editorial theory and biographical inquiry; manuscript and print; models of desire; ideas of darkness; memory and repetition; relations with the plays; and the sonnets and *A Lover's Complaint*.

Vendler, H. (1997), *The Art of Shakespeare's Sonnets*. Cambridge: Harvard University Press. Detailed readings of all the poems.

Works Cited

Adams, S. (2002), 'Britain, Europe, and the world', in P. Collinson (ed.), *The Sixteenth Century*, pp. 189–216. Oxford: Oxford University Press.

Aers, L. and Wheale, N. (eds) (1991), *Shakespeare in the Changing Curriculum*. London: Routledge.

Ake, J. (2003), 'Glimpsing a "Lesbian" Poetics in *Twelfth Night*', *Studies in English Literature*, 43 (2), 375–94.

Alexander, C. M. S. and Wells, S. (eds) (2000), *Shakespeare and Race*. Cambridge: Cambridge University Press.

Armstrong, P. (2001), *Shakespeare in Psychoanalysis*. London: Routledge. Subtle and sophisticated exploration of the possibilities of psychoanalytic criticism.

Baker, D. J. (1997), 'Where is Ireland in *The Tempest*?', in M. T. Burnett and R. Wray (eds), *Shakespeare and Ireland: History, Politics, Culture*, pp. 68–88. London: Macmillan.

Baker, H. A., Jr (1986), 'Caliban's Triple Play', *Critical Inquiry*, 13 (1), 182–96.

Bakhtin, M. (1984), *Rabelais and His World*, trans. Helene Iswolsky. Bloomington: Indiana University Press.

Barber, C. (1997), *Early Modern English*. Edinburgh: Edinburgh University Press.

Barker, D. E. and Kamps, I. (eds) (1995), *Shakespeare and Gender: A History*. London and New York: Verso. Very useful anthology of representative pieces.

Barker, F. (1984), *The Tremulous Private Body: Essays in Subjection*. London: Methuen.

—— ([1984]; 1992), 'Hamlet's Unfulfilled Interiority', rpt in R. Wilson and R. Dutton (eds), *New Historicism and Renaissance Drama*, pp. 157–66. London: Longman.

Barker, F. and Hulme, P. (1985), 'Nymphs and Reapers Heavily Vanish: The Discursive Contexts of *The Tempest*', in J. Drakakis (ed.), *Alternative Shakespeares*, pp. 191–205. London: Methuen.

Barnfield, R. (1605), *Lady Pecunia, or The praise of money*. London.

Barthes, R. (1968), 'La Mort de L'auteur (The Death of the Author)', *Mantéia*, 5, 12–17.

Bate, J. (2000), 'Caliban and Ariel Write Back', in C. M. S. Alexander and S. Wells (eds), *Shakespeare and Race*, pp. 165–76. Cambridge: Cambridge University Press.

Bates, C. (1999), 'The Point of Puns', *Modern Philology*, 96, 1–22.

Bearman, R. (2002), ' "Was William Shakespeare William Shakeshafte?" Revisited', *Shakespeare Quarterly*, 53, 83–94.

Belsey, C. (1985), 'Disrupting Sexual Difference: Meaning and Gender in the Comedies', in J. Drakakis (ed.), *Alternative Shakespeares*, pp. 166–90. London: Methuen.

—— (1988), *The Subject of Tragedy*. London: Methuen.

—— (1996), 'Cleopatra's Seduction', in T. Hawkes (ed.), *Alternative Shakespeares*, Vol. 2. London and New York: Routledge.

Bentley, G. E. (1971), *The Profession of Dramatist in Shakespeare's Time, 1590–1642*. Princeton: Princeton University Press.

Berry, P. (1997), *Shakespeare's Feminine Endings*. London: Routledge.

Berry, R. (1980), 'Hamlet: Nationhood and Identity', *University of Toronto Quarterly*, 49, 283–303.

The Bible (1560), ed. and trans. W. Whittingham *et al.* Geneva.

Billings, T. (2003), 'Caterwauling Cataians: The Genealogy of a Gloss', *Shakespeare Quarterly*, 54 (1), 1–28.

Blayney, P. W. M. (1997), 'The Publication of Playbooks', in *A New History of Early English Drama*, ed. J. D. Cox and D. S. Kastan, pp. 383–422. New York: Columbia University Press.

Boose, L. E. (1994), ' "The Getting of a Lawful Race": Racial Discourse in Early Modern England and the Unrepresentable Black Woman', in M. Hendricks and P. Parker (eds), *Race, Women and Writing in Early Modern Europe*, pp. 35–54. London: Routledge.

Boose, L. and Burt, R. (eds) (1997), *Shakespeare, the Movie: Popularising the Plays on Film, TV, and Video*. London: Routledge.

Booth, S. (ed.) (2000), *Shakespeare's Sonnets*. New Haven and London: Yale University Press.

Bowers, F. (ed.) (1987a), *Dictionary of Literary Biography*. Vol. 62: Elizabethan Dramatists. Detroit: Gale Research.

—— (1987b), *Dictionary of Literary Biography*. Vol. 58: Jacobean and Caroline Dramatists. Detroit: Gale Research.

Boyd, B. (2004), 'Mutius: An Obstacle Removed in *Titus Andronicus*', *Review of English Studies*, 55, 196–209.

Bradley, A. C. (1904), *Shakespearean Tragedy: Lectures on Hamlet, Othello, King Lear, Macbeth*. London and New York: Macmillan (Harmondsworth: Penguin, 1991).

—— (1909), *Oxford Lectures on Poetry*. London: Macmillan. Contains Bradley's important essay on the rejection of Falstaff.

Bradshaw, G. (1993), *Misrepresentations: Shakespeare and the Materialists*. Ithaca: Cornell University Press.

Brannigan, J. (1998), *New Historicism and Cultural Materialism*. Basingstoke: Macmillan.

Bristol, M. (1996), 'Race and the Comedy of Abjection', in *Big-Time Shakespeare*. London and New York: Routledge.

Brome, R. (1652), *A Joviall Crew, or The Merry Beggars*. London.

Brontë, C. (1995), *The Letters of Charlotte Brontë*, Vol. 1: 1829–1847, ed. M. Smith. Oxford: Clarendon Press.

Brook, P. (1968), *The Empty Space*. New York: Atheneum.

Brotton, J. (1998), ' "This Tunis, sir, was Carthage": Contesting Colonialism in *The Tempest*', in A. Loomba and M. Orkin (eds), *Post-Colonial Shakespeares*, pp. 23–42. London: Routledge.

Brown, J. R. (2002), *Shakespeare and the Theatrical Event*. London: Palgrave. A detailed but accessible book on reading Shakespeare in performance by one of the pioneers of the field.

—— (2005). *Macbeth: A Guide to the Text and its Theatrical Life*. London: Palgrave.

Brown, P. (1985), ' "This thing of darkness I acknowledge mine": *The Tempest* and the Discourse of Colonialism', in J. Dollimore and A. Sinfield (eds), *Political Shakespeare: Essays in Cultural Materialism*, pp. 48–71. Manchester: Manchester University Press.

Bruster, D. (2003), *Shakespeare and the Question of Culture: Early Modern Literature and the Cultural Turn*. Basingstoke: Palgrave Macmillan.

Bullough, G. (1962), *Narrative and Dramatic Sources of Shakespeare*. London: Routledge and Keegan Paul.

Burney, F. (1988), *The Early Journals and Letters of Fanny Burney*, Vol. 1: 1768–1773, ed. L. E. Troide. Oxford: Clarendon Press.

Calder, A. C. (1987), ' "The Weasel Scot": Some Characteristics of Shakespearian Depiction in *Henry V* and *1 Henry IV*', in J. D. McClure and M. R. G. Spiller (eds), *Bryght Lanternis: Essays on the Language and Literature of Medieval and Renaissance Scotland*, pp. 459–72. Aberdeen: University of Aberdeen.

Callaghan, D. (2000), *Shakespeare Without Women: Representing Gender and Race on the Renaissance Stage*. London: Routledge.

—— (2001), 'Shakespeare and Religion', *Textual Practice*, 15 (1), 1–4.

Carlyle, T. (1840), *On Heroes, Hero-Worship and the Heroic in History*. London: Chapman and Hall.

Cartelli, T. (1987), 'Prospero in Africa: *The Tempest* as Colonialist Text and Pretext', in J. E. Howard and M. F. O'Connor (eds), *Shakespeare Reproduced: The Text in History and Ideology*, pp. 99–115. London: Methuen.

Cassirer, E. (1992), *An Essay on Man: An introduction to a philosophy of human culture* (originally published 1944). New Haven and London: Yale University Press.

Cattle, G. (1995), ' "The detested blot": The Representation of the Northern English in Shakespeare's *Henry IV Part One*', *Parergon*, n.s. 13, 25–32.

Cavell, S. (1987), *Disowning Knowledge: In Six Plays of Shakespeare*. Cambridge: Cambridge University Press.

Cavendish, M. (2004), *Sociable Letters*, ed. J. Fitzmaurice. Toronto: Broadview Editions.

Chambers, E. K. (1924–25), ' "The Disintegration of Shakespeare": The British Academy Annual Shakespeare Lecture Read 12 May 1924', *Proceedings of the British Academy*, 11, 89–108.

Chambers, E. K. et al. (eds) (1932), *The Shakespeare Allusion-Book*, I. London: Humphrey Milford / Oxford University Press.

Charles, C. (1997), 'Gender Trouble in *Twelfth Night*', *Theatre Journal*, 49 (2), 121–41.

Charlton, H. B. (1942), *Hamlet*. Manchester: Manchester University Press.

Charnes, L. (1993), *Notorious Identity: Materializing the Subject in Shakespeare*. Cambridge, MA: Harvard University Press.

Chedgzoy, K. (1995), *Shakespeare's Queer Children: Sexual Politics and Contemporary Culture*. Manchester: Manchester University Press.

Clark, S. (2007), *Vanities of the Eye: Vision in Early Modern European Culture*. Oxford: Oxford University Press.

Clegg, C. S. (2001), *Press Censorship in Jacobean England*. Cambridge: Cambridge University Press.

Clemen, W. (1951), *The Development of Shakespeare's Imagery*. Cambridge, MA: Harvard University Press.

Colebrook, C. (1997), *New Literary Histories: New Historicism and Contemporary Criticism*. Manchester and New York: Manchester University Press.

Collinson, P. (2002), 'Conclusion', in P. Collinson (ed.), *The Sixteenth Century*, pp. 217–42. Oxford: Oxford University Press.

Cordner, M. (2006), ' "Wrought with Things Forgotten": Memory and Performance in Editing *Macbeth*', in P. Holland (ed.), *Shakespeare, Memory and Performance*, pp. 87–116. Cambridge: Cambridge University Press.

Crewe, J. (1995), 'In the Field of Dreams: Transvestism in *Twelfth Night* and *The Crying Game*', *Representations*, 50, 101–21.

—— (2001), '*Black Hamlet*: Psychoanalysis on Trial in South Africa', *Poetics Today*, 22 (2), 413–33.

Dawson, A. B. (1995), *Hamlet*. Shakespeare in Performance. Manchester: Manchester University Press.

de Grazia, M. (1994), 'The Scandal of Shakespeare's Sonnets', *Shakespeare Survey*, 46, 35–49.

Derrida, J. (1992), ' "This Strange Institution Called Literature": An Interview with Jacques Derrida', in D. Attridge (ed.), *Jacques Derrida: Acts of Literature*, pp. 33–75. London: Routledge.

—— (1994), *Specters of Marx: The State of the Debt, the Work of Mourning, & the New International*, trans. Peggy Kamuf. London and New York: Routledge.

—— (1995), 'The Time Is Out of Joint', trans. P. Kamuf, in A. Haverkamp (ed), *Deconstruction is/in America*, pp. 14–38. New York and London: New York University Press.

deVries, J. (1984), *European Urbanization, 1500–1800*. Cambridge, MA: Harvard University Press.

Dollimore, J. (1983), *Radical Tragedy: Religion, Ideology and Power in the Drama of Shakespeare and his Contemporaries*. Brighton: Harvester Press.

—— (1989), *Radical Tragedy: Religion, Ideology and Power in the Drama of Shakespeare and his Contemporaries* (2nd edn). New York and London: Harvester Wheatsheaf.

—— (2001), *Death, Desire and Loss in Western Culture*. Harmondsworth: Penguin.

—— (2004), *Radical Tragedy: Religion, Ideology and Power in the Drama of Shakespeare and his Contemporaries* (3rd edn). Basingstoke: Palgrave Macmillan.

Dollimore, J. and Sinfield, A. (eds) (1994), *Political Shakespeare: Essays in Cultural Materialism* (2nd edn). Manchester: Manchester University Press.

Doran, S. (1996), *Monarchy and Matrimony: The courtships of Elizabeth*. London and New York: Routledge.

Drakakis, J. (ed.) (1985), *Alternative Shakespeares*. London: Methuen.

Dryden, J. (1679), 'The Preface to the Play', in *Troilus and Cressida, or, Truth found too late a tragedy*. London.

Duffy, E. (2005), *The Stripping of the Altars: Traditional Religion in England c.1400–c.1580* (2nd edn). New Haven and London: Yale University Press.

Duncan-Jones, K. (2001), *Ungentle Shakespeare*. The Arden Shakespeare. London: Thomson Learning.

Eaves, T. C. D. and Kimpel, B. D. (1971), *Samuel Richardson. A Biography*. Oxford: Clarendon Press.

Egan, G. (2004), 'The 1599 Globe and Its Modern Replica: Virtual Reality Modelling of the Archaeological and Pictorial Evidence', *Early Modern Literary Studies*, Special Issue 12 (Virtual Reality Modelling of Performance Spaces), http://purl.oclc.org/emls/ ISSN 1201–2459.

—— (2006), *Green Shakespeare*. London: Routledge.

Elam, K. (1996), 'The Fertile Eunuch: *Twelfth Night*, Early Modern Intercourse, and the Fruits of Castration', *Shakespeare Quarterly*, 47 (1), 1–36.

Eliot, G. (1998), *The Journals of George Eliot*, ed. M. Harris and J. Johnston. Cambridge: Cambridge University Press.

Ellmann, M. (ed.) (1994), *Psychoanalytic Literary Criticism*. Harlow: Longman.

Elton, G. R. (1991), *England under the Tudors* (3rd edn). London and New York: Routledge.

Erickson, P. (2000), ' "God for Harry, England, and Saint George": British National Identity and the Emergence of White Self-Fashioning', in P. Erickson and C. Hulse (eds), *Early Modern Visual Culture: Representation, Race, and Empire in Renaissance England*, pp. 315–45. Philadelphia: University of Pennsylvania Press.

—— (2002), 'Can We Talk About Race in *Hamlet*?', in A. F. Kinney (ed.), *'Hamlet': New Critical Essays*, pp. 207–13. London and New York: Routledge.

Erne, L. (2002), 'Shakespeare and the Publication of His Plays', *Shakespeare Quarterly*, 53, 1–20.

—— (2003), *Shakespeare as Literary Dramatist*. Cambridge: Cambridge University Press.

Felperin, H. (1992), *The Uses of the Canon: Elizabethan Literature and Contemporary Theory*. Oxford: Clarendon Press.

Ferguson, M. W., Quilligan, M. and Vickers, N. (eds) (1986), *Rewriting the Renaissance: The Discourses of Sexual Difference in Early Modern Europe*. Chicago: University of Chicago Press.

Fernie, E. (2005), 'Shakespeare and the Prospect of Presentism', *Shakespeare Survey*, 58, 169–84.

—— (2006), 'Terrible Action: Recent Criticism and Questions of Agency', *Shakespeare*, 2 (1), 95–118.

Fielding, H. (1974), *Henry Fielding: Contributions to The Champion and Related Writing*, ed. W. B. Coley. Oxford: Clarendon Press.

Findlay, H. (1989), 'Renaissance Pederasty and Pedagogy: The "Case" of Shakespeare's Falstaff', *Yale Journal of Criticism* 3 (1), 229–38.

Fineman, J. (1986), *Shakespeare's Perjured Eye: The Invention of Poetic Subjectivity in the Sonnets*. Berkeley: University of California Press.

—— (1991), *The Subjectivity Effect in Western Literary Tradition: Essays Toward the Release of Shakespeare's Will*. Cambridge, MA: MIT Press.

Fitzpatrick, J. (2004), *Shakespeare, Spenser and the Contours of Britain: Reshaping the Atlantic Archipelago*. Hatfield: University of Hertfordshire Press.

—— (2007), *Food in Shakespeare: Early Modern Dietaries and the Plays*. Aldershot: Ashgate.

Fletcher, A. and MacCullough, D. (1997), *Tudor Rebellions* (4th edn). London and New York: Longman.

Foucault, M. (1969), 'Qu'est-ce Qu-un Auteur? (What is an Author?)', *Bulletin de la Societé francaise de Philosophie*, 63 (3), 73–104.

—— (1979), 'What Is an Author?', in J. V. Harari (ed.), *Textual Strategies: Perspectives in Post-structuralist Criticism*, pp. 141–60. London: Methuen.

—— (1987), *The History of Sexuality*, Vol. 1, *An Introduction*, trans. R. Hurley. New York: Random House.

—— (1990), *The History of Sexuality*, Vol. 1, *An Introduction*, trans. R. Hurley. Harmondsworth: Penguin.

—— (2002), *Power: Essential Works of Foucault 1954–1984*, Vol. 3, ed. J. D. Faubion. Harmondsworth: Penguin.

Foxe, J. (1597), *Actes and Monuments*, 2 vols. London. STC 11226a. Vol. 2.

Franssen, P. (2004), 'The Bard and Ireland: Shakespeare's Protestantism as Politics in Disguise', in C. M. S. Alexander (ed.), *Shakespeare and Politics*, pp. 185–97. Cambridge: Cambridge University Press.

Fraser, R. S. (2008), '*Henry V* and the Performance of War', in R. King and P. Franssen (eds), *Shakespeare and War*, pp. 71–83. Basingstoke: Palgrave Macmillan.

Freinkel, L. (2002), *Reading Shakespeare's Will: The Theology of Figure from Augustine to the Sonnets*. New York: Columbia University Press.

Freud, S. (1997), *Writings on Art and Literature*. Stanford: Stanford University Press.

Frye, R. M. (1967), *Shakespeare's Life and Times: A Pictorial Record*. Princeton: Princeton University Press.

Fukuyama, F. (1992), *The End of History and the Last Man*. London: Hamish Hamilton.

Gallagher, C. and Greenblatt, S. (2000), *Practicing New Historicism*. Chicago: University of Chicago Press.

Garber, M. (1987), *Shakespeare's Ghost Writers: Literature as Uncanny Causality*. London and New York: Methuen.

Gibson, R. (1998), *Teaching Shakespeare*. Cambridge: Cambridge University Press.

Goldberg, J. (1992), *Sodometries: Renaissance Texts, Modern Sexualities*. Stanford: Stanford University Press.

—— (1995), 'Hal's Desire, Shakespeare's Idaho', in N. Wood (ed.), *Henry IV Parts One and Two*, pp. 35–64. Buckingham: Open University Press.

—— (2003), *Shakespeare's Hand*. Minneapolis: University of Minnesota Press.

Grady, H. (2005), 'Shakespeare Studies, 2005: A Situated Overview', *Shakespeare*, 1 (1), 102–20.

Grady, H. and Hawkes, T. (eds) (2007), *Presentist Shakespeare*. Accents on Shakespeare. London and New York: Routledge.

Granville-Barker, H. (1930), *Prefaces to Shakespeare*. Vol. 1, Hamlet, King Lear, The Merchant of Venice, Antony and Cleopatra, Cymbeline. London: Batsford. Reprint 1961.

Green, R. (1592), *Greene's Groatsworth of Wit: Bought with a Million of Repentance*. London.

Greenblatt, S. (1976), 'Learning to Curse: Aspects of Linguistic Colonialism in the Sixteenth Century', in F. Chiappelli (ed.), *First Images of America: The Impact of the New World on the Old*, 2 vols, II, pp. 561–80. Berkeley: University of California Press.

—— (1980), *Renaissance Self-Fashioning: From More to Shakespeare*. Chicago: University of Chicago Press.

—— (1985a), 'Invisible Bullets: Renaissance Authority and its Subversion, *Henry IV* and *Henry V*', in J. Dollimore and A. Sinfield (eds), *Political Shakespeare: Essays in Cultural Materialism*, pp. 18–47. Manchester: Manchester University Press.

—— (1985b), 'Shakespeare and the Exorcists', in P. Parker and G. Hartman (eds), *Shakespeare and the Question of Theory*, pp. 163–87. London: Methuen.

—— ([1985]; 1992), 'Invisible Bullets: Renaissance Authority and its Subversion, *Henry IV* and *Henry V*' [1985], rpt in R. Wilson and R. Dutton (eds), *New Historicism and Renaissance Drama*, pp. 83–108. London: Longman.

—— (1988), *Shakespearean Negotiations: The Circulation of Social Energy in Renaissance England*. Oxford: Clarendon Press.

—— (1990), *Learning to Curse: Essays in Early Modern Culture*. London: Routledge.

—— (2004), *Will in the World: How Shakespeare Became Shakespeare*. New York and London: W. W. Norton.

Greenfield, M. (2002), '*1 Henry IV*: Metatheatrical Britain', in D. J. Baker and W. Maley (eds), *British Identities and English Renaissance Literature*, pp. 71–80. Cambridge: Cambridge University Press.

The Guardian (2008), <http://www.guardian.co.uk/uk/2008/sep/09/3>.

Gurr, A. (1988), 'Hamlet's Claim to the Crown of Denmark', in L. Cookson and B. Loughrey (eds), *Hamlet*, pp. 92–98. Longman Critical Readers. London: Longman.

Guy, J. (1988), *Tudor England*. Oxford: Oxford University Press.

Hadfield, A. (2003), 'The Power and Rights of the Crown in *Hamlet* and *King Lear*: "The King – The King's to Blame" ', *Review of English Studies*, n.s. 54 (217), 566–86.

—— (2004), '*Hamlet*'s Country Matters: The "Scottish Play" within the Play', in W. Maley and A. Murphy (eds), *Shakespeare and Scotland*, pp. 87–103. Manchester: Manchester University Press.

—— (2005), *Shakespeare and Republicanism*. Oxford: Oxford University Press.

Hall, K. F. (1995), *Things of Darkness: Economies of Race and Gender in Early Modern England*. Ithaca: Cornell University Press.

—— (1998), ' "These Bastard Signs of Fair": Literary Whiteness in Shakespeare's Sonnets', in A. Loomba and M. Orkin (eds), *Post-Colonial Shakespeares*, pp. 64–83. London: Routledge.

Halpern, R. (2002), *Shakespeare's Perfume: Sodomy and Sublimity in the Sonnets, Wilde, Freud, and Lacan*. Philadelphia: University of Pennsylvania Press.

Hamilton, P. (1996), *Historicism*. London and New York: Routledge.

Hawkes, T. (1986), *That Shakespeherian Rag*. London: Methuen.

—— (1991), 'Comedy, Orality, Duplicity: *Twelfth Night*', rpt in G. Waller (ed.), *Shakespeare's Comedies*, pp. 168–74. London: Longman.

—— (1992), *Meaning By Shakespeare*. London: Routledge.

—— (2002), *Shakespeare in the Present*. Accents on Shakespeare. London: Routledge.

Hayes, A. (1992), *Invisible Power: The Elizabethan Secret Services, 1570–1603*. New York: St Martin's Press.

Heinemann, M. (1985), 'How Brecht Read Shakespeare', in J. Dollimore and A. Sinfield (eds), *Political Shakespeare: Essays in Cultural Materialism*, pp. 202–30. Manchester: Manchester University Press.

Henslowe, P. (1961), *Henslowe's Diary*, ed. R. A. Foakes and R. T. Rickert, with supplementary material, Introduction and Notes. Cambridge: Cambridge University Press.

—— (2002), *Henslowe's Diary* (2nd edn), ed. R. A. Foakes. Cambridge: Cambridge University Press.

Highley, C. (1990), 'Wales, Ireland, and *1 Henry IV'*, *Renaissance Drama*, 21, 91–114.

—— (1997), 'The Tyrone Rebellion and the Gendering of Colonial Resistance in *1 Henry IV'*, in *Shakespeare, Spenser, and the Crisis in Ireland*, pp. 86–109. Cambridge: Cambridge University Press.

Hindle, S. (2002), *The State and Social Change in Early Modern England, c. 1550–1640*. New York: St Martin's Press.

Hirst, D. (2002), 'Text, Time, and the Pursuit of "British Identities" ', in D. J. Baker and W. Maley (eds), *British Identities and English Renaissance Literature*, pp. 256–66. Cambridge: Cambridge University Press.

Hiscock, A. and Hopkins, L. (eds) (2007), *Teaching Shakespeare and Early Modern Dramatists*. London: Palgrave Macmillan.

Hodgdon, B. (2006), 'Shopping in the Archives: Material Memories', in P. Holland (ed.), *Shakespeare, Memory and Performance*, pp. 135–67. Cambridge: Cambridge University Press.

Holderness, G. (1992), *Shakespeare Recycled: The Making of Historical Drama*. London: Harvester Wheatsheaf.

Holland, P. (1997), *English Shakespeares: Shakespeare on the English Stage in the 1990s*. Cambridge: Cambridge University Press.

—— (2001), *Shakespeare Survey 54, Shakespeare and Religions*. Cambridge: Cambridge University Press.

—— (2006), *Shakespeare, Memory and Performance*. Cambridge: Cambridge University Press.

Honigmann, E. A. J. (1985), *Shakespeare: The 'Lost Years'*. Manchester: Manchester University Press.

Hope, J. (1999), 'Shakespeare's "Native English" ', in D. S. Kastan (ed.), *A Companion to Shakespeare*, pp. 239–55. Oxford: Blackwell.

Hunt, M. (1999), 'Be Dark but Not Too Dark: Shakespeare's Dark Lady as a Sign of Colour', in J. Schiffer (ed.), *Shakespeare's Sonnets: Critical Essays*, pp. 368–89. New York and London: Garland.

Hutson, L. (2001), 'Not the King's Two Bodies: Reading the "Body Politic" in Shakespeares' *Henry IV*, Parts 1 and 2', in L. Hutson and V. Kahn (eds), *Rhetoric and Law in Early Modern Europe*, pp. 166–98. New Haven: Yale University Press.

Irace, K. O. (1994), *Reforming the 'Bad' Quartos: Performance and Provenance of Six Shakespearean First Editions*. Newark: University of Delaware Press.

Jameson, A. (1901), *Shakespeare's Heroines*. London: Dent (first published as *Characteristics of women, moral, poetical, and historical*, 1832).

Jameson, F. (2002), *The Political Unconscious*. London: Routledge.

Jardine, L. (1983), *Still Harping on Daughters: Women and Drama in the Age of Shakespeare*. Sussex: Harvester Press.

Johnson, S. (1968), *Preface to Shakespeare. Works of Samuel Johnson: Johnson on Shakespeare*, Vol. 7, ed. A. Sherbo. New Haven: Yale University Press.

—— (1977), 'Preface to Shakespeare', in *Samuel Johnson. Selected Poetry and Prose*. Berkeley: University of California Press.

Jones, E. (1949), *Hamlet and Oedipus*. London: Victor Gollancz; New York: Norton.

Jones, P. (ed.) (1977), *Shakespeare: The Sonnets*. London: Macmillan. This collection includes many important essays on the Sonnets up to the early 1970s.

Joseph, Sister M. (1947), *Shakespeare's Use of the Arts of Language*. New York: Columbia University Press.

Joughin, J. J. (ed.) (1997), *Shakespeare and National Culture*. Manchester: Manchester University Press.

Kastan, D. S. (1991), ' "The king hath many marching in his coats", or, what did you do in the war, Daddy?', in I. Kamps (ed.), *Shakespeare Left and Right*, pp. 241–58. London: Routledge.

—— (1999), *Shakespeare after Theory*. London and New York: Routledge.

King, R. (2005), *Cymbeline: Constructions of Britain*. Basingstoke: Ashgate.

—— (2008), ' "The Disciplines of war": Elizabethan War Manuals and Shakespeare's Tragicomic Vision', in R. King and P. Franssen (eds), *Shakespeare and War*, pp. 15–29. Basingstoke: Palgrave Macmillan.

Kliman, B. (2004). *Macbeth: Shakespeare in Performance* (2nd edn). Manchester: Manchester University Press.

Knight, G. W. (1930). *The Wheel of Fire*. London: Oxford University Press.

Knights, L. C. (1946), *Explorations*. London: Chatto & Windus.

Kozuka, T. and Mulryne, J. R. (eds) (2006), *Shakespeare, Marlowe, Jonson: New Directions in Biography*. Aldershot: Ashgate.

Kunzle, D. (2002), *From Criminal to Courtier: The Soldier in Netherlandish Art 1550–1672*. History of Warfare, Vol. 10. Leiden and Boston: Brill.

Kurland, S. M. (1994), '*Hamlet* and the Scottish Succession?', *Studies in English Literature*, 34 (2), 279–300.

Lamb, C. (1818), *The Works of Charles Lamb in Two Volumes*. London: C. and J. Ollier.

Laroque, F. (1988), *Shakespeare's Festive World*, trans. J. Lloyd. Cambridge: Cambridge University Press.

Lawson, N. (2004), *Feast: Food That Celebrates Life*. London: Chatto and Windus.

Leach, S. (1992), *Shakespeare in the Classroom*. Buckingham: Open University Press.

Lever, J. W. (1971), *The Tragedy of State*. London: Methuen.

Levine, L. (1994), *Men in Women's Clothing: Anti-Theatricality and Effeminization, 1579–1642*. Cambridge: Cambridge University Press.

Liebler, N. C. (1995), *Shakespeare's Festive Tragedy: The Ritual Foundations of Genre*. London and New York: Routledge.

Linklater, K. (1992), *Freeing Shakespeare's Voice: An Actor's Guide to Talking the Text*. New York: Theatre Communication Group.

Loades, D. (1987), *The Tudor Court*. Totowa, NJ: Barnes & Noble.

—— (1997), *Tudor Government: Structures of Authority in the Sixteenth Century*. Oxford: Blackwell.

Lockyer, R. (2005), *Tudor and Stuart Britain: 1485–1712* (3rd edn). Harlow: Longman.

Loomba, A. (1996), 'Shakespeare and Cultural Difference', in T. Hawkes (ed.), *Alternative Shakespeares*, II, pp. 164–91. London: Routledge.

—— (2002), *Shakespeare, Race and Colonialism*. Oxford: Oxford University Press.

Lusardi, J. P. and Schlueter, J. (2003), ' "I Have Done the Deed": *Macbeth* 2:2', in F. Occhiogrosso (ed.), *Shakespeare in Performance: A Collection of Essays*, pp. 71–83. Newark: University of Delaware Press.

Macdonald, R. R. (1995), 'Uses of Diversity: Bakhtin's Theory of Utterance and Shakespeare's Second Tetralogy', in N. Wood (ed.), *Henry IV Parts One and Two*, pp. 65–91. Buckingham: Open University Press.

Maguire, L. E. (1996), *Shakespearean Suspect Texts: The 'Bad' Quartos and Their Contexts*. Cambridge: Cambridge University Press.

—— (2004), *Studying Shakespeare: A Guide to the Plays*. Oxford: Blackwell.

Mahood, M. M. (1957), *Shakespeare's Wordplay*. London: Methuen.

Maley, W. (1997), *Salvaging Spenser: Colonialism, Culture and Identity*. London: Macmillan.

—— (2007), ' "A Thing Most Brutish": Depicting Shakespeare's Multi-Nation State', *Shakespeare*, 3 (1), 79–101.

Marotti, A. F. (1982), ' "Love is Not Love": Elizabethan Sonnet Sequences and the Social Order', *English Literary History*, 49, 397–428.

Marshall, T. (1998), '*The Tempest* and the British Imperium in 1611', *The Historical Journal*, 41(2), 375–400.

Masten, J. (1997), *Textual Intercourse: Collaboration, Authorship, and Sexualities in Renaissance Drama*. Cambridge Studies in Renaissance Literature and Culture, 14. Cambridge: Cambridge University Press.

Maunsell, A. (1595), *The first part of the catalogue of English printed bookes: vvhich concerneth such matters of diuinitie, as haue bin either written in our owne tongue, or translated out of anie other language: and haue bin published, to the glory of God, and edification of the Church of Christ in England . . . The second parte, which concerneth the sciences mathematicall and also phisick and surgerie*. London. http://www.cerl.org/web/en/services/estc.

McAlindon, T. (2001), 'Perfect Answers: Religious Inquisition, Falstaffian Wit', in P. Holland (ed.), *Shakespeare Survey 54, Shakespeare and Religions*, pp. 100–7. Cambridge: Cambridge University Press.

McCluskie, K. (1985), 'The Patriarchal Bard: Feminist Criticism and Shakespeare: *King Lear* and *Measure for Measure*', in J. Dollimore and A. Sinfield (eds), *Political Shakespeare: Essays in Cultural Materialism*, pp. 88–108. Manchester: Manchester University Press.

McCoy, R. C. (2001), 'A Wedding and Four Funerals: Conjunction and Commemoration in *Hamlet*', in P. Holland (ed.), *Shakespeare Survey 54, Shakespeare and Religions*, pp. 122–39. Cambridge: Cambridge University Press.

—— (2004), ' "The Grace of Grace" and Double-Talk in *Macbeth*', in P. Holland (ed.), *Shakespeare Survey 57, Macbeth and its Afterlife*, pp. 27–37. Cambridge: Cambridge University Press.

McDonald, R. (2001), *Shakespeare and the Arts of Language*. Oxford: Oxford University Press.

McMillin, S. (1972), 'Casting for Pembroke's Men: The *Henry VI* Quartos and *The Taming of a Shrew*', *Shakespeare Quarterly*, 23, 141–59.

Meads, C. (2001), *Banquets Set Forth: Banqueting in English Renaissance Drama*, Manchester: Manchester University Press. A close study of banquet scenes in Shakespeare with extended discussions of banquets in *Macbeth* and *The Tempest*.

Merriam, T. (2005), *The Identity of Shakespeare in 'Henry VIII'*. Renaissance Monographs 32. Tokyo: The Renaissance Institute of Sophia University.

Michelakis, P. (2002), *Achilles in Greek Tragedy*. Cambridge: Cambridge University Press.

Montrose, L. (1986), 'Renaissance Literary Studies and the Subject of History', *English Literary Renaissance*, 16, 5–12.

Neill, M. (1994), 'Broken English and Broken Irish: Nation, Language, and the Optic of Power in Shakespeare's Histories', *Shakespeare Quarterly*, 45 (1), 1–32.

Newcombe, D. G. (1995), *Henry VIII and the English Reformation*. London and New York: Routledge.

Ngugi wa Thiong'o (1993), *Moving the Centre: The Struggle for Cultural Freedoms*. Oxford: James Currey.

Nicholls, M. (1999), *A History of the Modern British Isles, 1529–1603: The Two Kingdoms*. Oxford: Blackwell.

Norbrook, D. (1992), ' "What Cares These Roarers for the Name of King?": Language and Utopia in *The Tempest'*, in G. McMullan and J. Hope (eds), *The Politics of Tragicomedy: Shakespeare and After*, pp. 21–54. London: Routledge.

Novy, M. (1995), 'Shakespeare and Emotional Distance in the Elizabethan Family', in D. Barker and I. Kamp (eds), *Shakespeare and Gender: A History*, pp. 63–74. London: Verso.

Orgel, S. (1975), *The Illusion of Power: Political Theater in the English Renaissance*. Berkeley: University of California Press.

—— (1989), 'Nobody's Perfect: Or Why Did the English Stage Take Boys for Women?', *South Atlantic Quarterly*, 88 (1), 7–29.

—— (1994), 'Prospero's Wife', *Representations*, 8, 1–13.

—— (2001), 'Cymbeline at Santa Cruz', *Shakespeare Quarterly*, 52, 277–85.

Orkin, M. (1997), 'Whose Things of Darkness?: Reading/Representing *The Tempest* in South Africa after April 1994', in J. Joughin (ed.), *Shakespeare and National Culture*, pp. 142–69. Manchester: Manchester University Press.

Palfrey, S. (2005), *Doing Shakespeare*. London: Thomson Learning.

Palfrey, S., and Stern, T. (2007), *Shakespeare in Parts*. Oxford: Oxford University Press.

Palmer, J. (1912), 'The Winter's Tale', *Saturday Review*, 23 Nov.

Parker, P. (1996), *Shakespeare from the Margins: Language, Culture, Context*. Chicago: University of Chicago Press.

—— (2003), 'Black *Hamlet*: Battening on the Moor', *Shakespeare Studies*, 31, 127–64.

Patterson, W. B. (2000), *King James VI and I and the Reunion of Christendom*. Cambridge: Cambridge University Press.

Pechter, E. (1995), *What Was Shakespeare? Renaissance Plays and Changing Critical Practice*. Ithaca: Cornell University Press.

—— (2003), 'What's Wrong with Literature?', *Textual Practice*, 17, 505–26.

Pendergast, J. S. (1995), 'A Nation of Hamlets: Shakespeare and Cultural Politics', *Extrapolation*, 36 (1), 10–17.

Pequigney, J. (1995), 'The Two Antonios and Same-Sex Love in *Twelfth Night* and *The Merchant of Venice'*, in D. Barker and I. Kamps (eds), *Shakespeare and Gender: A History*, pp. 178–95. London: Verso.

Platt, P. G. (1999), 'Shakespeare and Rhetorical Culture', in *A Companion to Shakespeare*, ed. D. S. Kastan, pp. 277–96. Oxford: Blackwell.

Poole, A. (2004), 'Caliban and Ireland', in *Shakespeare and the Victorians*, pp. 220–24. Arden Critical Companions. London: Thomson Learning.

Pope, A. (1986), 'The Preface to the Editor', in *The Prose Works of Alexander Pope*, Vol. 2: 1725–1744, ed. R. Cowler. Oxford: Blackwell / Shakespeare Head.

Porter, C. (1990), 'Are We Being Historical Yet?', in D. Carroll (ed.), *The States of Theory: History, Art, and Critical Discourse*, pp. 27–62. Stanford: Stanford University Press.

Rackin, P. (1989), 'Androgyny, Mimesis, and the Marriage of the Boy Heroine on the English Renaissance Stage', in E. Showalter (ed.), *Speaking of Gender*, pp. 113–33. London: Routledge.

Reynolds, P. (1991), *Teaching Shakespeare*. Oxford: Oxford University Press.

Robins, E. (1900), 'On Seeing Madame Bernhardt's Hamlet', *North American Review*, 171 (December), 908–19. Text presented on http://www.jsu.edu/depart/english/robins/docshort/onseeham.htm.

Robson, M. (2008), *Stephen Greenblatt*. London and New York: Routledge.

Ronayne, J. (1983), 'Style', in A. Gurr, J. Orrell and J. Ronayne (eds), *'The Shape of the Globe': Report on the Seminar Held at Pentagram Limited London By the International Shakespeares Globe Centre (ISGC) on 29 March 1983*, pp. 22–24. The Renaissance Drama Newsletter Supplements 1. Coventry: University of Warwick Graduate School of Renaissance Studies.

—— (1997), 'Totus Mundus Agit Histrionem [The Whole World Moves the Actor]: The Interior Decorative Scheme of the Bankside Globe', in J. R. Mulryne, M. Shewring and A. Gurr (eds), *Shakespeare's Globe Rebuilt*, pp. 121–46. Cambridge: Cambridge University Press.

Rose, J. (1985), 'Sexuality in the Reading of Shakespeare: *Hamlet* and *Measure for Measure*', in J. Drakakis (ed.), *Alternative Shakespeares*, pp. 95–118. London: Methuen.

—— (1995), 'Hamlet – the *Mona Lisa* of Literature', in D. Barker and I. Kamps (eds), *Shakespeare and Gender: A History*, pp. 104–19. London: Verso.

Royle, N. (2005), *How to Read Shakespeare*. London: Granta.

Ryan, K. (1995), 'The Future of History in *Henry IV*', in N. Wood (ed.), *Henry IV Parts One and Two*, pp. 92–125. Buckingham: Open University Press.

—— (ed.) (1996), *New Historicism and Cultural Materialism: A Reader*. London: Arnold.

Sacks, D. H. (1999), 'The Countervailing of Benefits: Monopoly, Liberty, and Benevolence in Elizabethan England', in D. Hoak (ed.), *Tudor Political Culture*, pp. 272–91. Cambridge: Cambridge University Press.

Sanders, J. (2001), *Novel Shakespeares: Twentieth-Century Women Novelists and Appropriation*. Manchester: Manchester University Press.

Sawday, J. (1996), *The Body Emblazoned: Dissection and the Human Body in Renaissance Culture*. London and New York: Routledge.

Schalkwyk, D. (1994), ' "She never told her love": Embodiment, Textuality, and Silence in Shakespeare's Sonnets and Plays', *Shakespeare Quarterly*, 45 (4), 381–407.

—— (2005), 'Love and Service in *Twelfth Night* and the Sonnets', *Shakespeare Quarterly*, 56 (1), 76–100.

Schoenbaum, S. (1975), *William Shakespeare: A Documentary Life*. New York: Oxford University Press (in association with Scolar Press). Presents facsimiles of all extant documents pertaining to the life and career of Shakespeare, accompanied by detailed explanations of how such documents were viewed at the time they were produced.

Schwyzer, P. (2002), 'The Bride on the Border: Women and the Reproduction of Ethnicity in the Early Modern British Isles', *European Journal of Cultural Studies*, 5 (3), 293–306.

Scott, Sir W. (1972), *The Journal of Sir Walter Scott*, ed. W. E. K. Anderson. Oxford: Clarendon Press.

Sedgwick, E. K. (1985), 'Swan in Love: The Example of Shakespeare's Sonnets', in *Between Men: English Literature and Male Homosocial Desire*, pp. 28–48. New York: Columbia University Press.

Seed, P. (2000), ' "This island's mine": Caliban and Native Sovereignty', in P. Hulme and W. H. Sherman (eds), *'The Tempest' and Its Travels*, pp. 202–11. London: Reaktion Books.

Shakespeare, W. (1603), *[Hamlet] The Tragicall Historie of Hamlet Prince of Denmarke*. London. STC 22275 (Q1).

—— (1948), *Titus Andronicus*, ed. J. D. Wilson. The New Shakespeare. Cambridge: Cambridge University Press.

—— (1997), *The Norton Shakespeare*, ed. S. Greenblatt et al. New York and London: W. W. Norton.

—— (2004), *Pericles*, ed. S. Gossett. The Arden Shakespeare. London: Thomson Learning.

—— (2006), *Hamlet*, ed. A. Thompson and N. Taylor. London: Thompson Learning.

Shakespeare, W. and Middleton, T. (2004), *Timon of Athens*, ed. J. Jowett. The Oxford Shakespeare. Oxford: Oxford University Press.

Shapiro, J. (2005), *1599: A Year in the Life of William Shakespeare*. London: Faber and Faber.

Sharpe, J. A. (1997), *Early Modern England: A Social History 1550–1760* (2nd edn). London and New York: Arnold.

Sheils, W. (2004), 'Catholics and Recusants', in R. Tittler and N. Jones (eds), *A Companion to Tudor Britain*, pp. 254–70. Malden, MA and Oxford: Blackwell.

Shelley, P. B. (1954), *Shelley's Prose, or The Trumpet of a Prophecy*, ed. D. L. Clark. Albuquerque: University of New Mexico Press.

Showalter, E. (1985), 'Representing Ophelia: Women, Madness, and the Responsibilities of Feminist Criticism', in P. Parker and G. Hartman (eds), *Shakespeare and the Question of Theory*, pp. 77–94. New York and London: Methuen.

Sinfield, A. (1992), 'Masculinity and Miscegenation', in A. Sinfield, *Faultlines: Cultural Materialism and the Politics of Dissident Reading*, pp. 127–42. Berkeley: University of California Press.

Singh, J. G. (2003), 'Caliban versus Miranda: Race and Gender Conflicts in Postcolonial Rewritings of *The Tempest*', in A. Thorne (ed.), *Shakespeare's Romances*, pp. 205–25. New Casebooks. London: Palgrave Macmillan. [Reprinted from V. Traub, M. L. Kaplan and D. Callaghan (eds), *Feminist Readings of Early Modern Culture*, pp. 191–209. Cambridge: Cambridge University Press, 1996.]

Skrebels P, and van der Hoeven, S. (eds) (2002), *For All Time?: Critical Issues in Teaching Shakespeare*. Kent Town, S. Aust.: Wakefield Press.

Sleights, J. (2001), 'Rape and the Romanticization of Shakespeare's Miranda', *Studies in English Literature*, 41 (2), 357–79.

Smith, B. R. (2000), *Shakespeare and Masculinity*. Oxford: Oxford University Press.

Smith, G., Stephen, L. and S. Lee (eds) (1937–38), *The Dictionary of National Biography: From the Earliest Times to 1900*. Vol. 14: Myllar-Owen. 22 vols. Oxford: Oxford University Press.

Spurgeon, C. F. E. (1935), *Shakespeare's Imagery and What It Tells Us*. Cambridge: Cambridge University Press.

Strier, R. (1995), *Resistant Structures: Particularity, Radicalism, and Renaissance Texts*. Berkeley: University of California Press.

Suzuki, M. (2000), 'Gender, Class, and the Ideology of Comic Form: *Much Ado About Nothing* and *Twelfth Night*', in D. Callaghan (ed.), *A Feminist Companion to Shakespeare*, pp. 121–43. Oxford: Blackwell.

Taylor, G. (1993), 'The Structure of Performance: Act-intervals in the London Theatres, 1576–1642', in G. Taylor and J. Jowett (eds), *Shakespeare Reshaped 1606–1623*, pp. 3–50. Oxford Shakespeare Studies. Oxford: Clarendon Press.

—— (1995), 'Shakespeare and Others: The Authorship of *Henry the Sixth, Part One*', *Medieval and Renaissance Drama in England*, 7, 145–205.

—— (2000), '*Hamlet* in Africa 1607', in I. Kamps and J. Singh (eds), *Travel Knowledge: European 'Discoveries' in the Early Modern Period*, pp. 211–48. New York: St Martin's Press.

—— (2004a), 'Shakespeare's Mediterranean *Measure for Measure*', in T. Clayton, S. Brock and V. Fores (eds), *Shakespeare and the Mediterranean: The Selected Proceedings of the International Shakespeare Association World Congress at Valencia 2001*, pp. 243–69. Newark: University of Delaware Press.

—— (2004b), 'Shakespeare's Midlife Crisis', *Guardian*, 3 May, p. 11.

Taylor, J. (1630), *All the workes of John Taylor*, London.

Tennenhouse, L. (1986), *Power on Display: The Politics of Shakespeare's Genres*. London: Methuen. Classic piece of New Historicist criticism.

Thompson, A. (1995), ' "Miranda, where's your sister?": Reading Shakespeare's *The Tempest*', in D. Barker and I. Kamps (eds), *Shakespeare and Gender: A History*, pp. 168–77. London: Verso.

—— (1998), ' "Miranda, Where's Your Sister?": Reading Shakespeare's *The Tempest*', in A. T. Vaughan and V. M. Vaughan (eds), *Critical Essays on Shakespeare's The Tempest*, pp. 234–43. New York: G. K. Hall.

Thompson, A. and Roberts, S. (eds) (1997), *Women Reading Shakespeare, 1660–1900: An Anthology of Criticism*. Manchester: Manchester University Press.

Tibbets, T. (2004), 'Teaching Shakespeare through Performance', in P. Skrebels and S. Van Der Hoeven (eds), *For All Time?: Critical Issues in Teaching Shakespeare*, pp. 36–43. Adelaide: Wakefield Press.

Tillyard, E. M. W. (1944), *Shakespeare's History Plays*. London: Macmillan.

Tittler, R. (1998), *The Reformation and the Towns of England: Politics and Political Culture, c.1540–1640*. Oxford: Clarendon Press.

Traub, V. (1992), *Desire and Anxiety: Circulations of Sexuality in Shakespearean Drama*. London: Routledge.

—— (1997), 'Response to Richard Levin's "(Re)Thinking Unthinkable Thoughts" ', *New Literary History*, 28 (3), 539–42.

—— (1999), 'Sex without Issue: Sodomy, Reproduction, and Signification in Shakespeare's Sonnets', in J. Schiffer (ed.), *Shakespeare's Sonnets: Critical Essays*, pp. 431–54. New York and London: Garland.

Trollope, A. (1951), *The Letters of Anthony Trollope*, ed. B. A. Booth. Westport, CT: Greenwood Press.

Tucker, P. (2001), *Secrets of Acting Shakespeare: The Original Approach*. London and New York: Routledge.

Urkowitz, S. (1988), ' "If I Mistake in Those Foundations Which I Build Upon": Peter Alexander's Textual Analysis of *Henry VI Parts 2 and 3*', *English Literary Renaissance*, 18, 230–56.

Vaughan, A. T. and Vaughan, V. M. (1991), *Shakespeare's Caliban: A Cultural History*. Cambridge: Cambridge University Press.

Veeser, H. A. (ed.) (1989), *The New Historicism*. London and New York: Routledge.

Vendler, H. (1997), *The Art of Shakespeare's Sonnets*. Cambridge, MA: Belknap Press of Harvard University Press.

—— (1968), *The Artistry of Shakespeare's Prose*. London: Methuen.

—— (ed.) (1975), *Shakespeare the Critical Heritage vol. 3, 1733–1752*. London and New York: Routledge.

Vickers, B. (2002), *Shakespeare, Co-author: A Historical Study of Five Collaborative Plays*. Oxford: Oxford University Press.

Vygotsky, L. S. (1978), *Mind in Society*. Cambridge, MA: Harvard University Press.

Ward, J. (2004), 'Metropolitan London', in R. Tittler and N. Jones (eds), *A Companion to Tudor Britain*, pp. 347–62. London: Blackwell.

Webb, D. (2000), ' "Pageants truly played": Self-dramatization and naturalistic character in *The Jew of Malta*', *Renaissance Forum*, 5 (1) (http://www.hull.ac.uk/renforum/v5no1/webb.htm).

Webster, J. (2006), *The White Devil*, ed. C. Luckyj. London: A. & C. Black / New Mermaids reprint.

Weimann, R. (1974), 'Shakespeare and the Study of Metaphor'. *New Literary History*, 6, 149–67.

—— (1996), *Authority and Representation in Early Modern Discourse*, ed. D. Hillman. Baltimore and London: John Hopkins University Press.

Wells, S. (1984), *Re-editing Shakespeare for the Modern Reader*. Oxford: Clarendon Press.

—— (2002), *Shakespeare: For All Time*. London: Macmillan.

—— (2006), *Shakespeare & Co*. London: Penguin.

Wells, S., Taylor, G., Jowett, J. and Montgomery, W. (1987), *William Shakespeare: A Textual Companion*. Oxford: Oxford University Press.

Wentersdorf, K. (2006), 'The Winchester Crux in the First Folio's *1 Henry VI*', *Shakespeare Quarterly*, 54, 443–49.

Werstine, P. (1990), 'Narratives about Printed Shakespeare Texts: "Foul Papers" and "Bad" Quartos' *Shakespeare Quarterly*, 41, 65–86.

—— (1999), 'A Century of "Bad" Shakespeare Quartos', *Shakespeare Quarterly*, 50, 310–33.

White, R. S. (1987), *Keats as a Reader of Shakespeare*. London: Athlone Press.

—— (1999), *The Tempest: Contemporary Critical Essays*, New Casebooks. Basingstoke: Macmillan.

Williams, R. (1983), *Keywords: A Vocabulary of Culture and Society*. London: Oxford University Press.

Wilson, J. D. (1943), *The Fortunes of Falstaff*. Cambridge: Cambridge University Press.

—— (1962), *Shakespeare's Happy Comedies*. Evanston: Northwestern University Press.

Wilson, R. (1997), 'Shakespeare and the Jesuits: New Connections Supporting the Theory of the Lost Catholic Years in Lancashire', *Times Literary Supplement*, 4942, 19 December, pp. 11–13.

—— (2004a), ' "Every Third Thought": Shakespeare's Milan', in T. Clayton, S. Brock and V. Fores (eds), *Shakespeare and the Mediterranean: The Selected Proceedings of the International Shakespeare Association World Congress at Valencia 2001*, 416–24. Newark: University of Delaware Press.

—— (2004b), 'Shakespeare in Hate', *Poetica: Zeitschrift fur Sprach- und Literaturwissenschaft*, 36 (1–2), 149–67.

—— (2004c), *Secret Shakespeare: Studies in Theatre, Religion and Resistance*. Manchester: Manchester University Press.

—— (2007), *Shakespeare in French Theory: King of Shadows*. London and New York: Routledge.

Wilson, R. and Dutton, R. (eds) (1992), *New Historicism and Renaissance Drama*. Hemel Hempstead: Harvester Wheatsheaf.

Wilson, S. (1995), *Cultural Materialism: Theory and Practice*. Oxford: Blackwell.

Winstanley, L. (1921), *'Hamlet' and the Scottish Succession: Being an Examination of the Relations of the Play of 'Hamlet' to the Scottish Succession and the Essex Conspiracy*. Cambridge: Cambridge University Press.

Wollstonecraft, M. (1979), *Collected Letters of Mary Wollstonecraft*, ed. R. M. Wardle. Ithaca and London: Cornell University Press.

Womack, P. (1995), *'Henry IV* and Epic Theatre', in N. Wood (ed.), *Henry IV Parts One and Two*, pp. 126–61. Buckingham: Open University Press.

Worster, D. (2002), 'Performance Options and Pedagogy: *Macbeth'*, *Shakespeare Quarterly*, 53 (3), 362–78. Worster explores various performance possibilities in *Macbeth*.

Wright, E. (1984), *Psychoanalytic Criticism: Theory in Practice*. London and New York: Methuen.

Wright, G. T. (1988), *Shakespeare's Metrical Art*. Berkeley: University of California Press.

—— (1999), 'Hearing Shakespeare's Dramatic Verse', in *A Companion to Shakespeare*, ed. D. S. Kastan, pp. 256–76. Oxford: Blackwell.

Wrigley, E. A. and Schofield, R. S. (1981), *The Population History of England, 1541–1871: A Reconstruction*. Cambridge, MA: Harvard University Press.

Wymer, R. (1999), *'The Tempest* and the Origins of Britain', *Critical Survey*, 11 (1), 3–14.

Zeffirelli, F. (1990), *Hamlet*. Motion Picture. Warner / Le Studio Canal+ / Carolco / Icon / Marquis / Nelson.

Ziegler, G. (2008), 'Suppliant Women and Monumental Maidens: Shakespeare's Heroines in the Boydell Gallery', http://www.shakespeare-gesellschaft.de/publikationen/boydell-katalog/georgianna-ziegler.html, accessed 1 September, 2008.

Index